Sing a
New Song

Sing a New Song

Portraits of Canada's Crusading Bishops

Julie H. Ferguson

Foreword by
The Most Reverend A. Hutchison,
Primate of Canada

THE DUNDURN GROUP
TORONTO

Copy-editor: Patricia Kennedy
Design: Andrew Roberts and Jennifer Scott
Printer:Friesens

Library and Archives Canada Cataloguing in Publication

Ferguson, Julie H., 1945-

   Sing a new song : portraits of Canada's crusading bishops / Julie H. Ferguson.

  Includes bibliographical references and index.

ISBN-10: 1-55002-609-7
ISBN-13: 978-1-55002-609-2

   1. Hills, George, 1816-1895. 2. Somerville, David, 1915-. 3. Hambidge, Douglas. 1927– 4. Ingham, Michael. 1949– 5. Anglican Church of Canada--Bishops--Biography. 6. Bishops--Canada--Biography. 7. Bishops--British Columbia--Biography. I. Title.

BX5619.F47 2006   283.092'271   C2006-901340-3

1 2 3 4 5   10 09 08 07 06

We acknowledge the support of the **Canada Council for the Arts** and the **Ontario Arts Council** for our publishing program. We also acknowledge the financial support of the **Government of Canada** through the **Book Publishing Industry Development Program** and **The Association for the Export of Canadian Books**, and the **Government of Ontario** through the **Ontario Book Publishers Tax Credit program**, and the **Ontario Media Development Corporation**.

Care has been taken to trace the ownership of copyright material used in this book. The author and the publisher welcome any information enabling them to rectify any references or credits in subsequent editions.

J. Kirk Howard, President

Printed and bound in Canada.

www.dundurn.com

Dundurn Press
3 Church Street, Suite 500
Toronto, Ontario, Canada
M5E 1M2

Gazelle Book Services Limited
White Cross Mills
High Town, Lancaster, England
LA1 4XS

Dundurn Press
2250 Military Road
Tonawanda, N.Y.
U.S.A. 14150

Sing a
New Song

TABLE OF CONTENTS

LIST OF ILLUSTRATIONS

PART THREE — DOUGLAS W. HAMBIDGE

PART FOUR — MICHAEL C. INGHAM

FOREWORD

In the service for the ordination of a bishop, the bishop-elect stands facing the bishops who have gathered to participate in the consecration and the celebrant says,

> *A bishop in God's holy Church is called to be one with the apostles in proclaiming Christ's resurrection and interpreting the Gospel, and to testify to Christ's sovereignty as Lord of lords and King of kings.*
>
> *You are called to guard the faith, unity, and discipline of the Church; to celebrate and to provide for the administration of the sacraments of the new covenant; to ordain priests and deacons, and to join in ordaining bishops; and to be in all things a faithful pastor and wholesome example for the entire flock of Christ.*
>
> *With your fellow bishops you will share in the leadership of the Church throughout the world. Your heritage is the faith of patriarchs, prophets, apostles, and martyrs, and those of every generation who have looked to God in hope. Your joy will be to follow him who came not to be served but to serve, and to give his life a ransom for many.*

Sing a New Song is the story of four people who have fulfilled that call in a marvellous way, and now their stories, which are central to it, can be shared with the Church.

I have had the privilege of working closely with two of the bishops in this book and consider them friends. I have met and talked with a third and admired the courage and tenacity of a fourth. To my knowledge there has not been a great deal written about the Church's history in British Columbia. In so many ways this book is a valuable historical record of the first Bishop of British Columbia through to a living and ongoing history of the current Bishop of New Westminster.

It is important for us to know the lives of these bishops, not only from an historical point of view, but also in terms of faith. They are all very creative and fiercely independent people. The author herself points out that geography may explain some of this pioneering spirit, but I think it is something more than that. These four bishops have used the gifts God has given them to enable ministry in new and exciting ways. The wonder of this book is in learning how God has called them and used them as creative agents of change.

Perhaps each of us can learn something about our own faith development from their lives and witness.

I am very thankful to Ms. Julie Ferguson for her work on this project, as there is always a danger that we will lose an important part of our past without the dedication and hard work of researchers and authors like her. I commend *Sing a New Song* to you, that through your awareness of the past your faith in the future will be strong.

+Andrew

The Most Reverend Andrew S. Hutchison
Archbishop and Primate
September 2005

PREFACE

"**Never place a period where God has placed a comma.**"

Gracie Allen, 1902-1964
American comedienne

For those readers who are disappointed not to find their favourite bishop included between these covers, I can only say that I considered many. Some did not meet my criteria for this book; others had too little material available about them to fill more than a couple of pages; one or two suitable bishops are already the subjects of fine books (Ted Scott, a former Canadian Primate, is a prime example); and still more served during times that did not grapple with the great issues that occupied humankind in western countries for the last century and a half. However, the bonus created by culling the list to four means I have left other authors a surplus of intriguing and sometimes eccentric bishops who need to have their stories recorded for future generations.

Although social justice is the major theme of *Sing a New Song*, this was not one of the criteria I imposed when selecting candidates — leaders of all faiths are, or should be, motivated by social justice. Instead I chose as my main criterion bishops who, by pushing the envelope of equality rights in Canada, became mirrors of, or change agents for, society's attitudes, both here and in other nations. Oddly enough, all four subjects ministered in British Columbia. My other criteria included:

- the bishops had to be Canadian;
- the bishops had to be Anglican;
- the bishops had to have faced opposition to the positions they espoused.

My journey started about four years ago when a couple of publishers suggested I write a biography. But who to choose? The search for an ideal subject hovered constantly but not urgently in my consciousness until I was listening to a panel of international freelance writers at Vancouver's "Word on the Street" in 2003. Inspiration struck with a wallop and I knew instantly I had identified the perfect person to write about — he was Canadian, controversial, and accessible. The idea was also a good fit for my publisher, Dundurn Press — in fact, so good, it was breathtaking. Dundurn's publisher, Kirk Howard, agreed with me, and so I eagerly went to seek the subject's permission to write his story. He refused, and for very good reasons. Disappointed, I shelved the idea.

Sing a New Song flowed from the original inspiration and satisfied my desire to write a biography, though in a less intimidating format: four short ones, instead of one long one. However, I did not anticipate the difficulty of composing biographies a quarter of the usual size when each of these bishops could fill a full-length book. I had to omit quantities of fascinating anecdotes, colourful examples of their characters, and lesser issues that illustrate their ministries. So severely did I have to abbreviate the run-up to and the fallout from the adoption of the blessing of same-sex unions in the Diocese of New Westminster that the cutbacks hurt. Indeed, I had to leave out so much about the very full lives of three of these four bishops that the outcome of *Sing a New Song* may well be three full-length biographies. Also time constraints meant I could not talk to all those I felt necessary to this story, which frustrated me. However, I bequeath the detailed story of how the issue of human sexuality played out in the Diocese of New Westminster, the Anglican Church of Canada, and the Anglican

Communion to others more qualified to do it justice than I. Despite the challenges of this book's format, the pleasure of again delving deeply into Canadian history has sustained me throughout the project, along with the sincere encouragement of many individuals, most of whom are named in the Acknowledgements.

I need to explain my credentials — first by telling who I am not. I am not a theologian, I am not a priest or deacon in the Anglican Church of Canada, and I am not a scholar. I am simply an ordinary Anglican parishioner compelled to tell four stories that anyone can enjoy — whether a Christian or not, whether a churchgoer or not. Readers also need to know that, over time, I have arrived at a liberal position on the great issues that beset these bishops through reading, discussion, and reflection, as well as guidance from the clergy of my parish. I have tried to present both sides of the matters discussed, but inevitably write with some bias, just as the subjects of these short biographies also lean one way or another. Although I have never written church history before, my two previously published books on Canadian naval history met with some acclaim, so I hope the skills of research and interviewing are transferable and that I have accomplished them satisfactorily for this book too.

While I have had to set the issues adopted by these four bishops into context, I have done so simply. Other authors have recorded these settings and the pro and con arguments in such detail that I felt it pointless to repeat their work. Their books are listed in the selected bibliography at the back for those who are stirred to pursue more reading.

A word about terminology: giving labels to people and things creates stereotypes, which is an action most try to avoid. However, *Sing a New Song* proved impossible to write without using adjectives or nouns to indicate the positions that individuals or groups espoused in the great debates. My use of these words neither provides the breadth and variety of thought each one inevitably contains nor recognizes the fact that not all catholic Anglicans are liberal or protestant Anglicans, conservative. So, having explained that, I have tended to use the following interchangeably, especially in the last three sections:

- liberal/progressive/catholic
- conservative/traditional/evangelical/protestant.

Most authors, when they write a non-fiction book, know that their words are their own and that they are free to make whatever judgement of individuals and interpretation of events they desire. This book is different. Each of the three living bishops read their sections of the manuscript, made suggestions and corrections, and approved every word. Why? I wanted their input, so that *Sing a New Song* would contain their truth for posterity, not mine. However, any remaining errors definitely fall on my shoulders.

As always, the team behind this book has been exemplary — without them, *Sing a New Song* would not have seen the light of day. No author could ask for better assistance or support.

Julie H. Ferguson
Port Moody, B.C.
September 2005
www.beaconlit.com

ACKNOWLEDGEMENTS

The Great Thanksgiving . . .

As with any book, this one has required the input and work of many individuals, and they deserve my recognition. Each has given of time, talents, and knowledge with a generosity of spirit that has heartened me and for which I give my humble, but enormous, thanks. Furthermore everyone's patience with me as I accelerated up to speed was commendable. *Sing a New Song* is as much a product of their diligence as it is mine.

First I must acknowledge the three living bishops, each of whom submitted to countless interviews. With infinite good humour, they let me wire them up and talked for hours with candour, honesty, and amazing recall. I am greatly indebted to Archbishops David Somerville and Douglas Hambidge and to Bishop Michael Ingham for their cooperation, and especially for their witty "sound bites," which have enlivened *Sing a New Song*. Of course, if you can preach a good sermon, you can tell a fine story, and all did. I am also grateful for their painstaking work on the manuscript; all three checked their sections for mistakes and omissions, as well as making some excellent suggestions that have enhanced the final result. Bishop

Michael's contribution needs to be described in a little more detail — he identified and introduced me to many whom I needed to meet and/or interview. He provided a small office whenever I was in the synod office, and, last but not least, he allowed me to include him in the book. This was a gift I dearly wanted but dared not expect. Although he did not know me at the outset, he encouraged the project — a leap of faith, if ever there was one! And, most of all, he trusted me. Thanks be to God!

Next I must thank all the many others who agreed to provide background interviews, either in person or on the phone. They are listed in the back of the book, not because they are less important, but simply because that's where the publisher put the list. I appreciated every word they offered and could not have written such detailed biographies without their insights.

Now I must honour the many individuals who have played other roles in the project. In no particular order: the Reverend Doctor Catherine Hall, the rector of St. John's, Port Moody, who stimulated my thinking, served as a theological coach, and even critiqued the final manuscript on a vacation; Neale Adams, the editor of the diocesan newspaper, *Topic*, and communications officer of the Diocese of New Westminster, who cheerfully dug up articles and photographs from the past, made valuable suggestions, and whose comprehensive Web site management saved me many hours of research; Doreen Stephens, provincial and diocesan archivist (retired), who ministered for hours as a treasure hunter for me in a temporary office no bigger than a closet; all the archives' volunteers; the Reverend Eileen Nurse, who runs Bishop Ingham's office and helped with hard-to-find documents and other minutia; Doctor Norman Knowles, an historian who improved my understanding about the 1500s and 1600s and wrote an endorsement; Joan Scott, of my parish, who meticulously transcribed over thirty-five hours of interviews; Steve Schuh, president of Integrity Vancouver, who patiently answered my many questions; Roberta Bagshaw, who offered her knowledge of Bishop George Hills and First Nations when I was unsure; the primate of Canada, the Most Reverend Andrew Hutchison, for writing the foreword; Archbishop David Somerville, the Reverend Doctor Richard Leggett, Dr. Patricia Bays, and the Reverend Canon Herbert O'Driscoll for writing endorsements; my Education for Ministry group, where supportive fellow students and my mentor provided me with encouragement and unflagging interest throughout; and lastly my Port Moody Writers' Group, led by Eileen Kernaghan, which as always provided solid and constructive criticism of the manuscript. I give you all my heartfelt thanks.

I have nothing but admiration for both my husband, James, and for my friend, Jan Williamson. They lived with my creative fog for the year of the writing phase and my rising anxiety as the deadline approached. Jan, especially, ensured that I took one day a week to relax by inviting me to play golf every Wednesday. Now that the fog is dissipating, perhaps you will trust me to drive the golf cart again?

The team at Dundurn also deserves my thanks and praise: Kirk Howard, publisher, for believing in my idea and giving me the contract *without* the need of a book proposal (heaven on Earth for any author!); my editor, Patricia Kennedy, who hunted down my errors and improved the book immensely; and Jennifer Scott, Dundurn's art director, who is responsible for the book's appearance and stunning cover.

Blessings to all!
JHF

For all those who struggle for equality rights

INTRODUCTION

"The church is human, not divine"

Christianity, in all its guises, has been grappling with what it all means since about 33CE. The processing of what happened so long ago and how we apply it to our cultures and lives has occupied theologians and scholars through the centuries. This inquiry will never end because we have a religious tradition that requires constant exploration to be a living faith. The current bishop of New Westminster, Michael Ingham, sees theology as "a clash of ideas, an engagement of opposites . . . an evolving discipline" if we want to keep Christianity out of museums. This ongoing effort causes uneasiness, as new ideas and positions move the faithful out of their comfort zones.

Dissent, division, and difficulty with its theology are not new to the Anglican Church, whether in Canada or around the world. In his address to the Synod of the Diocese of New Westminster in 2004, the Bishop of Olympia remarked, "The Church was born broken." Bishop Vincent Warner was referring to Judas's betrayal of Jesus the night before he was crucified. Later dissent divided Christianity into east and west; the Protestant Reformation split the western Roman Catholic Church; and denominations regularly broke off thereafter as the believers processed their faith and decided they did not agree with others' interpretations or practice. Often the divisions took place over the authority vested in a leader or leaders, but they also happened regularly over theological positions.

Modern Anglicanism accepts a broad spectrum of practice and beliefs — from very Protestant and Word-centred to remarkably Catholic. It is this freedom that not only attracts adherents but also leads to strongly held viewpoints and disagreements. These differing positions have caused difficulties throughout the Church's history and continue to do so today. Healthy Anglicans cherish this freedom to sort out their own beliefs and worship practices, as well as engage in the debates that arise. But controversial issues also tend bring out bigotry, hatred — and the wackos. The Church is human not divine.

Over the last hundred odd years, in a world church that unites vastly different cultures, contexts, and customs among its members, Anglicanism has faced dissent among its clergy and laity over many issues, including prayer-book reform, Christian initiation, the ordination of women to the priesthood and episcopate, divorce, and the remarriage of divorced persons. None has split the world church, although it teetered over the ordination of women to the priesthood — some ecclesiastical provinces still ordain only male priests. But today the divisive issue of homosexuality is the outward and visible sign of something more. This issue is being used as the scapegoat for a serious internal power struggle for control of the Anglican Church between the protestant conservatives and the more progressive liberals. This battle for control really does threaten the unity of the Anglican Communion worldwide, and many informed observers predict a division will result. That being said, homosexuality is neither the first issue that the church has struggled with as society has evolved, nor will it be the last. Once it is resolved, at least in North America, another question will surely come along to rattle the *status quo* again.

What has changed the face of this most recent Anglican conflict are modern communications. Television and computers have allowed the debates within the church to reach everyone all over the world almost instantaneously. Add to that is the fact that the media thrive on conflict of any kind, and the stand for equality rights for gays and lesbians in the Diocese of New Westminster has been a good story, drawing global secular interest. Much of this journalism has focused on the internal clashes and has unfortunately failed to balance the reports of dissension with stories of the mission and ministry the church achieves on a daily basis. So, whereas the debate over the ordination of women was relatively slow to penetrate the population, the effect of the current controversy has been immediate and significant.

The Archbishop of Canterbury may "lead" the Anglican Church around the world, but he cannot, as the Pope can, tell his flock of seventy-seven million faithful or the ecclesiastical provinces and their dioceses what to do. Neither can he prescribe uniformity of doctrine or practice; Anglican dioceses are autonomous. Anglican bishops cannot interfere in another's diocese either. This has been the system since the 1500s, and the provinces of the Anglican Communion have lived together by agreeing to disagree — until now.

Significant controversy has dogged the episcopates of all four bishops chosen for *Sing a New Song*. All have faced severe opposition; one was involved in the only Anglican schism in Canadian history; two jeopardized their careers; and one was voted the sixth most important person of the twentieth century, one whose world view has transformed the wider society. To meet this quartet of sharply contrasting and fearless bishops, who fought for and won rights for women, aboriginals, blacks, and gays and lesbians, read on!

ART ONE

"The West Is Destined to Be Great and Powerful…"

**The Right Reverend George Hills,
First Bishop of British Columbia, 1859–92**

Imbued with the uncompromising values of Victorian England, classically educated, and single, the new bishop of British Columbia strode eagerly down the gangplank of his ship after a ten-week journey from England. It was 1860, and George Hills had arrived in Esquimalt on southern Vancouver Island in the northwest Pacific, a place as remote and cut off from civilization as London was its epicentre. Hills was on a mission to bring Christianity, Church of England–style, to the immigrants, gold miners, and First Nations peoples of the frontier.

In the mid-1800s the Church of England was aggressively promoting its version of the Gospel in all four corners of the British Empire. This active evangelism of the period, mostly funded by the laity in the Mother country, needed priests and lay missionaries, directed by bishops, to convert the "heathen," plant churches, and prevent other Christian denominations in the colonies from winning the competition for souls. Those in England who administered this endeavour selected candidates for colonial bishops (and other clergy) who had the same qualifications as those who led the structured, established dioceses, and churches in Britain. The church leaders lacked essential knowledge of the colonies to which they appointed staff, little of their geography, their populations and languages, and the living conditions with which their clergy had to contend. Many in the Mother church imagined that life in the colonies was similar to living in English villages, and tended to select genteel bishops who were more suited to the sophisticated, slow-paced cathedral closes of Britain. However, the new frontier needed tough outdoorsmen with an innate sense of survival, an unwavering faith, and a gift for languages and listening. The colonial bishops who travelled to the far-flung, untamed outposts to spread the Word were, for the most part, upper-class men with degrees in the Classics from Oxford and Cambridge. That many managed to adapt and flourish, as well as embrace their ministries with wisdom and compassion, is one of God's miracles. Life in remote regions was never easy, and sometimes it was life-threatening.

Like his selection committee, George Hills displayed ignorance about his destination when he remarked in London, on accepting his position, "May we be able to plant there no meagre seedling of our beloved Church, but . . . its full institutions . . . our scriptural formularies . . . our system of Church government."[1] These preconceived notions of the region for which he was ecclesiastically responsible were exposed on arrival. Isolated, uncivilized, rugged, and vast beyond an Englishman's imagining, his new diocese of British Columbia covered an area larger than France and Spain combined and included the Colony of Vancouver Island and the newer Colony of British Columbia on the mainland. But whatever the bishop must have felt, he did not run from the situation.

I have no wish to move from a position of interest

Five years before Hills set foot in Victoria, Vancouver Island had an estimated population of 744 non-Native immigrants, most of whom were under forty years of age. Scattered throughout the island and mainland were over thirty thousand First Nations' peoples who spoke eleven languages and many dialects.[2] In 1858, when the gold rush poured twenty-five thousand rough-and-ready prospectors through a small and unprepared Victoria on their way to the mainland, the governor of the Colony of Vancouver Island realized that immediate action was necessary to secure the mainland as both British and Church-of-England Christian. Sir James Douglas petitioned the Imperial government in London to act, and also alerted the Church to the need for clergy to minister to the influx of miners and settlers. The British government responded and turned the mainland into the Colony of British Columbia in 1858, appointing Douglas its governor, as well as that of Vancouver Island. Douglas promptly made the chief justice of Vancouver Island, Matthew Begbie, the new colony's chief justice too, thus wrapping up the authority of the British holdings in one neat package. The Church responded by determining the Pacific Northwest was ready for more clergy, as well as a bishop.

The wealthy Miss Angela Burdett-Coutts not only donated £15,000 as an episcopal endowment for the new see, but also identified the ideal candidate for the job. With encouragement from Hills's cousin, Sir Harry Verney,* she nominated Hills for the post. Hills protested the nomination: "I have no wish to move from a position of interest."[3] His reaction was not surprising, for taking up the post was indeed a risky career move. If the appointment failed, and he returned to England, Hills's episcopal career was over. Colonial bishops never served as bishops in the United Kingdom after serving overseas. The Church had been forced to take this action to reduce the rising number of episcopal resignations when bishops' pioneering spirits repeatedly faltered in the harsh realities of the frontier. But despite the obvious risks and the solicitous advice of colleagues, Hills accepted the offer. He was consecrated at Westminster Abbey as the first Bishop of British Columbia in February 1859, responsible for the Church of England in both colonies, Vancouver Island and British Columbia.

The Society for the Propagation of the Gospel (SPG) administered the endowment fund, and, with Burdett-Coutts as a member

---

* Sir Harry Verney served as a liaison between Hills and Burdett-Coutts after Hills took up his bishopric. Hills spent his honeymoon at the Verney estate, and the two men corresponded regularly until Hills retired in 1892.

of its board, Hills was acutely aware that continued funding rested on his performance in the new diocese, a realization that coloured some of his subsequent decisions. His relationship with his sponsor started off well, but was not to last. As all colonial bishops were expected to do, Hills spent the year after his consecration in England raising more funds for the diocese through his newly established Columbia Mission Fund. He also recruited two priests, who arrived in Victoria in the summer of 1859, well ahead of him. One was the Reverend R. J. Dundas, destined for a second parish in the Victoria area, and the other was the Reverend John Sheepshanks. The latter was surprisingly well suited for New Westminster in the new colony, then a small clearing among the huge fir trees on the banks of the Fraser River. Sheepshanks relished the hardships and the challenge of operating with no church, no stipend, and no lodging.

Despite his comfortable livings in England, George Hills was neither cowardly nor effete, but simply astonished by a land that barely registered on any map — and of which few of his acquaintance had even heard. He was a man who lived his responsibility — to God, to his sponsors, and to himself. Toughened by an unkind father and sensitized by his devoutly Christian mother, Hills would display an intense duty to his episcopate, extraordinary fortitude, as well as significant internal insecurities, throughout the thirty years he would devote to British Columbia.

Born in Egthorne, Kent, George Hills had a boyhood that was unhappy and filled with disappointments. Denied the usual education of an upper-middle-class family by his admiral father, Hills made do with the local school and universities that were considered second rate. But despite his unremarkable beginning in a society where breeding and "the old school tie" mattered so much, he made his mark in the church through hard work and adherence to duty, ending up as a canon* of Norwich Cathedral and the popular vicar of a large, prosperous parish in Great Yarmouth on the east coast of England. It was here, where he was contentedly established, that Burdett-Coutts found him.

By the time the SPG selected Hills for the remote diocese, he had matured into an energetic, orderly adult who was experienced in

---

* In England in the late 1800s, a canon was a member of a cathedral chapter who could participate in the selection of bishops.

urban parish work. Representative of his class and time, he genuine-ly believed he was called to transform the new colonies and their populations into a replica of British life, because he considered the Church of England and British society superior to any others. Tall at six feet four inches, slim, and good looking in his younger years, the new bishop was also conforming, mostly humourless, and not adept at judging character. His later portraits show an unsmiling man with thin, tight lips, deep-set eyes, bushy eyebrows, and receding hair that curled over his ears. Hills was always close-shaven, never growing a

The Right Reverend George Hills, Bishop of British Columbia, just after his consecration in England, 1859. (BC Archives A-01366)

beard or the mutton-chop whiskers that many men of the time adopted. His face looks closed, because Victorians rarely faced a camera with a smile.

While Hills was known to lack understanding and empathy for his peers, a deficiency that caused him much heartache later on, he certainly displayed compassion for the less fortunate. His contemporaries, however, believed this empathy stemmed more from his sense of duty than from his heart. Today we would describe the new bishop as lacking the common touch, but he was a typical Victorian bishop. Outsiders saw him as a cultured and scholarly man, because of his library of fifteen hundred books and his degrees, although others have disputed this impression. He was certainly an administrator of considerable skill and devotion, perhaps bordering on the compulsive. Those closest to him remembered Hills as a man unyielding in his opinions, who stood his ground when opposed, and his episcopal actions certainly confirm this trait. His uncompromising stands would provide sporadic fireworks during his term as bishop, some of which resulted in valuable outcomes — though one unfortunate incident would end in an antagonistic division within the Church of England on the Pacific Coast.

Revive the church spirit

George Hills arrived in his new land, along with his servants, on the Feast of the Epiphany 1860; he was met by the Reverend R. J. Dundas, and they chose to walk the three miles from Esquimalt to Victoria after Hills's disembarkation from the ship. The new bishop struggled through puddles well over his ankles, but was rewarded with his first glimpses of Indian villages. The pair slogged on into Victoria, "the rambunctious, muddy little settlement"[4] where Hills was to live and minister.

Hills's early impressions of Victoria and its citizens were understated in his diary, but meticulously described in his correspondence to his sponsor. His reaction to the living conditions, scenery, and people's attitudes penetrates every word. Hills's diary noted that Victoria was much more spread out than he expected. Translated, this meant it was not the established town he had envisaged. The

Victoria: A "muddy little settlement" when Hills arrived. (BC Archives G-6073)

town had no sidewalks or even boardwalks; its houses were built of wood,* and indeed Hills's first home was a small wood-frame building with few comforts. He liked the natural scenery, which had a wild and romantic beauty, but he found the governor of the two colonies, Sir James Douglas, stiff, defensive, and married to "a half caste."[5] Worse yet, the Church was "in a feeble state."[6]

Hills's first letter to the SPG, eight pages long and written four months after his arrival, shows he clearly recognized the strategic importance of the new colonies — they were the only British possession on the west coast of all the Americas, both north and south. He wrote about the land's attributes being "highly attractive to the . . . enterprise of our race."[7] Hills recorded surprise that the majority of Victoria's citizens were not British, but emigrants from California, who were a "strange mixture of all nations, most difficult to reach."[8] Many were unchurched and, early on, he deemed them worthy targets for evangelizing. From the beginning, Hills thought that the aboriginal Indians strongly desired "to be like the whites,"[9] imitating their worst vices to be sure, but also wanting to adopt the dress and manners of British society. The new bishop also complained of a severe lack of servants and the exorbitant price of goods and services, but he admitted that land was cheap.

The incumbent of Christ Church, the only Church of England church in Victoria, was the Reverend Edward Cridge, who had arrived in the colony five years before. He had mixed feelings upon the arrival of the bishop, for suddenly he had to take direction after

---

* In England, only the poor built their homes of wood — the middle and upper classes lived in brick or stone houses.

a long period of autonomy; indeed canon (ecclesiastical) law demanded his obedience to the new bishop. The two men were at opposite ends of the Anglican spectrum: Cridge was a low churchman with "ultra protestant views," and Hills was a moderate high churchman, who favoured the sacramental church in which the Eucharist was celebrated every Sunday as the central act of Christian worship. Both clerics held their positions with strong conviction, but the gulf that separated them was bridged by civility in their early relationship. At their first encounter, Hills found Cridge amiable and enthusiastic about any changes that he might want to make. And there were several of these changes the next day — Hills's first Sunday in the diocese.

The new bishop preached at the 11 a.m. Eucharist, which was celebrated at his request instead of Morning Prayer. Men comprised nearly 80 per cent of that first congregation, because non-Native women were few on the fringes of civilization. Hills saw "some coloured people" in the congregation and a "few Indians stood near the door."[10] Only a handful took communion. The bishop also recorded in his diary that the service at Christ Church and preaching in Esquimalt in the afternoon moved him greatly, but he was referring to his longing for his old parish in Yarmouth.

The bishop lost no time in shouldering the burden of increasing the profile of the Church of England in Victoria and beyond. On his fifth day in Victoria, Hills announced his intention to plant a new church, which caused surprise amongst the Christ Church parishioners, who felt it would dilute their congregation. Hills, however, was certain his plan would do the opposite, as well as clearly demonstrate his intent to "revive the church spirit"[11] of Victoria. Since an iron church that he had purchased in England was already on the high seas heading for the West Coast, and Hills had formed a committee on January 23 to handle its erection, it seems the laity's views were unlikely to sway his plans. By his eleventh day on the job, Hills was visiting the First Nations people (Songhees) in Esquimalt and checking to see how much they knew about Jesus and the Christian faith. Three weeks into his post, and he was pitching Church of England schools for the non-Native children to the chief justice to lessen the hold the Catholic missionaries had on education in his diocese. A few months later Hills's mission for the aboriginal people in Esquimalt had opened, and included a school and an ordained missionary, who also taught the children. Hills was nothing if not vigorous in his approach to his calling on the frontier.

As the Church of England bishop, Hills was automatically on the top rung of society in Victoria, dining frequently with the governor, who was reserved and sombre, the chief justice, who was gregarious and witty, and the commanding officers at the Royal Naval station. Quickly he found himself being consulted on myriad issues of importance. The bishop was well received by those with whom he dined and consulted — they thought him a definite asset. Not having to earn his social standing and being considered the local representative of God, Hills had immediate influence on the politics, moral tone, and law and order of the two colonies. The leaders of other Christian denominations present in Victoria did not enjoy the same position of authority — not even the Roman Catholic bishop. Hills understood his God-given entitlement and took full advantage of his unique situation.

Five weeks after stepping off the ship on Vancouver Island, the bishop had his first experience of the neighbouring colony. He took a steamer from Victoria up the Fraser River to New Westminster, the capital of the new Colony of British Columbia, which had expanded to a population of four hundred souls since Sheepshanks had arrived the previous summer. The steepness of the slopes, the dense forest with towering evergreens, overwhelmed the bishop, who was used to the rolling hills, neat fields, and oak trees of England. Despite the wilderness, however, he foresaw "a vast city [that] may one day pursue world wide commerce."[12] He fervently prayed that he would have a part in ensuring that it would start out Christian.

Pentecost (late May) saw Hills travelling again, heading upcountry on the mainland — a journey vastly different to the easy trips he had made by train around Britain while fundraising for his diocese. On his way, he again visited New Westminster and laid the foundation stone for Holy Trinity, later to become a cathedral, before boarding the boat that was to take him as far as Hope. Sheepshanks, the governor, and the chief justice accompanied him on the week-long voyage, with a stop at Fort Langley. From Hope, with its rough prospectors and lone missionary, Hills and his retinue pushed on by

The Reverend John Sheepshanks, 1860. (BC Archives F-05146)

canoe to Yale, where he was well received by another Church of England missionary, who asked for a church and a school. The bishop celebrated the Eucharist in a store with a congregation of forty, but only three communicants. Next, the men visited Spuzzum, Boston Bar, Lytton, and finally Lillooet. The bishop travelled on horseback and on foot for most of this section of his visit, dressed in his clericals despite soaring temperatures and swarms of mosquitoes, and never once let his stately manner slip. But one day, when he

Holy Trinity, New Westminster, in 1860, Sheepshank's parish church.
Note the small shed (L) which was the rectory. (DNW1-8)

Hills as he would have looked on his episcopal journeys through his diocese.
(BC Archives 52145)

could no longer tolerate Sheepshanks's cheerful whistling, the bishop told him that such behaviour was most "undignified."[13] Although Hills must have experienced considerable strain throughout his introduction to the Colony of British Columbia, being inexperienced in the wilderness and unaccustomed to lying on the ground wrapped in a blanket, he roughed it well enough. Much to his surprise, Hills wore out his clothes and a pair of new boots on this sixty-day, 826-mile, apostolic adventure.

The bishop's purpose was not only to acquaint himself with his diocese and to meet the clergy and missionaries who were already working in various places, but also to get a feel for the Christian needs of the aboriginals and miners from many nations. It was an eye-opening expedition for the Victorian bishop; Hills found life primitive even in the settlements. There were few clergy and no churches, hymnals, or prayer books. The roads were the barest of trails, distances great, and travel often hazardous — for example, the road from Boston Bar to Lytton was only ten inches wide in parts, with a vertical drop to the Fraser River on one side. The bishop remarked on the lack of women in the interior, but actually meant "white" women, for he simply did not count the many First Nations women he had met. In so doing, Hills demonstrated the prevailing attitude of Europeans to indigenous peoples: to him, they were on the outside of the religion and culture he was trying to establish, unless they adopted Victorian customs and Church of England Christianity.

Hills had difficulty communicating directly with the majority of his flock. Early in his episcopate, he could speak no First Nations' languages, Chinook (the trading patois), other European tongues, or Chinese, and had to rely on interpreters. He discovered in the bars and shacks he visited that most of the miners were not interested in God or were too busy surviving to have time for religious observances; many were unruly and anti-establishment types, there being no one in authority to restrain their behaviour. Hills also learned that the First Nations men and women had already met Jesus, through itinerant Roman Catholic priests, in a way he found inadequate and annoying. Hills's detailed notes do not record much, if anything, about the traditional spirituality of the First Nations. Likely, he never inquired about it, or, if he did, considered his findings were not important enough to document. Despite these absorbing experiences in the wilderness, Hills seemed more concerned by the low numbers taking Holy Communion than anything else, a clear indication of his doctrinal position.

Bishop Hills strove to firmly establish the Church of England in the two colonies as soon as possible. He had the iron church erected in north Victoria and consecrated it to St. John. He travelled regularly around Vancouver Island by hitching rides on Royal Navy gunboats

St. John's parish church, Victoria, known locally as the Iron Church, which Hills ordered from England, c. 1870. (Detail of BC Archives A-02788)

and on the mainland, evangelizing the miners and settlers as well as meeting his clergy. And always, everywhere, he endeavoured to convert the First Nations people before anyone else did. Within six months of arriving, Hills also founded a private school in Victoria for immigrants' sons, and, three months after that, another for girls, both endowed by Burdett-Coutts. All of these activities, Hills dutifully reported to his sponsors, the Society for the Propagation of the Gospel, who probably never truly grasped the challenges and hardships that their pioneering bishop endured.

After writing his first report to the sponsoring society in May 1860, Hills listed his achievements in his diary, as if to reassure himself that he was making progress. But underneath them, he also wrote, "I have had more vexations and troubles than in all my ministerial life before. . . . I have felt deeply how unequal I am to combat my difficulties and have seen cause to regret in consequence my acceptance of the sacred office I hold."[14] Even so, Hills did not mention returning permanently to England, at least in his diary, though perhaps he did consider it in his heart. Stoically, he wrote that he trusted everything to God and surrendered to his will. Then he carried on.

One of the vexations early in Hills's first year was the widespread discrimination against Blacks and the effect it had on Victoria's community. This is the first time we see him courting criticism and taking an unpopular stand in the face of fierce majority opposition.

I have had more vexations and troubles...

In 1858 a group of Blacks, seeking relief from the severe prejudice against them in California, visited Sir James Douglas, the governor, and inquired about immigration to the colony. Reverend Cridge warmly welcomed them on arrival, and Douglas actively encouraged their plans. He told them that they could buy land on Vancouver Island and, after seven years' residency, could become British citizens. Just before Hills stepped off the gangplank, four hundred Blacks had arrived in Victoria and many began worshipping in the Congregationalist Meeting House, which had two ministers and a large number of American worshippers. It did not take long before the Americans in that congregation objected and demanded a separate seating arrangement for the new immigrants. Emotions ran so high amongst the church members that they caused a bitter split in the congregation and between the Reverends William Clark and Matthew Macfie.

Hills kept a low profile on the issue during his first few weeks in Victoria, as he listened to the debate swirling through the population and as Macfie, the minister who supported segregation, opened a separate church. At the end of January, Hills's position became clear when Reverend William Clark, who was in favour of inclusion, called to talk it over. The bishop "thanked him for the stand he had made in respect of the coloured people."[15]

March saw Hills stepping into the fray more publicly; not so much because he chose to do so, but more because prominent citizens on both sides of the issue sought to influence him. His journal that month is full of entries about the subject, sometimes short but mostly lengthy, as he grappled with what he saw as a nasty injustice facing the baptized Blacks.

On visiting a couple from Christ Church on March 15, the bishop discovered that the wife was an American Episcopalian and her husband was English (later he would become the lieutenant-governor of the colony). Mrs. Trutch immediately brought up the "colour question," as Hills called it, making it clear that she opposed segregation in churches, as she believed all were equal in the sight of God. But Hills quickly learned that she was an exception to the prevailing attitude, and most Americans in Victoria chose not to attend Christ Church, because Blacks were not segregated in its congregation. The Trutches then regaled him with stories of Black slavery in the deep South and informed him that the wife of the Bishop of Oregon still owned slaves. Hills recorded, "Just the thought sickens me."[16] The new bishop's eyes were opening wider, and his heart began to ache for the Victoria Blacks, whom he believed would not be free "even on British soil."[17] Worse was to come, and it was to threaten his plans for the expansion of the Church of England in Victoria, as those in opposition declined to support that work financially.

But first Hills learned from a Black the details of the division in the Congregationalist church that resulted in the dismissal of the minister, Mr. Clark, who opposed segregation. Then Clark himself told the bishop how upset his community was at the events that took place after the Reverend Matthew Macfie took the largely American congregation away and set up a new church, funded from an American source. This left Mr. Clark running the original church that the Congregational British Colonial Society financed and to which they had appointed both ministers. When Clark appealed to this homeland society for a ruling, they told him to leave Victoria forthwith. Hills commented sadly that he thought exclusive principles would prevail, and then attempted to persuade Clark to consider being received into the more welcoming Church of England. He was unsuccessful.

The cruel situation escalated, infecting other institutions and other denominations. Immigrant citizens began asking for more segregation — parents of non-Native students attending the Roman Catholic school threatened to remove their children if they were not separated from the "coloured"* students. When the sisters opened a separate classroom, the "coloured" parents withdrew their children, disconcerting everyone involved. Hills saw this as an added incentive for the Church of England church to open a non-segregated school as soon as possible, a long-held desire of his, and he again informed the community that his church would never make any distinction. The battle lines were drawn and, by now, those who disagreed with the bishop, including the editor of one of the Victoria newspapers, began to ostracize him for his unwavering support of the Blacks and First Nations people. Hills was not deterred.

On March 23, a Black woman visited Hills. Mrs. Washington was a communicant at Christ Church, and the bishop came to admire her. On one of the rare occasions that colonial clergy stopped to listen — probably because she was Christian — Hills asked her questions and recorded all her responses in his diary. Her tears discomfited him when she spoke of the injustice done to Blacks. Hills encouraged her to cheer up, because the Church of England could be relied upon to ensure no discrimination would occur in their sphere of influence.

Three days later Hills had another visitation — this time from two Black men who came to services at Christ Church, though not by choice. They told the bishop they would prefer to attend the Congregationalist church but for the situation there, and were letting him know that they were also excluded from the YMCA and other organizations in Victoria. Hills exclaimed, "from whatever society [you] were excluded, I was excluded also, for I should belong to nothing where such unrighteous prejudices existed."[18] Then he inquired why the two men thought they were being treated this way. Perceptively, they told the bishop, "There is, deeply seated in human nature, an [inclination] to hate those you injure."[19]

Dinner with a visitor on Easter Saturday 1860 once again demonstrated to Hills the entrenched attitudes he was opposing. A New Yorker, whom he met on his journey to Victoria and considered worthy, discussed the "colour question" frankly after he had attended a service at Christ Church and found "coloured people sitting in all

---

* This term was used in this instance to refer to both Black and First Nations children.

parts of the church."[20] Mr. Caitlin told the bishop, "it was not intended they should be equal."[21] Hills carefully rebutted all the American's arguments, including that of the dangers of intermarriage, and sadly commented afterwards, "[his] objection was grounded not upon reason but upon a prejudice of caste."[22]

Hills continued to object with rising anger to the escalating discrimination, and began to take action. He had, by now, purchased the unused Congregationalist Meeting House for the diocese after Clark left town. He wrote at least one scathing letter about the issue to the British newspapers, indicting the Congregationalist minister Macfie who backed the discriminatory wishes of his white American congregation. Hills may have actually used the pulpit in support of the Blacks in Victoria, though it cannot be said with any certainty. There is one entry in his diary during that time, indicating that he delivered a sermon on "the scandal." The bishop's first report to his sponsors in London mentions the situation briefly and makes it clear that the Church of England was the "only religious body which has stood out for [Blacks'] equal rights, especially in the House of God."[23]

How did the Blacks and First Nations people see the bishop? One of Hills's priests wrote home in October 1860, "They perfectly worship the Bishop."[24] Small wonder, as he not only fervently believed and spoke for their equality, he willingly took the risk of society's alienation on their behalf at the very beginning of his episcopate.

Hills made his last entry on this issue in his diary on October 18, 1860, when Mr. Macfie paid a surprise visit to persuade him to "modify [his] opinion."[25] Apparently the Congregationalist minister took exception to some of the bishop's remarks about the prejudicial stand he took against Victoria's Blacks that were published in English newspapers. Macfie addressed the bishop at length, denying that he ever supported or practised segregation. Hills realized immediately that he was lying and sharply told Macfie that he had no one but himself to blame, for, after all, it was he who opened a new chapel to accommodate the members of his congregation who did not want Blacks integrated. The bishop believed that Macfie got what he deserved. He lost his reputation in England, if not in Victoria, because he followed the line of least resistance and expediency. Hills had no patience with such behaviour.

I did not dream of resting upon the state

In a region so far removed from its administrating government, the colonial leaders learned quickly that, if they requested advice from England, responses could take six months to return, by which time the problems had either evaporated or changed. Often these officials did not ask, but simply acted. The isolation meant that western leaders had few limitations imposed on their actions, consequently getting away with things that, had they been closer to centres of government, would never have been allowed. One excellent example of this phenomenon is the attempt of Sir James Douglas, governor of the two colonies, to interfere with and continue his control of the Christian churches.

Just before George Hills arrived, the governor had given Crown land and authorized public funds to build a Church of England church in Langley. The editor of the *Daily Colonist* alerted the Victoria citizens to the scheme and explained some of the dangers inherent in governments sponsoring religion. The editorial was enough to slow Sir James Douglas down and allow one of the Congregationalist ministers to step in and force him to abandon the scheme. But the issue was not buried; Douglas, keen to keep it alive, had revived it in a new format when the newly established Colony of British Columbia superseded the previous authority of the Hudson's Bay Company (HBC) in 1859.

Douglas was not only the governor of both colonies; he also retained his appointment as an official of the HBC. In 1855, in the latter capacity, he had contracted Reverend Edward Cridge as a HBC chaplain for a renewable five-year term. The company had provided Cridge with a house, land, and his stipend. In April 1860 the contract became due, and, although the HBC no longer had authority, Douglas as governor was still in a position to renew it. This meant that the state was about to provide Cridge's living. Enter the new bishop, who had just stepped off the boat!

Hills was horrified that any civic official, however senior, could be in a position to hire and fire ordained clergy, and even more shocked that the government was about to provide land for the Church. The bishop reacted swiftly and decisively. In an early sermon at Christ Church, he took an unequivocal stand, proclaiming "I did not dream of resting upon the state."[26] He demanded an immediate meeting with Douglas, and got it. During several more visits, Hills managed to persuade Douglas to change his mind, largely because his principle argument was that Cridge believed the property provided by the HBC belonged to him personally and not to the HBC, the Church, or the new diocese. Hills then transferred the property's ownership to a church board of trustees and negotiated a reduction in its size, effectively cutting out Cridge and the state. Additionally, he ensured the governor understood that only the bishop could license (hire and fire) Church of England clergy, clearly demonstrating that his episcopal authority superseded the governor's in all matters pertaining to the Church. It also meant that Cridge reported solely to the bishop of British Columbia, and no longer to the HBC and Douglas.

The major winner of the confrontation was Hills, or, more correctly, the Church. In a fundamental and important victory, the bishop's firm stance and immediate action ensured the Church's independence from the state. A minor winner was Douglas, who no longer had to control the disaffected Cridge. The losers were Cridge, who was left without the house and land that he believed he owned, and the relationship between the two men. The bishop noted afterwards in his diary, "[Cridge] thinks he is ill used."[27] Cridge lost no time in petitioning the bishop for compensation, but Hills refused to discuss the matter.

Douglas, having lost that battle, continued to try to win the war. He attempted to gain some control over the Christian churches in the two colonies under the guise of generosity. He summoned Hills to a meeting and announced he was making one-hundred-acre land grants to the four major Christian denominations in regions where there were enough people to justify building a church. Hills was infuriated again, and on two counts: first, that Douglas had tried once more to exert the power of the state upon the church when Hills thought he had backed off, and, second, because Douglas had delayed informing him about the grants until it was too late to stop them. But the board of the Columbia Mission Fund in London, which Hills had set up to help fund the diocese before he left, was less antagonistic over the grants, and wrote that denying state endowment would cause financial difficulties for the new diocese. Hills ignored their concerns, but the board was proved correct over the years.

When the small communities of Lillooet and Port Douglas (near Yale) showed interest in building Church of England churches, the governor had the temerity to offer each the grant, knowing full well the bishop's opposition. Hills immediately wrote to the church committees, offering to increase their diocesan funding if they refused the government aid. Lillooet's congregation could not resist the land grant and took it, whereas Port Douglas declined it — at least initially. Hills discovered, on meeting the governor again shortly afterwards, that the Port Douglas congregation had reversed their refusal, informing the governor that, if they still qualified for the grant, they would take it. In another twist, several months later, the members of the Lillooet committee changed their minds and declined theirs. Once more Hills made his opinion clear, preaching, "From the State we seek no exclusive privilege — we ask only for liberty, a fair field, and no favour."[28]

Other denominations were less independent, accepting the land grants with alacrity, and, although the bishop had no jurisdiction over their actions, he continued to oppose the scheme fervently. However, his church committees' vacillation over the land grants had a less harmful effect on their bishop's efforts with the governor than would be supposed. Eventually Hills's persistence was rewarded, and Douglas ceased offering enticements to the infant churches of British Columbia.

Children of the forest who dwell among the tall trees

Hills was intensely interested and involved with the spiritual state of the First Nations inhabitants, who outnumbered the non-Native settlers and miners. He visited the aboriginal settlements wherever he journeyed in his vast diocese, and stayed in the villages, often for several days, checking out the Natives' knowledge of Christianity and seeing for himself the effect that colonialization was having on their way of life. The Songhee villages in Esquimalt, which he had seen from a distance on the day he arrived, provided him with his first experiences. Later he met many First Nations people at Lytton and Lillooet during his long journeys into the mainland interior. Riding the Royal Navy's gunboats at their invitation, the bishop would also regularly drop in on the peoples of the coast of Vancouver Island, and he subsequently opened missions for several bands, which the SPG funded.

One such visit occurred in October 1860, when Hills sailed into Barkley Sound for the first time on HMS *Grappler*. He was greatly moved by the heart-stopping beauty of the coastline. Here he discovered the aboriginals spoke a different language to the tribes of the eastern side of Vancouver Island and were still free from European influence. "Drunkenness is hardly known amongst them,"[29] he reported in a letter to his Columbia Mission Fund board. Naval personnel told Hills that the Tseshaht nation had been seeking revenge for a chief whom the Songhees (from Esquimalt) had killed. When told that they must not take such action, because British law now prevailed and would avenge them, the Tseshaht replied that they could not put their faith in laws they knew nothing of, inferring they would apply their own remedy. The aboriginals also took the opportunity to complain that the white man had not provided teachers for them, as he had for neighbouring tribes, and that they remained illiterate. The bishop seized the chance to delve deeper into the tribe's situation while he was there, and what he learned led to him to ask for money from the Columbia Mission Fund to open a mission for them.

Grappler then steamed up the long inlet to Port Alberni, where a London shipping firm was establishing a lumber business. Forty Europeans were settling in, and the bishop immediately took two services for them in a store. A week later, Hills gathered the First Nations people in the same location and spoke to them about God, creation, Jesus, and heaven and hell. Apparently he used their language and addressed them as "Children of the forest who dwell among the tall trees."[30] A local settler remarked that the two chiefs present probably understood some of what Hills said to them. Presents were exchanged. Then three Tseshaht, a naval lieutenant, and Hills took a canoe trip to their village, which Hills described in vivid detail in his diary. He sent a copy of his entry to the Columbia Mission in November 1860:

> *We passed two small rivers: on either side were rich prairies and meadows, covered with grass, ready for herds of cattle. Varied trees bowed down upon the*

water. Noble Douglas pines, 150 or 200 feet, cedars, maples with the brightest yellow tints of [autumn], the nider, and a tree with leaves of deep crimson, lined the bank. Wild-fowl flew around in abundance — geese and ducks innumerable. The river literally swarmed with salmon. They swam against the canoe, they scrambled out of the way, they rushed up to shoal water, where they foundered about; the Indians struck them in the side, and knocked them on the head. I saw many caught or speared; their average boat load of salmon weighed each from fifteen to twenty-five pounds. The river is about one hundred yards wide. The gentle winding of the stream, its placid flow, with the noble trees and meadows, reminded us of the Thames between Richmond and Windsor.

After some time we came to the . . . village. We visited the lodges, which are square boarded houses, of roof and sides. The people are a fine race, but meanly clad; men and women all but naked, and very shy. They were somewhat alarmed, but, on the whole, pleased to see us. Great quantities of salmon were in all stages of preparation for winter use, some open and undergoing the process of smoking. The women were making oil, and cooking, and mat-making. They have no metal pot. Instead of boiling the pot over the fire, they have wooden boxes, the sides of which are sewn together. In them are placed the articles to be cooked, then water, then red-hot coals.[31]

Hills was moved to frustration and sadness during the smallpox epidemic of 1862 that decimated the aboriginals of British Columbia (some tribes like the Haida lost as many as 80 per cent of their people, but the average loss was about 30 per cent). He described the disease as "raging with violence" with "bodies cast out"[32] around Victoria. When he journeyed into the Cariboo that summer, Hills ran into a similar scene in Yale and wrote about the "importance [of giving] the Indian the benefit of vaccination."[33]

British Columbia, isolated by the Rockies, handled Indian land title differently from the rest of the country. Whereas the First Nations in the east continued to claim ownership of their land until they signed formal treaties with the governments, the B.C. government, after the Hudson's Bay Company's authority expired in 1859, claimed all land for the Crown. Joseph Trutch, a member of the B.C. legislature, speaking in 1864 on B.C. aboriginal policy, gives an idea of West Coast thinking on the subject: "The Indians have really no right to the lands they claim, nor are they of any actual value or utility to them, and I cannot see why they should . . . retain these lands to the prejudice of the general interest of the colony."[34]

In 1867, the British North America Act created Canada, giving the federal government responsibility for the aboriginal peoples and the provinces jurisdiction over lands and resources. A year later, a federal act passed that legalized the white man's efforts to "civilize" and assimilate the First Nations peoples by establishing small reserve lands that did not reflect their traditional tribal territories and by replacing their tribal governments with puppet band councils. Trutch would become responsible for squeezing the indigenous peoples of British Columbia into reserves and seizing their traditional lands.

The population of non-Natives in British Columbia had exploded since Hills arrived and, just after Confederation, equalled that of the aboriginal peoples. This significant white invasion into First Nations traditional territories had strained relations between the two. By the time the federal Indian laws extended to British Columbia in 1874, after the province joined Confederation, the provincial government awarded only 21,000 acres out of 218 million acres of land to the aboriginals, and the remnants of understanding between the two cultures disintegrated. The Nisga'a of the Nass Valley in northern British Columbia journeyed south to remonstrate with Trutch, who was now the lieutenant-governor of the province. He refused to meet them. The Earl of Dufferin, the governor general of Canada, publicly condemned British Columbia's land grab, and clergy and missionaries of various denominations, who had always supported the First Nations position, actively sought justice on their behalf. Two Methodist ministers became so vociferous that the B.C. government banned them from the subsequent land-claim hearings. Although Hills clearly supported indigenous peoples, he was consumed with an internal church matter at the time, and he did not record the events in his diary. However, he explained the injustice of the reserves and the heartache he felt over them in a speech he gave in England during one of his visits.

Church-funded residential schools for the education of First Nations children were another essential part of the plan to assimilate the aboriginals into Victorian culture and to squash their "heathen" practices. Early on, the churches and governments learned that day schools were ineffective in facilitating the assimilation. Students did not attend regularly because their tribes followed the game that provided their livelihoods and took their children with them; students continued to speak their Native language at home and at school; and boys and girls were still exposed to traditional spiritual practices and tribal ceremonies. Government and church leaders saw residential schools as the only solution to these problems. Some schools were already operating in British Columbia during Hills's episcopate, supported financially by the main Christian denominations through their mission societies. As a conforming product of his era, Hills would have supported the concept of residential schools, and may even have helped to fund them. The bishop certainly visited several on his later journeys around his diocese and conducted services for the students and staff. However, the schools Hills was so proud to start in Victoria were not for aboriginal children: the two he established were only for non-Native students whose parents could afford the fees; his mission schools in the Native villages served the aboriginal children. Roman Catholic nuns ran the Victoria school, founded in 1858 for First Nations children.

Early residential schools catered only to aboriginal boys, and it was not until the late 1870s, after Hills's huge diocese was divided into three, that similar schools opened for girls. The first school to accept both white immigrant and aboriginal students (an anomaly) was in Yale, in the newly created diocese of New Westminster. All Hallows in the West came into being in the mid-1880s through the efforts of Bishop Acton Sillitoe, who insisted that every girl had the right to be educated. Initially he had planned for separate schools, one for non-Native students and the other for aboriginal students. When funds fell short, however, Sillitoe combined them into one boarding school. The students learned together — except, when the non-Native students studied music and art, the aboriginal girls tackled household subjects and gardening. The immigrant families paid $15 per month for their sons and daughters to attend, and the Native children performed chores to cover their expenses, which inevitably led to the impression that the First Nation students were acting as servants. They got up an hour earlier than their non-Native peers to do cleaning chores, set the tables for lunch during recess, and spent the rest hour before dinner preparing vegetables. After ten years, the bishop reported equal academic results for both non-Native and aboriginal students. Soon after this, the immigrant parents demanded strict segregation of the students, and their wishes were implemented.

Before Hills retired, an amendment to the Indian Act in 1884 went even further. This law prohibited potlatches and other gatherings, ceremonies, including the raising of totem poles, and the wearing of traditional regalia, effectively annihilating aboriginal culture. Any Indian who engaged in these outlawed events could be jailed. This repressive law would not be repealed until 1951, when the oppression of the First Nations people began to ease a little.

Desperately . . . parochial

One year after Hills descended the gangplank to his new see, he was able to report to his Columbia Mission Fund board that his clergy had grown in number from one to fifteen, three churches had been built and their organizations regularized, he had undertaken several journeys to minister to the First Nations and miners in both colonies, had established two schools (for immigrants' students), and had founded and staffed an Indian mission and school in Esquimalt. The bishop was proud of these achievements in his first year, but the churches still had to be subsidized and money was needed to support an increase in clergy before there could be further expansion.* Hills made plans to return to England in 1863 to fundraise, the first of many visits "home" that were to punctuate his entire episcopate.

---

* Burdett-Coutts's endowment paid only the stipends of the bishop and archdeacons; monies for everything else in the diocese came from three mission societies, including the one that the bishop founded before he set sail.

Mary Hills, the bishop's wife, 1870. (BC Archives A-01368)

During that first visit to England, the bishop married Vice-Admiral Sir Richard King's daughter Mary. They honeymooned at the estate belonging to Sir Harry Verney, who had recommended Hills to Burdett-Coutts. Their marriage would not produce any children, but it seems to have been a happy and fulfilling relationship. Mary apparently idolized George and, for his part, Hills regularly mentions in his diaries how delighted he was to be married and what an asset Mary was to him and his ministry. She taught Sunday school, aided in Indian school work, and raised funds for the missions. Mary was also an avid gardener, and her efforts annually produced "one of the sights of Victoria."[35] Hills and Mary returned to England every three years or so for a year at a time to fundraise for his diocese and its missions to the First Nations, to report to Burdett-Coutts and the SPG, to renew acquaintances, and to enjoy the civilized society that they both missed. British Columbia in the late 1800s was still a cultural desert, according to the correspondence of the period, and life on the frontier without the refinements of culture was difficult to adapt to successfully. It was "desperately . . . parochial"[36] bemoaned the wife of the first bishop of New Westminster in 1880.

Only as an act of justice to the senior clergyman of the diocese

Deans (rectors) of cathedrals and their bishops commonly have variances of opinion, and sometimes downright disagreements, but few of these relationships break into open conflict, with subsequent lawsuits suits and division in the Church. When the rector of Christ Church, Edward Cridge, and the first bishop of British Columbia initially worked together, they did so politely, but with little connection or warmth. As the years progressed, evidence of increasing friction exists in both their papers, which flared into confrontation in 1872.

When Hills selected Christ Church as the cathedral of the Diocese of British Columbia in 1865, he named Cridge as dean, despite their clear disagreement on doctrinal matters. There is some evidence to suggest that Cridge promised to follow the rubrics (specific "stage directions") of the Church of England prayer book if he got the position. Even today Hills's reluctance to appoint Cridge shouts from the pages of one of his letters: he writes that he recognized Cridge as dean "only as an act of justice to the senior clergyman of the diocese."[37] Hills may have hoped this appointment would narrow the wide differences in their theologies and personalities; would ease his earlier denial of the house and land that Cridge believed were rightfully his and not the diocese's; and would allow Cridge to feel rewarded. Or perhaps the bishop simply had miscalculated the severity of the grudges that Cridge bore him because he failed to get to know him well enough.

Cridge did not much like the bishop either; the hostility between the two men was evident in his diaries too.[38] When Hills offered his dean the Archdeaconry of Vancouver in 1868, Cridge stubbornly refused the promotion, as he saw it as a means of getting rid of him. He may have been right.

Christ Church Cathedral was rebuilt after being destroyed by fire in 1869. The imposing edifice was more worthy of the title of cathedral, and it was a proud bishop who consecrated the new building on Thursday, December 5, 1872. The cathedral was packed, with all the

In 1874 Christ Church Cathedral stands on the hill after it was rebuilt following a fire; in the left foreground stands the Reformed Episcopal Church of Our Lord that Cridge established after Hills revoked his licence. (BC Archives A-04991)

local dignitaries and visiting clergy in attendance, and the Bishop of Oregon preached the sermon. At evensong that same evening, which Cridge conducted, every seat was taken.

All Cridge's unspoken resentment and unresolved issues, which had increasingly disaffected him since Hills had entered his world, exploded at the service. The Archdeacon of Vancouver, the Venerable William S. Reece, at the invitation of the dean, preached the sermon from St. Luke's Gospel, 24:52-53, "And they worshipped him, and returned to Jerusalem with great joy; and they were continually in the temple blessing God." Reece used this text to show mild support for the return of more sacramental worship in the Church of England. At the homily's conclusion, instead of announcing the closing hymn, Dean Cridge rose and protested "in an impassioned manner,"[39] flinging his arms about with agitation. In a voice he could scarcely control, the dean condemned the sermon,

> *My dearly beloved friends, it is with the greatest shame and humiliation that as a matter of conscience I feel it is my duty to say a few words to you before we part.*
>
> *As your pastor, after what we have just heard I feel it is my duty to raise up my voice in protest against it. . . . During the seventeen years that I have*

*officiated as your Pastor in this spot, this is the first
time Ritualism has been preached here; and I pray,
Almighty God, it may be the last. So far as I can prevent it, it shall be the last.*[40]

The congregation, sympathetic and willing to show it, applaud-
ed Cridge and stamped their feet. Some ladies hastily walked out,
including Hills's wife, who undoubtedly was unable to deal with
the tension crackling through the air. Another fainted. The clergy
shifted uneasily in their pews. Hills, stunned, conferred quietly with
the visiting bishop and managed to realize that this was not the
moment to intervene. The incident cast "a sad gloom"[41] over what
should have been a very happy day for the bishop. News of Cridge's
outburst roared through the community and provided sensational
newspaper headlines for several days; later letters to the editor
revealed strong lay support for Cridge's low-church practices. The
following Sunday, the bishop stood in his pulpit and preached tolerance to a nearly empty cathedral.

The causes of Cridge's startling explosion were far more complex
than a dean's resentment of his bishop, however much that was a
contributing factor. Indeed its genesis can be traced back to Henry
VIII's split with Rome and Elizabeth I's later commitment to a
national Church* within her kingdom that would eventually accept a
wide range of Christian theological belief, excepting those of the
most Papist or most fanatical Puritan doctrines. Her royal promise
heralded diversity of belief in Anglicanism, the scope of which produced centuries of tension and dissent. The diversity and dissent still
exist today — a truly double-edged legacy.

The move to Protestantism originating in the Reformation,
which was led by Luther and Calvin amongst others, got under way
in Europe in the sixteenth and seventeenth centuries in response to
the profligacy and corruption of the Roman church. The Puritans,
who followed Calvin, sought to purify the English church from with-

---

* While one of Elizabeth's motivations was political (national unity), other reformers in western Europe sought doctrinal change.

in by removing all hint of Roman Catholic influence that remained after Elizabeth's leniency. The most extreme Puritans relied solely on the Word (Scripture), forbade frivolity, opposed the sacraments and liturgy in favour of very simple worship, and denied the historic episcopate. Less severe forms of Protestant reform resulted in unadorned churches and clergy, a focus on the Word, the recognition of Church tradition, including bishops, and a rejection of the Catholic doctrine of transubstantiation.*

Following the restoration of the British monarchy in 1660 and the intellectual Enlightenment, the Church of England evolved into a more upper-class and educated defender of the "Anglican" *status quo*. These scholars and clerics sought to keep their church free from both the evangelical pietism prevalent in continental Europe and from Roman superstition while society gained more liberty after the strict rule of Oliver Cromwell and the Puritans.

English reformers of the eighteenth century capitalized on the poverty and pastoral neglect of the Church's less-fortunate parishioners, and another wave of change ran through the parishes of England. The Wesley brothers, for example, preached that everyone could approach their God directly, without the go-between of a priest, and this immediately struck a chord amongst the working classes. Wesley won large followings and, when unable to effect change from within, broke away from the Church of England in frustration. His Methodists strongly supported the primacy of the Word, de-emphasized the need for ritual, but also maintained baptism and the Eucharist. Those "Anglicans" that did not join the new movement, but leaned towards it, preferred a low-church approach to worship in their parish churches. They also believed that humankind was filled with sin but capable of redemption through a personal relationship with God, rather than through the sacraments. These "evangelicals" were a significant force in the Church of England from the late 1700s through the 1850s, though not the only one.

Intellectuals, who remained in the Church of England and were still influenced by the Enlightenment, gave rise to a group known as the broad church, which, although small in number and unorgan-

---

* The belief that the bread and wine changes into Christ's actual body and blood during the Eucharist.

ized, exerted considerable influence on the disorganized Church of the time. They are credited with keeping the low- and high-church adherents in the fold by widening the doctrines of the *via media* sufficiently to satisfy both factions. The high-church proponents, mostly scholarly divines in universities, also embraced a more liberal interpretation of the Scriptures, causing considerable upheaval when they published their position that the Bible was not to be taken as true in every detail. This, of course, flew directly in the face of the low-church supporters, who took the Bible more literally.

So the Church of England of the early- to mid-nineteenth century, while maintaining diversity in practice and belief, comprised a minority of scholars who favoured high-church practices and a majority of parish clergy who were low-church evangelicals (with a small "e"). The latter downplayed the Eucharist in favour of Morning Prayer and Evensong, and viewed other sacraments, except Holy Baptism, as simply symbolic and as playing little to no part in an individual's salvation. This was the postion of both Cridge when he sailed for Victoria to be chaplain for the Hudson's Bay Company and that of his sponsoring society.

When the Oxford Movement emerged in English universities in the mid-1800s, intent on restoring a high church, with much of the trappings that the evangelicals equated with popery, the low churchmen of the day reacted by forming the Evangelical movement (with a capital "E") to fight it. The moderates in this group did not want to abandon the sacraments or the apostolic succession, but rather wanted a less Catholic approach. Others were much more extreme, including Cridge. Before he left for Vancouver Island, he was a member of the Evangelical movement at the far end of the conservative spectrum — a strict Sabbatarian who condemned dancing, novels, and playing cards amongst "other works of the devil." He saw the Bible as the revealed word of God, true in the tiniest detail. Yes, Cridge was less of a Victorian evangelical and more of a Calvinist at heart.

The Oxford Movement, which George Hills leaned towards, did not support returning to the papal fold. They wanted a restoration of support for the apostolic succession and the re-establishment of the doctrines and the rituals of the early Church, including a more sacramental approach. Emotions ran high in both factions and often overflowed. This sorry state of affairs led to conflicts in the pulpit, Parliament, the courts, and even on the streets of England. These conflicts revolved around several key disagreements:

> **The authority of Scripture**: the Evangelical movement took the Bible literally and believed it was the sole reference on which to base their faith and practice; the Oxford Movement similarly upheld the Bible, but were less fundamental in their interpretation and declared that tradition also had its part to play, received, as it was, directly from the Apostles through the early Church fathers and succeeding bishops.
>
> **The apostolic succession**: some Evangelicals believed this to be contrary to Scripture, and that Church leaders were only necessary for administration, not for the provision of grace. The Oxford Movement held that bishops were the successors of the apostles, carried the tradition, and provided the authority of the Church.
>
> **The sacraments**: some Evangelicals believed that men and women could reach God and forgiveness through faith alone; others supported the Eucharist and baptism. However, they did oppose the view that baptism washed away sins in a way that seemed to infer almost supernatural powers to the officiator. The Oxford Movement considered the sacraments to be central to worship, especially the Eucharist, which should be celebrated every Sunday.
>
> **Ritual**: this was most high-profile difference — and undoubtedly also the stickiest. This issue was responsible for the riots of 1848 and prosecutions of high-church clergy. Ritualism did not become part of the doctrine of the Oxford Movement until the movement expanded from intellectuals into the parishes. Ritual included the ceremonies and external ornaments, such as vestments, flowers, crosses, and crucifixes, incense, etc., that had fallen into disuse in worship since the mid-1700s. The Evangelicals preached simplicity and were convinced the reintroduction of ornaments would result in a return to Rome. The Oxford Movement argued

that these practices and ornaments were not innovations, but had always been a part of the Church of England, for they were included in the Book of Common Prayer under the "Ornaments Rubric" from its first printing.

This doctrinal disagreement eventually caused a split in the Church of England. Evangelicals who could not accept the theological diversity in the Church broke away and established new churches — in England, the Free Church of England in 1844, and the Reformed Episcopal Church in the United States in 1873, both of which continue to draw members to this day, though not in large numbers.*

Thus at the time that Vancouver Island was being settled, the Church of England was divided into the low-church Evangelicals and high/broad church adherents. This division was mirrored in the young colony, brought from the "old country" by immigrants, clergy from both camps, and zealous lay missionaries. A common form of Church of England worship in the "new world" was low church. Evangelical clergy celebrated the Eucharist only at Christmas and Easter, Pentecost, and Michaelmas. They did not wear vestments, and crucifixes were hidden away. Cridge's Christ Church — and he thought of it as his — was no exception. Its congregation had grown up with Morning Prayer and was used to Cridge's very Protestant position, which taught a suspicion of and discomfort with any ritual that leaned towards high-church practices. But a higher church was gaining acceptance at the parish level in England, and Cridge, although he did not see it coming, was about to be caught by the tide.

The first bishop of British Columbia *and* his sponsor, the Society for the Propagation of the Gospel (SPG), were at the other end of the Anglican spectrum, supporting more ritual and sacramental worship. Although by no means an advanced ritualist or an Anglo-Catholic — he never wore vestments, for instance — Hills had been influenced in university and later by several leading clerics

---

* For example, in 2004 the Reformed Episcopal Church had 13,500 members in 137 parishes in the United States, fifty of which were established in the previous decade. In Canada, four parishes exist in British Columbia and five in Ontario.

who supported the broad church and the Oxford Movement. As he matured, he clarified and internalized his own position on the issues — for example, he definitely wished to reinstate the Eucharist as the central part of worship every Sunday. The battle lines were drawn.

Hills was severely shaken by the dean's outburst and the reaction of Christ Church Cathedral's congregation. A stickler for order and clerical correctness, the bishop believed he had to respond and be seen to respond to this violation of church law. In the days immediately following the incident, he wrote letters to Cridge, outlining how he had broken the canons (laws) of the Church and the laws of the state and asking for, at the very least, an expression of regret. Typical of the era and his character, Hills did not demand or even suggest a meeting; if he had, he might have been able to uncover and address Cridge's motives and defuse the situation. Instead the bishop mulled it over alone and predicted in his journal that he would not get an apology. He noted that, if one were not forthcoming, he would be forced to take severe action against his dean. When neither apology nor contrition were contained in Cridge's written reply, the bishop sent back a letter of censure,* the least he could do canonically in light of Cridge's obduracy. In fact, Hills would have been within his rights to suspend his dean forthwith, but that would have exacerbated rather than quelled the growing scandal at that stage.

Archdeacon Reece, on the other hand, cannot be regarded as anything but imprudent to preach as he did at such an important occasion — Anglicanism tolerates, then as now, a diversity of opinions and doctrines, and the pulpit is open to them all. Some chroniclers have speculated that Reece set out to deliberately antagonize Cridge, but there is little to suggest that was true, especially considering that it was the dean who had extended the invitation to Reece to preach at the first Evensong in the newly consecrated cathedral.

However Cridge did not have to do what he did. He had several alternatives within church law open to him that provided appropriate ways to object to another's sermon. First, he could have brought Reece's action to the attention of his bishop (formally, in

---

* See Appendix for an excerpt.

writing), who then would have dealt with it according to ecclesiastical law. Second, Cridge was within his rights to preach a rebuttal at the earliest opportunity after Reece had left the colony, in this case probably the next Sunday. Third, he could have published his views. But Cridge chose to ignore these more measured ways of refuting Reece's sermon and instead boiled over in front of the visiting archdeacon and his bishop, distressing the congregation and clergy. In so doing, Cridge had breached both canon and statute law; he had committed a serious ecclesiastical offence, violating Canon 53, which forbids public opposition between clergy. This canon means priests must not criticize and cast doubt on the doctrine of another preacher in their presence. Cridge had also disturbed the order of public worship, a civil offence called "brawling."

Although Hills's diary then fell silent on the issue for the next seven months, his Synodal Notes and Memo Books[42] show he was busy seeking legal advice, boning up on ecclesiastical law, and worrying. What effect would all this have on Burdett-Coutts and the SPG? Would the diocese continue to receive funding? Would the congregation return? How far should he take the censure? Cridge initially believed that the bishop would eventually rescind the censure, and Hills no doubt prayed that he had tamed his unruly dean.

Hills took no more direct action with Cridge during these months. Cridge avoided meeting Hills, because he had removed himself to the outskirts of Victoria, where he and those that left the cathedral with him, including Governor Douglas, worshipped at Craigflower. The Reverend Gribell filled in as rector of the cathedral until 1875, while Cridge was still listed as dean and was paid his stipend. The next rector of Christ Church, the Reverend Sam Gilson, appointed in October 1876, lasted three months and was not replaced until 1878 by the Reverend George Mason. When Mason left the province in 1881, the bishop would assume the position of rector himself for the remainder of his episcopacy in British Columbia.

The next open confrontation between the bishop and his dean occurred in July 1873, when Hills announced in writing that his annual visitation to the cathedral would take place at a specified date and time. Cridge promptly replied that he could not attend. When the bishop arrived at the appointed hour, he found the cathedral doors locked against him and one warden hovering outside. After unsuccessfully trying to locate the sexton, Hills rearranged the visitation for 4:00 p.m. the next day and wrote to Cridge that his attendance was mandatory. Cridge showed up with bad grace, refused to hand over the parish registers, and asked permission to speak to the bishop. The dean announced he would obey the laws of the Church, but not his bishop, accusing Hills of creating a division in the cathedral's congregation over the matter of the first diocesan synod. Cridge then handed Hills a written statement that said, amongst other things, that "The bishop had arbitrarily and unjustly violated the just and scriptural purity of the Church in connection with Christ Church during the past year."[43] Both Cridge and the wardens then repeatedly asked Hills under what authority he was demanding to visit the cathedral. The bishop declined to answer. Hills then asked for clarification of the dean's statement, but Cridge would not respond to his questions. He did promise to let Hills know the specifics behind his statement, but, despite several reminders from the bishop, he never did.

The dean then took the first of many steps that prevented any hope of reconciliation and demonstrated that his major grievance was built on a false assumption: Cridge believed the bishop had actually censured him for his low-church principles, not for his canonical disobedience. Cridge gathered his supporters, who included over 75 per cent of Christ Church's congregation, to a meeting at which he "publicly repudiated the bishop's censure and admonition,"[44] calling it "arbitrary, unjust, and a great wrong."[45] He also accused the bishop of subverting the faith and leading the Church towards papal domination. Cridge then had the full text of this address published in Victoria's newspapers. Although his teaching and the publication of his low-church beliefs were not contravening any law, he certainly stood the risk of being sued for defamation of character over his words about the bishop. Cridge had thrown down the gauntlet.

For six months after the abortive visitation to the cathedral in July 1873, a lengthy correspondence, which is preserved, ensued between the bishop and his dean. Hills answered all of Cridge's objections, until he finally ran out of patience and wrote in December that he was not going to continue the unprofitable exercise. Sadly, the written debate between the two men then continued in public: Hills in the pulpit and Cridge rebutting the bishop's sermons in the newspapers. However, Cridge had the upper hand from the outset, and those in support of him increased daily. For example, he was publicly praised for his "manly stand. . . for Protestant principles," and the bishop was criticized as being "domineering [and] unpopular."[46]

If Cridge was not doing much to redeem himself in the eyes of his bishop, Hills was not moving to resolve the intensifying crisis either. Clearly, the bishop was reluctant to take the issue of canonical disobedience further, as that meant an ecclesiastical tribunal and he shrank from further confrontation almost as much as Cridge enjoyed provoking it. Instead, Hills sought refuge in late 1873 in planning his first synod to manage the diocese's affairs, an aspiration that he had deferred because there were too few parishes and laity in the early years of his episcopate.

This dream did not prove easy to accomplish, as the vengeful dean switched his focus to sabotaging Hills's every move towards the first synod. Cridge's next salvo was to write to two newspapers in January 1874 objecting to the synod, which prompted Hills to comment privately, "A very unhappy and ill-tempered effusion — the burden of it being dislike apparently to any authority, especially that of the episcopate."[47] In other shots, Cridge publicly accused Hills of selling religious favours, stacked the elections for the cathedral parish council with anti-synod nominees, wrote scurrilous letters to wardens protesting the plan, and continued preaching about Hills's unjust oppression of him. Cridge's actions served to heighten public interest in the synod and to force churchgoers to take sides. The bishop resorted to explaining from the pulpit why a synod was required.

When the bishop's call for the election of lay delegates came in February 1874, the dean reacted once again, and called his supporters together. At considerable length, he again presented his reasons to them for opposing the first synod. In short, Cridge feared that, in differing from his bishop regarding doctrine, he would be at the mercy of Hills, who had divine authority over his clergy. The dean also held the view that bishops should only administer the church and not trespass upon religious freedom of the clergy in the diocese. Cridge was afraid that the first synod would irrevocably establish this authority, and that religious freedom would be perpetually endangered.[48] Cridge was wrong on all counts. Hills was, in fact, in a far more autocratic position without a synod, being able to act independently without reference to his clergy and laity.

Clearly, a more serious division was developing, not only between the bishop and his dean, but within the cathedral's congregation as well. The annual vestry meeting, which elected the wardens and cathedral committee for the next year, was held two days after the election of lay synod delegates from Christ Church and showed just how deeply the rift was wounding the community of faith. Members of the outgoing committee were firmly pro-synod, and included such local luminaries as Lieutenant-Governor Trutch and several judges. However, Cridge rallied his supporters to attend the meeting, and they outvoted Hills's team, taking control and prompting resignations from the three pro-synod members who were left on the committee. Now the newly elected committee could freely and loudly protest against the lay representation of the cathedral for the first synod, the plans for the first synod, and Hills himself. From then on Cridge's tactics changed. The cathedral committee, with Cridge's guidance, began to question the legal basis of the synod and the bishop's right to convene it, stating that only Queen Victoria could do so. As precedents for convening synods without the monarch's assent existed in many other colonial dioceses, the dean and committee appealed to the Archbishop of Canterbury for a ruling. They were sadly disappointed when the primate took Hills's side in the conflict. The dean's incitement of the opposition to the synod, his refusal to allow his bishop to inspect his cathedral, and his initial explosion at the consecration of the new Christ Church all demonstrated his challenge to episcopal authority and his disobedience. Rather than lessening, Cridge's defiance was escalating.

After months of Cridge's perverse behaviour, Lieutenant-Governor Trutch and other leading citizens of Victoria, who strongly believed it must be stopped, began to pressure the bishop to sort out the mess once and for all. Trutch even threatened to leave the cathedral's congregation, as it had "lost its sacred character,"[49] if Hills did not take action. As Cridge's vindictiveness grew, Hills's ability to remain detached lessened. By July 1874, eighteen months after the initial incident, the rift between the two men of God had widened to a chasm that was unlikely to be bridged. The bishop sent one more letter offering Cridge a last opportunity to apologize, and then took the case to ecclesiastical tribunal in September 1874 and later to civil court.

Who was this man who obstructed his bishop with such rancour? How was he able to convince most of the cathedral's congregation to leave with him? What precipitated his risky behaviour? Was it a belief that he had been passed over for bishop? Or was it simply their difference in theology? Was he rational or paranoid, perhaps even delusional? Opinions of the day ran the full range.

Edward Cridge, born in 1817, was the academically gifted son of a Devon schoolmaster and a mother who died when he was still young. Encouraged by his father, he later went to Cambridge, where he earned a B.A. Early on, Cridge showed his talent for and love of teaching, as well as his compassion for the needy, when he energeti-

The Reverend Edward Cridge, 1855, the year he arrived in Victoria as chaplain to the Hudson's Bay Company. (BC Archives A-01205)

cally fundraised for the victims of the great Irish famine. He was also a musician of note, playing the cello well enough to perform regularly. Five years after his priesting in 1849, Cridge was offered the position of chaplain-schoolmaster for the Hudson's Bay Company in Fort Victoria, and he welcomed the opportunity to practise his dual calling. Galvanized by the chance he had been given, he also promptly proposed to and married his childhood sweetheart in the two weeks between accepting the post and setting sail on the eight-month voyage around Cape Horn.

At thirty-eight, Cridge was a man of vigour and robust health, who enjoyed long, daily walks or a game of tennis and was confident in his intellect and his myriad abilities. He could read Latin and some Greek, excelled at mathematics, and knew the Scriptures inside out. He never hesitated to speak his mind, even then. Larger than life, of medium build, and energetic, Cridge had a warmth that drew people to him. In 1855, he and his wife, Mary, accepted without complaint the hardships of life in a primitive town of barely two hundred souls that had no transportation or modern conveniences. A vast improvement on the previous two HBC chaplains, who whined frequently, Cridge quickly became known for his compassion and his dedication to preaching and teaching the Gospel. He worked relentlessly, leading services everywhere for everyone — on ships, in Nanaimo, anywhere a congregation could be seated — giving of himself tirelessly to the new frontier. A prominent citizen was moved to comment that he was one of the best and most conscientious men living.[50] Soon Cridge earned the title of "father of the Church in the colony."[51] For several years, he remained the only non–Roman Catholic ordained minister on Vancouver Island and the mainland, and he enjoyed the autonomy and his growing importance.

The Council of Vancouver Island quickly recognized Cridge as someone with solid experience in teaching and appointed him to a committee reporting on the three public schools already established in Victoria, Craigflower, and Nanaimo. The subsequent report demonstrated his avid support of free education for all, and especially for female and First Nations children. Soon Cridge was named Superintendent of Education and Inspector of Schools, an honorary position that he held until 1865. He did not neglect the sick either, and later was instrumental in founding what would become the Royal Jubilee Hospital, the first hospital north of San Francisco and west of Winnipeg.

Within a year of his arrival, the first church in Victoria was built on a hill overlooking the town and, with great pride, Cridge took possession of Victoria District Church, which he named Christ Church after his former parish in London. Wooden and typical of many colonial churches, the building served the rapidly growing population for thirteen years before it burned to the ground and was replaced by a more imposing edifice that became the cathedral.

The lack of a bishop was soon felt in the developing colony, because, without one, new churches could not be consecrated and no confirmations or ordinations could take place. It was the Gold Rush of 1858 that precipitated action on this front, and overwhelmed Cridge's capacity to minister. Many expected that he would be named the first bishop of British Columbia.

A good friend of the governor of Vancouver Island, Cridge backed Douglas's request to the Church of England leaders for ministerial help with the growing flock by asking the evangelical low-church Colonial and Continental Church Society for more clergy. Although it was in direct response to Cridge's appeal that the Reverend William B. Crickmer arrived to help a few months later, a bishop came as well. The latter was of a higher class, and more of the high-church variety. . .

Hence we have a portrait of a man who worked ceaselessly for God, who was devout, very Protestant in his background and theology, a man who was loved and held in high esteem by most Victorians, and one who could genuinely take credit for the growth of the church and schools on Vancouver Island. Perhaps most importantly, he was the Church of England's man of God, who got there *ahead of the bishop*. Likely, Hills's appointment discomfited Cridge from the outset. The bishop, stiff and aloof, may have been unconscious of the feelings of a colleague who had successfully led the Church of England in the Colony of Vancouver Island for five years and who suddenly must have felt that he was reverting to the status of a curate.

Cridge was on a mission, one he had been on for most of his life in holy orders. He was convinced that the doctrines of the high church were harmful and must be stamped out. When his antagonism overflowed after Reece's sermon in the cathedral, the dean conceivably could have backed off and apologized, but by doing so he would have felt he was abandoning his dearly held principles. Cridge's conscience could not allow him to follow that path, so he dug himself in deeper and deeper with every move he made and sealed his own fate. It was a recipe for disaster, given the inflexibility of the bishop.

On August 27, 1874, Cridge received his summons to appear before his bishop to answer for his actions, along with eighteen articles that detailed the case against him. The trial commenced in ecclesiastical court on September 10, when "things alleged, charged and propounded"[52] against the dean were examined. Hills presided, accompanied by "assessors" — two of whom were clergy and two were county court judges — who would judge the case. The prosecutor was Mr. J. McCreight, QC, under instruction from the bishop's registrar. Cridge represented himself, supported only by the churchwardens of Christ Church Cathedral and one member of the church committee, which led to some procedural challenges.

Hills opened the remarkable proceedings with a few words, and the four charges against the dean were read:

- that Mr. Cridge had offended against the laws ecclesiastical;
- that he had refused to acknowledge the bishop's authority;
- that he had neglected to comply with the bishop's lawful requests; and,
- that he had obstructed the bishop in the performance of his episcopal office and functions. [53]

The prosecution developed the charges using the eighteen articles, which had accompanied the summons served on Cridge, and detailed Hills's objections. First came Cridge's attack on Reece's sermon; second was the meeting called by the dean in March 1873, at which he had denounced the bishop's censure and had later published his address; third was Cridge's disparagement of the episcopacy; and fourth was his refusal to receive the bishop's visitation at the cathedral in July, at which Cridge had read a statement that was insulting and accused the bishop of secession from the Church of England. The case for the prosecution revolved around Cridge's violations of canon and state law and his defiance of the bishop's authority.

The dean's trial lasted four days, and several witnesses were called, myriad documents were read into the proceedings, and the fifty letters written between the two clerics were entered into evidence. Few citizens observed the trial for the first two days.

Cridge had presented no written defence prior to the trial and refused to answer questions in court. Instead, while denying the

Hills, at the time of the trials in the mid-1870s. (BC Archives A-01365)

charges against him, he vigorously protested the validity of the court and its right to judge him in several long extemporaneous speeches. The dean also complained at length about his inability to prepare, given such a short time (six months), asked for an adjournment, and pleaded for the court to sit only one day a week, so he could get on with his ministry. The prosecutor quickly quashed Cridge's assertions that the court had no validity, saying that he would not have made them had he been acquainted with the law as it applied to the church in the colonies. His request for more time was roundly denied, but Cridge kept nagging for adjournments throughout the prosecution's opening on the first day. On the second day, Mr. McCreight continued to lay out the case in great detail, using the correspondence between the bishop and the dean, letters to the newspapers, and other evidence to demonstrate Cridge's waywardness and defiance. When offered the chance to cross-examine witnesses, the dean refused, again citing the invalidity of the court. Cridge did not attend the third day, pleading church duties, while the prosecution continued, with the bishop on the witness stand.

On the last day of the proceedings, a large crowd of Cridge's supporters attended. The prosecution was about to sum up, but allowed the dean to deliver a protest to the court. Everyone listened to the dean explain his refusal to participate in the proceedings in a carefully composed speech: "I believe the bishop to be personally disqualified by any authority of Her Majesty to try this case by reason of his having denied the Queen's supremacy, and thus [he has] virtually seceded from the Church of England."[54] This statement brought a ripple of applause from those gathered in the public gallery. Then Cridge walked out, and most of the public left with him. The rest of the day was taken up with the prosecution's summation, which McCreight concluded by saying, "Something must be done to compel [Cridge] to submit to the authority of the church."[55]

The assessors considered the evidence for nearly twelve hours and found sixteen of the eighteen articles proven, including Cridge's obstinate disobedience to the lawful authority of his bishop. Their report also expressed a hope that "in administering this necessary discipline the past faithful labours of Mr. Cridge may be recognized to mitigate . . . the force of any judgment." [56] Hills agreed with the sentiment, "there is no intention or wish on my part to remove Mr.

Cridge permanently from Christ Church. It will rest with himself, not with me, whether he be moved from the parish or not."[57]

When the Bishop of British Columbia rose to deliver the dean's suspension on September 18, he was well aware that he had little public support for what he was about to do. Standing before the ecclesiastical court, he looked uncomfortable. The bishop faced a room packed with members of the press and the dean's supporters, about eighty all told, but no dean. As Hills revoked Cridge's licence as a minister in the Church of England and suspended him until he might be willing to submit to episcopal authority, the courtroom filled with hissing, groaning, and yelling from an angry crowd. Hills wrote "about half a dozen . . . tried to get up a disturbance."[58] Then the bishop announced that Cridge would be offered a subsistence allowance during the suspension, which clearly indicated that the door was still open to reconciliation. Afterwards, outside the courtroom, three cheers for Cridge reverberated down the street and many shouted, "God bless him!"[59]

Later that day, Hills took up his pen and wrote:

> *This has been a most painful and sad affair. Sad is it that instead of union in fighting against sin, we should be thus divided. It was thought better to conduct the proceeding in the openest way — but I doubt whether this is advisable under the circumstances of a rapid and unprincipled press, unhappy elements in disposition amongst the people and our impotency to control an assembly, or the press. . . . There is necessarily a great deal of feeling. The absence of Church teaching in the two Churches of the town for so long, the novelty of the sight of a Church Court coupled with a continuous detraction of the Episcopal Office which has been carried on by Mr. and Mrs. Cridge for some time past in connection with the Synod movement, and only likely to keep alive an unintelligent excitement.*[60]

The anger, lack of understanding, and vilification of the bishop did not end there. The ecclesiastical trial might have been concluded, but the crisis and expression of opinion were not. The Victoria newspaper editorials quickly pilloried the bishop. One wrote that, although he was never liked or respected, he was now hated and should resign. Another opined that he would have made a better lawyer. After Hills dismissed his dean, he informed the wardens of Christ Church Cathedral that they must take full control of the church property and announced that he would officiate at the services on the following Sunday. Unbeknownst to the bishop, the wardens had already written to Cridge, assuring him of their sympathy in the crisis and of their plan to fundraise to cover his legal expenses, and asking him to continue to take the services at Christ Church. Cridge exacerbated this awkward development by writing to Hills and telling him the suspension was not effective in civil law.[61] In other words, he would not go.

Once this state of affairs became known, most of the populace turned up for the morning service on the following Sunday in anticipation of a public clash. The dean, occupying his normal reading desk, waited for the appointed time to begin. All at once a shiver went through the congregation as it heard the bishop leave his house. Then a sigh of relief accompanied the sound of Hills's carriage driving past on its way to St. Paul's in Esquimalt. A battle might have been won in the courtroom, but a duel was still being fought.

The bishop's heart was heavy as he drove past his cathedral — he might have avoided a nasty confrontation, but he had lost much face. Cridge had succeeded once more in defying his authority and that of the Church. In fact, he continued to preside and preach in the cathedral, to occupy the dean's house provided by the diocese, and to marry couples (perhaps illegally). Hills wrote nothing in his diary about his situation.

The bishop appreciated that he had to take the conflict one step further. He needed to have the secular Supreme Court of British Columbia determine what was "lawful authority," and, if it was his, to provide an injunction that would dispatch Cridge once and for all. The registrar of the diocese, on the instruction of Hills, inquired of Cridge if he was willing to have the question decided "on a case to be stated as agreed upon by consent of both sides."[62] The case the bishop and dean agreed upon was probably one decided earlier in South Africa — and off they went to court again.

In mid-October 1874, Chief Justice Matthew B. Begbie, known to be a severe judge, sat in judgement on the case for three days. Previously friendly with Cridge, Begbie had fallen out with the dean in 1872 over his deliberate overspending on the cathedral reconstruction after the fire. The chief justice thought Cridge's plan to cover the financial shortfall with missionary funds from England was dishonest and, being involved with the building committee, promptly disassociated himself from the dean's impropriety. Oddly enough, after this Begbie sent Cridge a cheque for the building fund.

Begbie listened as the prosecution presented all Cridge's previous offences and his latest, which was ministering without a licence. Then the judge heard the argument that the bishop was legally justified in revoking the dean's licence and that the prosecution would prove the bishop's authority. Once that was achieved, the prosecution wanted to have the sentence of the ecclesiastical court upheld.

This time Cridge attended court and had a lawyer. His defence rested on the premise that the bishop had no right to revoke the dean's licence or to lay charges against him. Defence counsel offered spirited arguments, amongst which he claimed that English ecclesiastical law did not extend to British Columbia; by convening the first synod, Hills had opposed royal supremacy and was thus excommunicated, so he could not suspend the dean; and because Cridge's oath of obedience to his bishop did not contain explicit examples of unacceptable behaviour, it was null and void. Begbie gave the two parties time on the second morning to try to settle their differences — but it was to no avail. After that, the defence counsel irritated Begbie as he went round and round his arguments repeatedly. In the end, Begbie exclaimed that Cridge's position was untenable.

At the conclusion of the evidence, the judge remarked that the heart of the dispute lay in what constituted the bishop's lawful authority and provided one last opportunity for Cridge to apologize by letter to the bishop by adjourning the court until the next morning. Cridge did write a letter that night, but the bishop and the judge, on reading it before the court reconvened on the third day, felt it contained insufficient contrition and no promise that he would change his ways in future.

Then the judge wrapped up the proceedings. He clarified the question of a colonial bishop's authority in his judgement, using several legal precedents, especially similar cases in South Africa. He established the validity of the previous ecclesiastical court and the authority of the bishop over the dean. Begbie eloquently shattered Cridge's defence and upheld the previous decision of the ecclesiastical tribunal that was "better . . . than [Cridge] would have expected to find"[63] in British Columbia. Regarding the key point about Hills convening a synod when he should not, the judge destroyed Cridge's reliance on Canon 12 by stating that it did not apply to members of the Church of England. Then Begbie dealt with the issue of Cridge disobeying the decision of the ecclesiastical court by continuing to act as a clergyman at Christ Church. The judge noted that recourse in this event was only available in state courts of law, where the case was now being heard. This situation had arisen because the issuance of the bishop's Letters Patent, three years after representative government had been established in the colony, failed to provide Hills with *coercive* ecclesiastical or civil jurisdiction within the colony. For the Bishop of British Columbia to have such powers required the new legislature to pass an act and, as it had not, only a ruling from the Supreme Court could put into effect Hills's sentence to suspend the dean and rescind his licence.

With all that said, Begbie noted with some astonishment that Cridge had never denied his offences but indeed had gloried in them. He was also surprised that the bishop had not sought redress sooner, and praised his forbearance. The judge's written judgement concluded, "that the findings were true, and that the sentences and whole judgment [of the tribunal] reasonable and appropriate enough to the offence. It is therefore just that it should be carried out."[64] Begbie ruled that the terms of the injunction meant that the revocation of Cridge's licence was in effect until such time he apologized or another court ruled otherwise. Thus was Cridge restrained from preaching and officiating as a clergyman of the Church of England. On his way to England soon after the case ended, Begbie mailed a letter and a cheque[65] to Cridge to help defray his court costs, adding a reference from Deuteronomy 14: 26.*

---

* Spend the money for whatever you wish – oxen, sheep, wine, strong drink, or whatever you desire. And you shall eat there in the presence of the LORD your God, your and your household rejoicing together. (New Revised Standard Version)

The following Sunday, the citizens of Victoria and the diminished congregation of the cathedral again held their breath as they waited to see if Cridge would disobey the court order and defiantly appear to take the morning service as he had after the tribunal. This time Cridge blinked, not Hills, and he went off to preside at a service for a large congregation of his supporters. Just before Morning Prayer commenced in the cathedral that day, men and boys stripped the pews of the hymnals, prayer books, and hassocks belonging to the pew holders who had chosen to follow Cridge. In Christ Church, Hills's chaplain preached to twenty-five congregants.

Cridge made no attempt to regain his licence, despite pleas that he do so from leading citizens. Seven months later, in April 1875, the case went before the Assize Court to make the injunction permanent and to prevent the former dean from benefiting further from his former position. Up until then Cridge had still been living in the parsonage reserved for the incumbent rector of Christ Church Cathedral and receiving a small stipend. Neither Cridge nor his counsel attended the court hearing — by then Cridge had accepted the futility of continuing to oppose Bishop Hills and gone his own way. In Begbie's absence in England, Justice J. Hamilton Gray made the injunction permanent and Cridge responsible for legal costs of $1,400, saying Cridge was acting under "a delusion as to his own position."[66] A wealthy supporter sent a substantial cheque to pay most of these costs, because Cridge could not, and again it was none other than Begbie. The chief justice, in his accompanying letter, expressed his sadness and regret over the outcome of the whole affair.[67] Notably the former dean touched neither a cent of the defence fund raised by the cathedral committee for his legal expenses nor cashed the second of the two Begbie cheques.*

After Begbie had ruled against him and before the injunction was made permanent, Cridge lost no time in informing Christ Church's wardens and church committee that he was considering joining the newly organized Reformed Episcopal Church, so that he could continue to serve his God and minister to the needy. The war-

---

* In the mid-1960s, Cridge's descendents still had the second of Begbie's cheques in their possession, uncashed.

dens and all the church committee members, who had resigned their positions at the cathedral, joined Cridge, and together they called a meeting of supporters.

On October 29, 1874, this meeting was attended by 75 per cent of the cathedral's congregation. Speaking proudly and eloquently, Cridge encouraged everyone to follow him to the Reformed Episcopal Church and start a new church. Several resolutions were carried later that evening, including:

- that the congregation of Christ Church organize themselves into a church affiliated with the Free Episcopal Church of England, and the Reformed Episcopal Church of Canada and of the United States;
- that Cridge be asked to be their pastor;
- that Cridge open communications with Bishop Cummins of the Reformed Episcopal Church in the United States to prepare for the admission of this new congregation into the communion; and,
- that Cridge order two hundred copies of their prayer book.

Needless to say, Cridge accepted the position of pastor. Ironically, the following Sunday, November 1, 1874, Cridge preached in the room where the ecclesiastical tribunal had taken place. He drew 400 people to Hills's 150 at two services. Amongst Cridge's flock that day were the wardens and entire church committee from the cathedral, most of the choir, the organist, and the Sunday School superintendent and teachers, as well as Douglas, the former governor of the colony.

Hills stoically continued his episcopal duties and took most of the cathedral services himself. Within the week of Begbie's judgement, the vestry (cathedral's congregation) had elected new wardens and a church committee, both of which rapidly became functional. The prosecutor at the ecclesiastical trial and the lieutenant-governor of the colony both served the new administration.

Only occasionally had the bishop revealed his reactions and feelings to the protracted controversy. Hills did not open his heart in his diary, and the entries are mostly factual, giving little indication of any inner turmoil. When others involved in the unpleasant case dined with the bishop and his wife, Hills referred to their conversations on the topic but provided few details. But once in a while, Hills's words provided glimpses of his irritation. When one of his own clergy chose to back Cridge, Hills complained, "and now he sides with the [dean]!"[68] He was also still angered by the newspapers' "pernicious abuse"[69] meted out to him throughout the two-year crisis. On detailing the case in the Supreme Court, the diary more than once records the bishop's pleasure that the judge agreed with his handling of the tribunal on almost every point and that he did so in a fair and just manner. This validation meant a great deal to Hills and he commented that he was "thankful for this as it justifies my conduct throughout."[70] His first mention of the s-word came on the Sunday after Begbie brought down his judgement. Hills predicted a "grievous schism,"[71] with hundreds following Cridge and causing bitter division in Victoria's society and families. The bishop was deeply saddened at the prospect, but could not see how it could be avoided unless Cridge recanted and proved his loyalty to the Church of England and to him.

On November 20, 1874, Cridge heard that the Reformed Episcopal Church in the United States had made him presbyter of the new church in Victoria. The prayer books arrived shortly afterwards. In March 1875, Cridge formally applied for his congregation's admission to that denomination, and heard that the application had been accepted in April, around the time that the permanent injunction was brought down. A month later, he was elected missionary bishop with jurisdiction of the Pacific region (the colonies of British Columbia and Vancouver Island, plus Alaska), because the council of the Reformed Episcopal Church felt that the isolation on the Northwest Coast warranted the authority to ordain and confirm. But Cridge was not consecrated until a year later in Ottawa, due to the difficulty of getting sufficient bishops to Victoria. This denomination did not believe in the apostolic succession and divine order but, rather, appointed bishops for a desirable form of Church administration. The former governor of the colony, Sir James Douglas, donated land to enable Cridge's congregation to build a church, and later provided an organ for it, which is still in use today. The new church, finished in late 1875 and consecrated in January 1876, was called The

Cridge around the time of the ecclesiastic tribunal. (BC Archives A-01203)

Lord's Church initially and later, through common usage, became known as the Church of Our Lord. The Church of England was intolerant of Cridge's new affiliation, stating that it was "plainly hostile to the Church of England," [72] because it weakened the Church's influence, reduced its congregations, and declared Anglican doctrine to be mingled with error.

Cridge's Church of Our Lord is largely unchanged today.
(Julie H. Ferguson)

At Christ Church Cathedral, after the new cathedral committee had settled in and tempers cooled down, plans for the synod moved forward. With harmony restored and no further opposition from Cridge, Hills proudly presided at the first synod of the Diocese of British Columbia in December 1875. Although Hills repeatedly complained to his sponsors of insufficient clergy and funds — on one occasion in the mid-1860s, he had used several thousand pounds of his own money — by the time of the schism he was able to report that the diocese had thirty parishes, twenty-five churches, twelve clergy (including three deacons), 450 regular communicants, and 3,500 church members out of a total population of 60,000 settlers and First Nations people.

Yet, despite these statistics, Hills never fully recovered — both as a man and as a bishop — from the personal harm done by Cridge's trial and departure. For ten years afterwards, he took no part in public functions in Victoria apart from his diocesan obligations, and he cringed at any mention of the affair until he died. One observer remembered that he suffered cruelly.[73] Financial support from the Society for the Propagation of the Gospel and other fundraising schemes, which had been decreasing before the controversy, dropped alarmingly after it. Although Hills was assiduous in his pursuit of money to provide for his diocese, the SPG board increasingly alienated him and couched their curt refusals to increase funding in officialese. Hills's plans for mission expansions had to be shelved, and those that were established were either cut back or suspended. Casualties included the missions in the Cariboo and in Esquimalt, and the lack of money for converting the many interested First Nations peoples saddened the bishop deeply.

In 1879, the Church of England divided the Diocese of British Columbia into three: the southern half of the mainland became the Diocese of New Westminster and the northern half, the Diocese of Caledonia. All that Hills had left was Vancouver Island. By 1881, the SPG had withdrawn all support for his Diocese of British Columbia but was generously funding the new diocese of New Westminster, which must have been difficult for Hills to bear, though perhaps understandable. The Columbia Mission fund that he had set up in 1859 continued to provide some funds and clergy, but they were never enough. Canada's governor general, the Marquis of Lorne, sympathetic to the diocese's financial plight, took up the cause with the Archbishop of Canterbury and got nowhere. There is no doubt that Hills was personally discriminated against in the matter of funding from Britain, and that this stemmed from his conflict with Cridge and Cridge's ultimate separation from the Church of England. The bishop's letters to friends showed his bitterness over how the SPG had treated him and the effect reduced funds would have on the growing colony. Never one to shirk his duty, Hills attempted once more to turn the tide with SPG in person in 1884, only to be soundly rejected with a terse five-line written refusal.

Nobleness of character and Christian courtesy

By 1885, Hills was in poor health with high blood pressure, and his physician recommended giving up all work; he did not. When Mary, his wife, had a stroke in 1887 and died a year later, Hills was distraught, and wanted to retire immediately, but his clergy persuaded him to continue. The aging bishop spent 1888 in England, grieving the loss of his wife, visiting old friends, and attending the 1888 Lambeth Conference. He returned to the Pacific Coast in 1889, rested and refreshed but less motivated. By now Hills was a tall, but broad, courtly old man, who could still preach in clear, ringing tones, and carried "on his shoulders the care and responsibility of a struggling missionary church."[74] His remaining years as bishop in Victoria were quiet, and he gratefully retired in 1892 to England. By then his original diocese boasted eighty-four clergy, over twenty churches and parsonages, four mission chapels, and several schools. Hills had also personally baptized over five hundred First Nations peoples. This amazing productivity in a land of extreme hardship — and while surrounded by severe animosity — bore testament to Hills's astonishing resilience, faith, and his stoic attention to duty.

Hills suffered a severe stroke soon after he reached England, but recovered sufficiently to take on the parish of Parham in Suffolk in 1894. This living was offered to him by the Bishop of Norwich, who was none other than John Sheepshanks — Hills's first priest in New Westminster in 1860. Rural and pleasant, the peaceful country parish suited Hills in his final year; he found himself both comfortable and appreciated at last. When he died in 1895 at seventy-eight, Hills was laid to rest in Parham's churchyard.

Colleagues' eulogies were kind to Hills. Dundas, who met him the day he first strode off the ship in Victoria and who became rector of the iron church, remembered his "energy, indomitable courage,

Hills late in his episcopate. (BC Archives A-01364)

and strong faith."[75] Dundas also wrote later, "The whole controversy between the Bishop and the Dean, and the litigation to which it gave rise, brought out in a very striking way the Bishop's nobleness of character and Christian courtesy." Hills's first appointee, Sheepshanks of Holy Trinity in New Westminster, spoke of Hills's "fortitude in bearing physical and mental evil, his wonderful patience, his sense of justice."[76] Everyone agreed that he had been a good and faithful servant.

However, embittered feelings persisted in the colony for several decades after Hills died, which permanently stained his reputation and prolonged the deleterious effects of the division in Victoria. One casualty of the acrimony was a biography of Hills,[77] commissioned in 1909 to mark the fiftieth anniversary of his consecration, which was never published, because Hills's successor was reluctant to risk reopening the wounds caused by the schism. The angst lasted in Victoria until the deaths of those involved eliminated memories on both sides.

The schism resulted from a clash of ideologies and class differences that were perhaps inevitable given the era, the isolation of the Pacific Coast, and those involved. Poured into that mix were two personalities convinced of their moral rectitude. Cridge's obstinacy and Hills's unbending attitude only added to an already impossible situation. Other ingredients included Cridge's abhorrence of high-church doctrine and his determination to act on his conscience and Hills's acute sense of episcopal duty and determination to go by the book. If there had been any hope of reconciliation at the beginning, the archival documents fail to reveal it.

The bishop himself had not been close to his flock. Addressed as "My Lord," aloof and austere, Hills never achieved an affectionate bond with the people or empathy with his clergy. His wife, who might have been a catalyst for connection, was disliked in the colony. Adding to his natural distance, Hills was often completely absent, either touring his diocese or fundraising for it in England. Cridge as HBC chaplain and later as dean, by contrast, had married almost everyone, baptized all their children, and buried the majority of citizens who died in Victoria.* The former dean was well liked and admired long before Hills arrived, and had much to his credit, improving life on the frontier by establishing schools, an orphanage, and a hospital. All of Cridge's accomplishments and his closeness to many in Victoria influenced the citizens in his favour, including Chief Justice Begbie. Although many parishioners acknowledged that the bishop was legally justified in his actions, they still left the cathedral congregation. Most who defected did so because they were low-church sympathizers and had been in the colony longer than Hills.

---

* In the fifteen years since Hills had been in Victoria, Cridge had baptized 339, married 112, and buried 262 people; Hills had baptized 23 whites, married 15, and buried 1, though for bishops lesser numbers are not unusual.

From the beginning, Hills frequently preached at Christ Church, but Cridge, as dean and rector, continued to arrange and conduct services. The style of worship therefore did not change significantly with the bishop's arrival and remained low church in character. Although no evidence exists to suggest Hills either preached ritualism or practised its doctrines in the cathedral — he never made the sign of the cross or wore vestments — Cridge and others regarded the bishop as a threat. Cridge's repeated assertions that the congregation was endangered by high-church doctrine, which he considered heresy, and the pro-Cridge bias of the local newspapers, ensured the cathedral congregation was suspicious of Hills's motives.

Cridge was more a Calvinist than a Victorian Evangelical in his drive to "purify" the church. He would probably have found it increasingly difficult to minister within the Church of England as the Pacific frontier moved to a more progressive social order and a more liberal "Anglican" attitude. Cridge's exit to the Reformed Episcopal Church suited him; his consecration as bishop justified all that he had done and provided him with the stature he sought. Cridge lived until he was ninety-six, revered by his congregation at the Church of Our Lord, who still remember him today.

The first Bishop of British Columbia sacrificed himself to bring Christianity, in the style of Victorian England, to one of the most remote parts of the British Empire, and he succeeded with little support, either from people or financially, from 1872 onward. The unpublished biography summed up the effects of the controversy: "It is so sad to think what a noble work these two men united could have done, and what sad havoc was wrought in the Church by the wretched division." The author also noted that, "some good came out of the evil; discipline was established, the Synod was formally brought into being and met for the first time."[78]

Hills wrote many times of the potential of the West Coast of North America and especially of British Columbia. Early on, he recognized the possibilities in the vast natural harbour of Vancouver and the navigable rivers of the coast and, when he added to them the approaching trans-continental railroad, he foresaw the development of cosmopolitan cities that would support international trade of immense proportions. He understood the value of British Columbia's's natural resources immediately, and later he foresaw the waves of immigration that would carry out the expansion. Hills wrote, "The west . . . is destined to be great and powerful."[79]

An effigy commemorates Hills in the present Christ Church Cathedral, Victoria, B.C. (DNW5-A.15)

PART TWO

"Our Old Models of God Are Dead Indeed"[80]

The Most Reverend T. David Somerville
Sixth Bishop of New Westminster, 1971–1980
Seventh Metropolitan of British Columbia and Yukon, 1975–1980

Gentleman, quiet radical, rebel[81] are some of the words that have been used in the public domain to portray the sixth bishop of New Westminster and seventh metropolitan of British Columbia and Yukon. In reality, he has more to him than that — more layers, more colour. When he retired, this extraordinary archbishop left a legacy of transformation that still pervades the diocese and irrevocably changed the Anglican Church in Canada.

Already a legend to the Church and cherished by everyone who knows him, T. David Somerville reached ninety years of age in November 2005, with sixty-six years of ordained ministry behind him. He has seen more changes in his lifetime than most — from horse-drawn carts to space travel, from the telegraph to cell phones, from pianos in the parlour to television and the Internet — and he has embraced them all. Ordained in 1939, Somerville-the-priest lived through war, the turbulent sixties, flower power, the rise of women's lib, and the "coming out" of gays and lesbians later in the century. A priest always ahead of his time, Somerville understood the need others had to push the envelope, often pushing it himself. This attitude endeared him to the restless inside and outside the church, whose often-youthful rebellion he found energizing; it also mightily discomfited several of his clerical colleagues.

Somerville's unofficial logo must surely be a great blue heron or crane; paintings, photos, and small sculptures of these birds are scattered throughout the apartment he shares with his wife, Frances. Why? He has the longest neck and legs people have ever seen. He once described himself as so tall and thin that he could "hide behind a telegraph pole."[82] Nowadays the retired archbishop may be slightly stooped, but his mind remains nimble and inquiring. Somerville's broad grin and mischievous laughter are never far away, and neither are his hugs. Somerville meets even first-time visitors with his arms wide open, then wraps them tightly around the guest while cheerfully saying, "Welcome! You must be. . . . Come on in and meet Frances. Oh! Call me David, everyone does." He is talkative too, and knows it: "I'm a bit like a jukebox. Put a coin in my mouth and I'll talk non-stop for you!"[83]

Colleagues and friends who treasure Somerville shed more light on the man and priest. Unanimously, they mention his gentle and compassionate nature, his mischievousness, and his impeccable manners. Others are captured by his humility and strength. Those who watched him as archbishop remember his gritty determination, coupled with his non-anxious presence.

David Somerville the Renaissance man is also known for his eclectic taste in activities that have little to do with his calling. While still agile enough, he was a keen amateur botanist, rambling through the countryside hunting for specimens to add to his collection. He is a Joycean, passionately fond of the classic books by Dubliner James Joyce and his contemporaries. In his younger days, when his voice was strong and trained, he loved to sing lieder, German songs with piano accompaniment. Somerville has always driven a Mercedes, appreciating their fine engineering and reliability. In a less secular era, he was a radio broadcaster, discussing music and literature, as well as leading morning devotions — before television took a universal hold on home entertainment.

Somerville's knack of showing his genuine interest in everyone has influenced his relationships throughout his years. He listens intently, quickly identifies the heart of the conversation, and then responds in the other person's terms, often with humour and always with a twinkle in his eye. But he is no pushover; Somerville will firmly correct misconceptions or charmingly disagree with you, giving an apt explanation. He challenges without alienating, according to Michael Ingham, the current diocesan bishop, "causing people to stop and think, or rethink, without diminishing them in any way."[84]

Somerville's voice has a song in it, and he is naturally articulate. He has never written down one of the thousand or more sermons he has delivered during his years of ministry. Instead, Somerville thinks about his sermons ahead of time, works out mentally what he wants to say, and simply gets up and says it. "I'm not just waffling. I really have a message and I always use humour."[85] A recent sermon focused on angels, and Somerville began by telling the congregation that he believed in angels but had "great difficulty with their feathers, a sort of anatomic impossibility."[86] Laughter echoed round the cathedral.

"A tradition of utter service"

Somerville is a B.C. boy, born in Ashcroft. He lived with his parents in Lytton in the hot, dry interior of the province until his father, Thomas, a police officer, died prematurely in the influenza epidemic of 1918. His mother, drained from nursing him, gave birth to a stillborn son soon afterwards. With nothing left to hold them in Canada and nearly penniless, the young David and his mother, Martha, journeyed to England to care for his ailing grandmother. They stayed for three years, and David remembers little of the parish church in Ilfracombe, Devon. But he does remember walking out of his first Sunday-school session and never returning. Plymouth Brethren friends of Martha, distressed that David was not attending Sunday school, decided to take him to theirs. All went well until the leader would not allow the newcomer to join in the game the others were playing, concerning Joseph and his brothers. David was so incensed at his exclusion that he left and walked home. The manner of his leaving was quiet and without fuss, showing early the strength beneath his gentle exterior. Afterwards, he always stayed in their pew with his mother throughout the service. When his grandmother died in 1922, Martha and David, now aged seven and frail after undulant fever, returned to Canada, using a small legacy from his grandmother. They settled in Salmon Arm, renewing their contact with friends in Lytton. The countryside around his new home inspired David with his life-long love of nature.

David Somerville, about seven, in Salmon Arm after his return to Canada from England, May 1923. (Somerville collection)

David and his mother were very close — she was the first in a series of individuals who provided a strong formative influence on the maturing boy. Martha was Irish, and had a commanding presence. She lived her life with conviction and activity, filling their home with good books and the sound of music on a wind-up gramophone. Martha never remarried, and worked so she could provide the best for her son. In 1929, when she believed the school in Salmon Arm could not provide for David's increasing academic needs, she took a risk in the Depression years and uprooted them so he could attend Grade 9 onward in a high school in Vancouver. Martha rented a boarding house on arrival to support them both, and David took on a paper route and other odd jobs. He also discovered the joys of a well-stocked public library, and never again went short of books to read. David quickly became a top student at King George High School.

The move to Vancouver set in motion other events that changed the boy's life. Mother and son joined the congregation of St. Paul's in the West End. Canon Harold King, who was its rector, prepared David for confirmation and Archbishop Adam de Pencier confirmed him. It was also at St. Paul's that Somerville received his call to the priesthood when he was seventeen years old.

In adolescence, Somerville was certainly drawn to spiritual matters, but had actively questioned the faith he was born into, and admitted that, for a short while, he favoured Buddhism. In Grade 13, when he was seriously considering medicine as a career, he attended a Lenten mission at St. Paul's, conducted by the Reverend Wilberforce Cooper from the Anglo-Catholic parish of St. James' in Vancouver's Downtown East Side. Cooper demonstrated a kind of devotion for other people and for God that the teenager had not encountered before. A few Sundays later, during a service, Somerville received a strong call to the priesthood, which he discussed with Canon King. Not overly surprised by it, and discerning that it was a real call, Somerville immediately changed course to pursue his vocation. In the "dirty thirties," money was limited for university education for most, but in the Somerville family, it was non-existent. The principal of the Anglican Theological College at the University of British Columbia, impressed on meeting Somerville, arranged for bursaries to get him through his studies and employed him as a college caretaker during the summer vacations. Somerville earned his B.A. in 1937, and then completed two years of theological study.

Somerville did not enjoy his theological training much. He found the early lectures incomprehensible, which was mildly distressing, but enjoyed Church history. He now began to attend St. James' regularly for spiritual nourishment and for the high mass. He "managed to survive"[87] at ATC, where division still persisted between high-church Anglo-Catholics and low-church evangelicals and the Eucharist was not always celebrated at the main service on Sundays. Somerville earned his Licentiate in Theology in 1939. Archbishop Adam de Pencier, who had confirmed him, ordained him deacon on April 30, 1939, and, a year later, priest. After an enjoyable year as a deacon, learning the "trade" in the affluent parish of St. Mary's Kerrisdale, the new priest was sent to Princeton, B.C., in the fall of 1940, just after the shock of Dunkirk.

The desperate evacuation of the British Expeditionary Force from the beaches of northern France changed attitudes to the war, and Canadians joined the armed forces in a flood. Although priests were exempt from military service, many clergy signed up too, and served for the duration. Somerville's bishop advised him that he should not do so, that the time was not right for him. He felt Somerville, then only twenty-four, needed to get his first solo parish experience under his belt before he considered volunteering to minister to the troops. Somerville thought about it and agreed.

So Somerville found himself in a remote area of the Pacific province, inland from Hope. "It was not a bit like leafy Kerrisdale!"[88] he recalled, and the roads were unpaved. Martha joined her son in the small house the parish provided. The driving conditions were hazardous at all times of the year, and the old car he had inherited from the previous incumbent was wheezing its last. Somerville supplemented his minuscule stipend, which wouldn't stretch to the repeated car maintenance and repairs, by moonlighting at the post office sorting mail three nights a week. His new bishop, the Right Reverend Sir Francis C. C. Heathcote,* understood the problem, and occasionally slipped him extra money from the discretionary fund to keep the

---

* The Right Reverend Sir Francis C. C. Heathcote had succeeded de Pencier on his retirement at the end of 1940.

Somerville in Princeton while at his first parish, c.1940. (Somerville collection)

young priest afloat. Somerville was on the road much of the time; early on Sundays he would start with a morning service in Princeton, then drive to Hedley for 10 a.m. service; afternoons were spent in Copper Mountain or Allenby, and then he would race back to Princeton in time to take an evening service.

Somerville showed his innovational approach to ministry early. He brought the dramatic arts and music appreciation to the parish, not only to meet the interest expressed by the isolated parishioners, but also to develop their sense of community. The young priest regularly treated the boys' club to his passion for botany and birding with the help of the library in Victoria, which supplied the materials and donated the shipping costs. Despite the rigours of the parish, Somerville also enjoyed ministering to the miners up and down the Similkameen Valley; when he took services at the Nickel Plate Mine in winter the road was impassable and he was transported six thousand feet up the mountain in an ore bucket. Most importantly, however, he was learning to be a self-reliant parish priest.

Somerville with his mother, Martha, in Sardis, c. 1947.
(Somerville collection)

Archbishop Sir Francis Heathcote liberated Somerville after five years and assigned him to a parish in the Fraser Valley just after the end of the Second World War. The green and lush dairy-farming country was a welcome change from the isolated community in the mountains, and he spent five very different years as the incumbent of St. John's, Sardis, with responsibility for St. Peter's, Rosedale. The well-established community had the church deeply embedded into their everyday life, which Somerville found encouraging after the difficulty in focusing the Similkameen population on things spiritual. This parish also provided him with a more active social life than he had had in Princeton. He enjoyed being close enough to Vancouver to take voice lessons to develop his glorious singing voice — Somerville won his category in the first local music festival he entered. The large rectory garden in Sardis provided him an opportunity to grub around in the earth and grow vegetables and flowers and relax. Somerville also began broadcasting at the local radio station, foreshadowing an important ministry that would take off when he returned to Vancouver.

After the Sardis parish, a reassignment in 1949 delivered Somerville back to Father Cooper, the priest who had taught the Lenten mission at St. Paul's that had led to his vocation. Cooper had asked for Somerville twice, and Heathcote had turned him down initially, leaving the thirty-three-year-old caught in the middle. When Somerville had ten years' parish experience, the bishop of New Westminster finally relented. Somerville rejoiced in the opportunity, despite warnings from Heathcote that he would be labelled as an Anglo-Catholic and "never get anywhere."[89] With anticipation, Somerville packed up his belongings, and in 1949 moved into the clergy house of St. James' in Vancouver with the two much older priests, Cooper and Father Whitehead.

Somerville calls this period "his golden age," and he imagined he would stay at St. James' forever; this was his natural home and comfort zone. Father Cooper was the other major influence in Somerville's life, second only to Martha, who encouraged his calling as a teenager, taught him how to pray privately, and heard his first confession. He had a magnetic personality and continued to guide his protégé at St. James'. Somerville later recognized that Cooper became both his spiritual and surrogate father, as well as mentor.

St James', amid the "outcasts" of Vancouver, was liberal in its point of view, with a strong sense of ritual. Somerville's eleven years there followed "a tradition of utter service" in an atmosphere of "loving, evangelical catholicism."[90] Somerville appreciated the deeply devotional and sacramental atmosphere and the way of life that imitated the life of Christ. He was still single, and it suited him to live monastically, while sharing the parish work with the more experienced priests. "[St. James'] was very much alive," he recalls, and filled with much laughter and fun, immense amounts of praying, and lots of hard work. St. James' provided an oasis of intense inspiration, erudition, and deepening faith for Somerville as he ministered to the poor and disadvantaged, to youth, to the elderly, and to the drunks of skid row. After Somerville had joined the team, Cooper soon nicknamed him the "midnight son,"[91] because of his evening expeditions and late arrivals home, long after the older priests had fallen exhausted into bed.

Somerville when rector of St. James', Vancouver, c. 1955. (Somerville collection)

When Cooper and Whitehead retired, Somerville became rector of St. James' in 1952 and got into the habit of climbing the bell tower and looking out "like a gargoyle"[92] over the parish rooftops while reflecting on the best approach to ministry. The parish was unique, a collection of groups that did not mingle much. It comprised three different congregations in the fifties — drifters, locals who lived within the parish boundaries, and Anglicans from all over the Lower Mainland, who attended St. James' for its spirituality and Anglo-Catholic worship. Somerville's high-altitude reflections led him to conclude that one purpose of the parish was "to draw these groups into a helping relationship with one another,"[93] and he devised a way to do it. To the credit of the more well-heeled parishioners, everyone agreed to give it a try. Somerville picked a Sunday afternoon when the congregation would visit every house around St. James' and find out what the residents needed. He exhorted his helpers not to accept a drink or get into an argument during their visits.

Somerville did not participate in the visitations, because he knew, from his own pastoral visits, what the results would be. Most of those living nearby were impecunious male pensioners who lived without many necessities and needed low-rent housing. The parishioners returned after several hours, brimming over with their experiences: 90 per cent had had a wonderful time and learned their neighbours were delighted that St. James' was interested in them. After discussion and prayer, the parishioners started the Old Age Pensioners' Society (an acceptable name in those days). Soon a room below the church became the men's meeting place, where the fire was always alight and the kettle was always boiling. In the fifties, "it was the most wonderful outreach in the whole community,"[94] according to Somerville.

During this decade he began to recognize the indicators that predicted the change that would sweep through western society in the 1960s, and he worried that the Anglican Church was ill-prepared for the impending upheaval.

As rector, Somerville, in his turn, became a mentor for a new batch of young men who chose to worship at St. James', often after having distasteful experiences in their home parishes as university students. These men soon were referred to as "David's Boys," and one was Michael Peers, who was to become primate of the Anglican Church of Canada from 1986 to 2004. Recently Peers dropped

Somerville a note, in which he called him his "father" in the same sense that Somerville referred to Cooper. Peers also thanked his mentor for the affirming influence he had on his decision to become a priest, as well as Somerville's positive example of what a priest should be.[95]

It was at St. James' that Somerville's broadcasting ministry took flight. He became one of several priests and pastors on CBC radio who shared a daily inspirational talk. His skill at the microphone and popularity with listeners soon resulted in the CBC asking him to chair an interdenominational advisory board on religious matters. Another outcome was his own programs, one of which was *Music and Western Man*. Somerville derived considerable relaxation and relief from the demands of an inner-city parish with his regular broadcasting, and his name became known for the first time to Vancouverites outside the church community.

As the 1950s drew to a close, the economy slumped and unemployment rose, precipitating an escalation in the eastside community's demands on St. James' outreach. The door bell and telephone rang continuously, and the clergy worked unceasingly. The parish turned both the church and the church hall into a hostel for homeless men and, after the media exposed the need and reported on the work of St. James', the clergy provoked the city to take action too. Keeping the hostel going wore everyone out. Possibly due to exhaustion, Somerville had a serious car accident at this time that put him in hospital with head injuries. During his long convalescence, he realized that the strain of the relentless pressure of pastoral concerns was taking its toll, and he cautiously began to consider that a move might be wise after spending so long at St. James'.

As he was attracted to academe, and knew that the Dean of Residence at the Anglican Theological College (ATC) was leaving, Somerville asked the Most Reverend Godfrey P. Gower, the then-bishop of New Westminster, if he could join the faculty where he was once a student. When Gower agreed, Somerville left St. James' in 1960 to teach pastoral care to a new generation and to supervise the "hotel-end" of the school. He was forty-five that fall, and his mind and body recovered from the hectic demands of a slum parish in the more relaxed atmosphere that university life brought, including an apartment in the school. Somerville felt at home. He also relished the intellectual discourse with professors and fellow teachers, while thoroughly disliking the role of "house master" to the feisty students of the early sixties.

Somerville taught pastoral theology, as well as doctrine and church history, and found that he itched to make changes in the curriculum. He developed an internship program that had the students assigned to a parish during their final year to get a feel for what pastoral care was all about. Unfortunately, most ended up just reading the lesson and teaching an odd Bible class and were not able to put into practice all Somerville was teaching in the classroom. He dearly wanted his students take part in parish life and administration — to actually do marriage preparation, to do the baptismal classes, and care for those in need. To Somerville's surprise, his scheme ran into fierce opposition from faculty, who thought, for example, that students needed Greek more than a parish internship, and his program collapsed after a couple of years. However, several years later it was successfully revived, using his blueprint. Another scheme Somerville promoted, after he saw it in action in Oregon, was clinical pastoral training, in which the clergy and students spent three months in a hospital, ministering to the sick and their families, supervised by a chaplain. The program did not get under way during Somerville's time at the university.

The times, they were a-changing — just as Somerville had anticipated — and so was he. "I was exposed to a real heavy dose . . . of 'Why don't we change it; why don't we do something else?'" By the time he left ATC, the quiet, small-c catholic priest had morphed into a committed liberal and a progressive mover-and-shaker, who was saying, "Let's try to find out a better way for doing this."[96] His outward approach did not alter much — he remained the compassionate, gentle soul he always was — but now he was a man on a mission. The five years at ATC "altered [my] perspective and re-affirmed my hunches,"[97] Somerville commented in retrospect. The academic world had allowed him the time, opportunity, and materials to re-examine his theological positions and the church's place in a turbulent era. His findings kindled an acute desire for experimentation and reform that would reconnect a "fossilized"[98] church to the evolving society. Somerville was becoming a quiet but definite revolutionary. All he needed was some scope.

"It was the worst year of my life"

In the mid-1960s, the Anglican Church of Canada asked author and journalist Pierre Berton to write a Lenten devotional book for use in parishes. The work turned out to be unexpectedly different — Berton, instead, wrote a severe criticism of an outdated church that he believed had failed both its members and society. Somerville, in the minority, appreciated *The Comfortable Pew*, and wrote a review in the diocesan paper in which he supported Berton's call for much-needed reform. However, many in the Church objected to the licence Berton had taken and disagreed strongly with his observations about their beloved institution. The majority was tossed out of its complacency by the things that Berton wrote — his exposé was brutal.

Berton accused the Anglican Church of abdicating its leadership, of being more concerned with the institution itself than with its mission in the world outside, and of failing to communicate internally through stimulating sermons and externally with action. He seriously wondered if it was possible to save the church, though he thought an effort should be made; so did Somerville…

"The virus that has weakened the Church is apathy,"[99] wrote Berton, who described religious proponents as passionless and indifferent to the great issues of the day. In the 1960s many members of Christian denominations, especially the youth and young adults, were bored, irritated, and unable to find a purpose or meaning in attending services on Sundays. Berton recognized that the years after the Second World War had become a new Christian era — quite different from the biblical period, from the Middle Ages, and from Victorian times — and needed a new approach. He was not shy about making suggestions either: he wanted a new kind of church that would commit to reaching the hearts and souls of the people of the new age; he wanted it to move out of the four walls of church buildings and to minister to the greater world outside "The church will have to flock to the people,"[100] Berton wrote. He also called for new ministries and new liturgies. Berton urged the Anglican Church to conduct a thorough, painful examination of itself, as well as to look closely at how inclusive it really was; so did Somerville…

The year that saw *The Comfortable Pew* published also saw Somerville move to Toronto. During a 1965 vacation in Europe, messages piled up at home for him. Most were from Church House in Toronto, seeking him for General Secretary of the General Board of Religious Education (GBRE) to replace Michael Creal, who had been instrumental in commissioning Berton's book and who had resigned unexpectedly. Creal's visionary shoes were a difficult fit for anyone who had to follow him: the GBRE was sizzling with exciting ideas for reform, and Creal was much admired by his staff. Somerville accepted the position, knowing that he needed to cool the fires while maintaining the energy, but he was unaware of how demoralized the department was.

Several factors contributed to the GBRE's turmoil. One, *The Comfortable Pew* was not the book everyone had expected — instead of being a devotional work, it was an attack on the Anglican Church — and the Church establishment blamed the GBRE. Two, the GBRE's *New Curriculum*, which was being developed for Sunday schools and adult education with much anticipation, was not yet finished when Somerville arrived. When it was finished, it failed to revolutionize parish life as it was expected to do. Three, the members of GBRE felt abandoned by Creal's departure, and resented that they had no input in the selection of Creal's successor. Four, reorganization of the Church's administrative structure was sweeping over the GBRE and reducing its clout. So Somerville, who arrived with little idea of the depth of the underlying angst, was expected to downsize the department, and found all his energies directed to damage control. Nothing he tried eased the awkward situation, and the staff remained hostile to him, despite his deep commitment to educating the laity and increasing lay participation in all facets of parish life. At the end of an unrewarding year, Somerville was at low ebb: "It was the worst year of my life."[101]

However, change was rattling Christian denominations everywhere in the mid-1960s, and the Anglican Church was no exception, giving Somerville some hope that the Church could be revitalized. The reorganization of the national Church's administration was one of many reforms implemented to bring the Church up-to-date, and Somerville was in the thick of it. Church House sent him on a change-management and leadership course run by the Episcopal Church in the United States, which introduced Somerville to the par-

ticipatory style of management. He took to it, and immediately started to practise what he had learned. "In the 1960s, everything seemed
possible. We put a man on the moon. We dreamed dreams,"[102] said
Somerville in 2002, describing the enthusiasm of the times, but he
recalled, with some regret, that it was not enough to accelerate a
slow-moving institution like the Anglican Church of Canada.

Relinquishing his role in GBRE in 1966, Somerville became
Director of Planning and Research, one of several responsible for
steering the reform of the administration. In the same way that
many large corporations hired consulting firms in the sixties to
assist their rigorous self-examination and guide them in modernizing, so did the Church. Price Waterhouse, the management
consultants, produced the Netten Report for Church House,
some of the recommendations of which turned out to be a mixed
blessing. For example, one suggestion, which was implemented,
was that the primate should relinquish diocesan responsibilities
and become a full-time CEO — a boon to the primate, who
could focus his energies better, but a move that delivered a huge
increase in executive power, which some bishops fought for
years. Another recommendation dissolved the empire-building,
old Church of England–type bureaucracies of education, missions, and social service, which vied for budgets, time, and staff,
and led to a more corporate-like system that, it was hoped,
would serve Anglicans in Canada better. But there was a dark
side to the streamlining — this reform left the bishops out of the
management loop and gave them another reason to feel excluded. As the reforms took shape and were approved by General
Synod, Somerville became the Executive Director of Program,
leading the newly arranged departments of parish and diocesan
services, national and world program, and communications.
During the upheaval, he "let [his] staff boil away and keep
going, as long as they boiled openly."[103] By now Somerville had
stopped feeling miserable, as he sensed the heartbeat of change
strengthen; at last he was at the "sharp end" and becoming a
change agent. He discovered that he liked it — a lot. Somerville
felt that dioceses and parishes were ready for a change in leadership style. He felt compelled to rid the Church of its patriarchal,
authoritarian methods and implement participatory leadership.

His personal deliberations and "hunches" from his ATC years were surfacing rapidly, and he saw that he might have an opportunity to try some out. It was in 1966 in Toronto that Somerville delivered an early "sound bite" to the media that demonstrated he was serious about his mission for change: "Our old models of God are dead indeed."[104]

"Now you can ride the balky horse for a while"

For several years his mother had experienced a recurrent dream in which she saw a procession in Christ Church Cathedral in Vancouver with Somerville at the end. When he was in Toronto, Martha began to nag him gently about returning home to "be bishop." Her son probably paid little attention to her pressure until he was nominated for co-adjutor* bishop of New Westminster in 1968. Somerville agreed to let his name stand, mainly because he thought he would enjoy being back in Vancouver, but he did not believe for one moment that he would be elected. He was wrong. T. David Somerville was elected on the second ballot with the greatest majority in the history of the diocese, 294 to 46 for his closest competitor. His years of broadcasting on CBC Radio and teaching at ATC meant the laity and clergy all felt they knew him. Somerville accepted the church's call and got into position to start putting his "hunches" into practice.

Somerville broke tradition immediately by being consecrated bishop at the Agrodome instead of in Christ Church Cathedral in downtown Vancouver. Inclusive to the point of obsession,[105] he was determined that everyone participate in a big public celebration, and he drew over four thousand on a snowy January day in 1969. On a phone-in show on CJOR radio before the event, Somerville was criticized for choosing a "cow palace," and smoothly retorted that he thought the location was most appropriate — after all, the origin of Christianity was in a stable. Then he chuckled.

---

* Co-adjutor is a bishop-in-waiting, with the right of succession when the diocesan bishop steps down. Co-adjutors differ from suffragan bishops, who are assistants to the incumbent bishops and do not automatically succeed.

Martha Somerville's amethyst set into the new episcopal ring.
(Somerville collection)

Martha Somerville did not live long enough to know that her son became bishop; sadly she died four months before his election. However, they were united again by a particularly special consecration gift: a large amethyst of hers became the stone for his episcopal ring. Close friends who knew of her dream offered to set the gem for the new bishop. Somerville took it to Toni Calvelti, the famous Vancouver jeweller, who set it in gold with the words *love, joy, peace, faith,* and *hope* engraved around the setting. Many who knew Martha remarked on her "presence" at Somerville's consecration, including the outgoing bishop, Godfrey Gower. Certainly in the new bishop's mind, his mother was definitely there, filled with pride in her son.

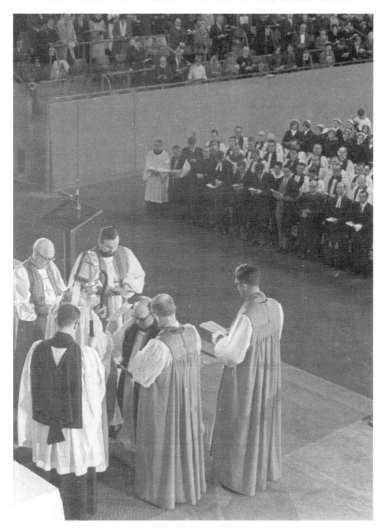

Archbishop Godfrey Gower consecrates Somerville as co-adjutor of New Westminster in the "cow palace," January 1969. (PSA 8-74)

Participants remember that the event went well, a stately and spiritual ceremony, with a beautiful liturgy. Another gift steeped in history and significance was presented to Somerville at his consecration. Archbishop de Pencier's son gave him the stole that his father had worn the day Somerville was confirmed. Somerville gave a clear indication of the style he would bring to his episcopate, while at the microphone. After an interruption from an overexcited congregant, he looked up and said words that conveyed, "I hear you, I affirm you, and I'm listening to you."[106] At the end of the service, in the excitement, Somerville was forgotten and found himself almost alone in the empty Agrodome after saying thank you and goodbye to all who attended. He had not taken his car, and no one had been asked to transport him to the dinner hosted for him by the attending bishops. Had it not been for Father Lloyd Wright of St. James', who was helping with the clearing up, Somerville would have missed the special gathering in his honour.

Somerville mingles with his flock after the consecration and is nearly forgotten.
(PSA8-77)

Archbishop Godfrey Gower, the diocesan bishop of New Westminster as well as the metropolitan of the ecclesiastical Province of British Columbia and Yukon, immediately handed over his office to Somerville and provided him with the opportunities he needed to learn the job, including sending him to "Bishop School" in Banff just after his consecration. The two men built on their earlier relationship during Somerville's tenure at St. James' and ATC, working well together as partners and friends. Over regular lunches, Gower graciously allowed his co-adjutor to tell him how he would run the diocese, and he gave Somerville the responsibility for committee work, inductions, and the confirmations in the diocese. Although an able administrator, Somerville chose to rely on two strong executive archdeacons during his tenure, so he could focus on his pastoral role with the clergy. Gower's parting words to his successor were "Well, David, now you can ride the balky horse for a while!"[107]

Somerville was installed as the sixth Bishop of New Westminster at Christ Church Cathedral on Sunday July 11, 1971, having been "in-waiting" for two and a half years. He was fifty-six, still single, and filled with energy for his mission. The new bishop immediately broke tradition for the second time and decided not to live in Bishopthorpe, the official residence on West 49th Avenue, choosing instead to live in an apartment thirty storeys above English Bay with spectacular views through its floor-to-ceiling windows. Colleagues nicknamed it the "episcopad," and once more Somerville could survey his domain from on high as he used to do from the bell tower of St. James' when he was rector.

It was the era of long hair and beards, flower power and beads, youth on the move in psychedelic vans, and free love. Woodstock had taken place in 1969, and soon became the seminal event to describe the Age of Aquarius. Churches began experimenting with rock masses and folk services in the hopes of connecting with the youth and slowing the plummeting attendance on Sundays.

Somerville loved the youth of the day, admired their ability to nail the discrepancies that lay between the Church and the world outside, and supported many of their desires for change. Mostly he listened to them when many of his generation did not. His involvement in a dispute at Christ the King in Burnaby showed where his sympathies lay. The rector of the parish had opened the church basement as a hostel for backpacking hippy couples (unmarried, of course) and failed to separate the sexes. Although the rector's warden approved the plan, the rest of the parish council were on vacation and were not consulted. When they returned, they abruptly shut the hostel, huffing and puffing about the moral turpitude of the young. The congregation instantly took sides, and much acrimony resulted. Somerville was asked to chair a parish meeting to sort out the division. He did not remove the rector, as some parishioners demanded, but quietly suggested that a curtain dividing the men and women might have been a good idea. By then it was too late to restore the hostel, and the hippies moved in with parishioners who were sympathetic to their plight. (Did they provide separate bedrooms…?)

Somerville admired a former Archbishop of Canterbury, William Temple, known for his progressive approach to social justice. Temple once said that the Church is *the only organization that exists for those who are* not *its members.* These words stayed with Somerville for much of his ministry and, once he was bishop, he often pushed and prodded parishes and their members by saying:

> *Are we going to be the "holy huddle" that just gathers together on Sunday or are we going to get to work trying to meet the needs of the community in which this building stands? What's the building for? Does it look like a filling station where you come and get your gas tank full on Sunday and then don't go back again or have anything more to do with it? Or is it in some way a support . . . helping you to vision what the possibilities could be in your life?*[108]

In a letter written early in his episcopate, Somerville put a bomb under the parishes. He told them to get away from maintenance and to identify what they could do *outside* the walls of their parish churches. Later, in retirement, Somerville reviewed his actions: "I think that a diocese needs to be stirred up every now and then because we fall into habits and patterns that we just want to repeat and repeat. The temptation always is to say, 'That's the way we've always done it' or 'We've never done it that way before,' which means the whole thing gets stale. I was wanting imagination; I was wanting some pioneering spirit."[109] He got it from some parishes, and those that took up the challenge received much support from both their bishop and the synod office.

Pastorally inclined towards all and eager to develop a strong leadership, Somerville pledged to spend a week in every one of the eighty parishes in the diocese of New Westminster. "It nearly killed me, but I did it,"[110] he recalled later. He stayed with each incumbent and his family, often sharing his bed with their children and pets, visited the parishioners, and took communion to the sick. The bishop held a "free-for-all" at each church, which anybody could attend and ask whatever they wanted. Somerville greatly enjoyed those sessions when he could sense the pulse of the people. He was probably one of the few bishops who knew his clergy and their spouses really well; pastorally he took great care of them, and addressed their problems as soon as he was able.

One outcome of his progress around the diocese was Somerville's annual clergy conference (later he added one for clergy wives too*), where eminent speakers gave presentations on a broad spectrum of issues and the bishop encouraged his clergy to expand their views. Another of his innovations was the Ministry Committee; it advised the bishop on parish appointments, which were now advertised for the first time. One more outcome of Somerville's leadership was his implementation of quarterly meetings for the regional deans. Gathering at the abbey in Mission in the Fraser Valley, they hashed out the issues concerning the diocese and its parishes, as well as receiving training in leadership, management by objective, budgeting, and con-flict management. Increasingly the clergy were dealing with conflicts arising from the looming reforms. For example, many priests and church members in the diocese were fearful of and/or opposed to the revision of the *Book of Common Prayer* and the proposal to admit young children to communion, to say nothing of the spectre of ordaining women to the priesthood.

"The Anglican grovel"

"I was always wanting to do something to brighten up the service,"[111] said David Somerville, remembering the old liturgy, which he had experienced while he was growing up.

Anglicans live through their liturgy; it defines them. Tinkering around with the words, music, and other parts of the way they worship has historically sent some Anglicans in the pews and at the altar into a tailspin; they like their services to be familiar and representative of the centuries of proud tradition since Henry VIII

---

* In the first half of Somerville's episcopate, there were only clergy wives — the ordination of women had not yet taken place.

broke from Rome and their Anglican predecessors pursued the *via media.**

Most liturgical churches came to grips with modernizing their orders of service in the sixties and seventies but, when the proposal to revamp the Anglican prayer book surfaced, it was met with anguish, resistance, and opposition from both clergy and parishioners throughout Canada. Renewal of the liturgy meant changing the Anglican Church's long-held identity, which was considerably out of date, and it was a long process, not completed during Somerville's episcopate. But Somerville, never one for sitting on the fence, wasted no time in embracing the opportunity for reform and, according to his dean, Canon Herbert O'Driscoll, set a courageous example of experimentation within his diocese, not only in liturgy but also in music and art. These trials allowed many of the faithful to realize that renewal could be transforming and not frightening. The bishop's example and willingness to try had a positive impact on the whole Church in Canada. Somerville stated, "The old idea of uniformity that all Anglicans in the world should do the same thing, out of the same book, at the same time, on the same day [and], that wherever you went in the world, you would find something you used at home, DIED."[112]

When he went to parishes to conduct confirmations, Somerville used to take copies of a new American confirmation service with him, which caused some of his clergy to balk. He said that he overcame the struggles by pulling rank on them! This and other manifestations of Somerville's mission for reform led to a recurring question from his episcopal colleagues in eastern Canada: "What are you crazy people out West doing now?" He would reply mischievously, "Just you wait. You'll be doing it yourselves before long!"[113] Somerville is not alone in believing that the Rockies are the cause of British Columbia's freedom to try new things and its fierce independence — all four bishops featured in this book have observed the same phenomenon. British Columbia is a relatively "new province without the burden of a long tradition,"[114] and the mountains separate it from the seats of power by just enough to allow British Columbians to try innovations before being stopped.

---

* "The middle way" between Protestantism and Roman Catholicism

The problems the Anglican Church wanted and needed to correct in the *Book of Common Prayer*, which dated back to 1549, were many. The Canadian prayer book, based on the 1662 English version, had been revised only twice, once in 1918 and again in 1962. The original and the revisions reflected a former society — one in which Christianity was the centre of the cosmos and the church had considerable influence on the state. The *BCP* used an archaic, though beautiful, language that was not only male-dominated but also difficult for many to understand. Worse, it had a medieval, penitential air about it and condemned those of other faiths, not at all in keeping with the new scholarship or the modern, pluralistic society. Somerville irreverently called it "the Anglican grovel."[115] Furthermore, the rubrics (instructions on how to perform the services) had the priest doing everything and the congregation watching passively. Somerville yearned to ramp-up lay participation and make worship more inclusive. He also wanted the liturgy to convey joy, mystery, and spirituality.

The real work started on the *Book of Alternative Services (BAS)* in 1972, just after Somerville succeeded Bishop Godfrey Gower to New Westminster and Archbishop Ted Scott became the primate. Scott encouraged the revision process and approved several experimental liturgies for trial (though not the notable *Trail Liturgy* of his former Diocese of Kootenay, which was used before 1972). Somerville did not work on the new liturgies himself but made his diocese a proving ground as the revision proceeded. While some parishes delivered the contemporary liturgies well, accompanied by education, some did not, and this increased the anxiety and opposition among some congregants.

The *BAS* took over a decade to produce and, before it was published, the *Third Canadian Order*, known as the "Blue Book," exposed many congregations to a more modern form of worship. The *BAS* was finally approved in 1985, but only as an option; in the classic Anglican way of compromise, the Church voted to keep the prayer book of 1959 as the official liturgical text of Canadian Anglicans and allowed the *BAS* to be used, as its name suggests, as an alternative with approval of diocesan bishops. Now widely used, the *BAS* is the more inclusive of the two prayer books and better reflects the church's focus on social justice, peacemaking, and lay participation. Newcomers to the faith can understand the contemporary language more easily and be spiritually nourished rather than scolded for their sinfulness.

In the beginning, the liturgical changes sometimes led to parishes having two congregations who never met each other — each would attend only the service for which "their" prayer book was used. Clergy, like Michael Ingham, the current bishop of New Westminster, who wrote a book[116] in 1986, explaining the *BAS* and modelling the integrity in both traditions, had more success with acceptance of the new *BAS*. Bishop Somerville's clear example of letting go of the old ways and his forthright encouragement of the modern liturgies meant that the new prayer book was generally well received in the churches of the New Westminster diocese.

In churches that adopted the *BAS* exclusively at the beginning, some congregants walked out and never came back; they missed the splendid English and imagery of the *BCP* and disliked the "bland" worship offered by the *BAS*. But their reluctance to adjust to a new form of worship did not prevent the wheels of change rolling ahead. Next came rock and folk music in church, guitars and clapping, and . . .

"To grow up in the sacrament"

Somerville remembers a lively discussion that took place at General Synod in 1971 at Niagara Falls, Ontario, on a motion that proposed allowing children to take Holy Communion before they had been confirmed. The long lineups at the microphones were mainly made up of mothers asking, "Why not? I want this for my children," and describing how they came up to the altar rail for communion and their "children just got a pat on the head" (a blessing). General Synod defeated the motion then, but did decide to study it. At this moment, Bishop Somerville took up the cause on behalf of the mothers, repeatedly using the comment "First baptism, then confirmation, then first communion, followed by disappearance."[117] Somerville was surprised how hard the struggle proved to be, especially given that the Orthodox churches had been giving Holy Communion to children for centuries and the neighbouring Diocese of Alaska had no problem with it.

Most clergy had experienced youngsters at the altar rail saying, often quite loudly, "Why can't I have any?" and their parents asking for an explanation. Somerville knew the scenario all too well, and had long been frustrated because all he could reply was "It's never been done." But once theologians began to argue that, if baptism makes one a full member of the church, then surely it is the doorway to communion too, Somerville felt momentum in the right direction and pushed harder for change. For years he had said, "I found confirmations almost heartbreaking, because I knew that . . . most of them in a year's time would have disappeared from the church."[118] Somerville hoped that earlier participation in the Eucharist would instill a greater sense of belonging in youngsters once they had reached adolescence, and keep them in the church longer. He also dearly wanted them all to "grow up in the sacrament,"[119] because it was so supremely important to him. So, before the 1973 General Synod voted on the issue, Somerville permitted children to receive Holy Communion in his own diocese, as long as the clergy and parish agreed. He also issued instructions that, from then on, the sacrament of Holy Baptism should "take place in the midst of the congregation so that new members [could] be welcomed."[120]

Of course, Somerville met opposition, mostly the argument that "the children won't understand." He handled that deftly enough by telling his critics that he didn't understand communion either, as it is one of the great mysteries. Others worried that the children would misbehave. Somerville disagreed, and time proved him correct — as long as they were old enough to "mind their manners" there were few problems.

Although the bishop of New Westminster had embraced and encouraged the admission of children to Holy Communion in his diocese, others in the House of Bishops were not so convinced. Some wanted to maintain the old way of Christian initiation — baptism with water, instruction, confirmation, then first Communion; others sought to run both systems in parallel, so parents could choose. Somerville wanted none of that and went ahead on his own decisively, while other bishops waited for the national House of Bishops to provide guidance, even though they supported the change. Somerville chose to avoid the delay caused by "studying issues to death." He said that any hint of change in the Church creates disagreement and "We fly into an academic mode," which, in his opinion, means "delaying tactics." He also said, "In the meantime, we are bleeding."[121]

The next General Synod in 1973 resolved to admit all to Holy Communion after baptism. At the same time, Synod voted to restore baptism as a principal service of the day in front of the whole community, rather than conduct it as a private rite, just as Somerville had decreed in his diocese two years before. The bishop of New Westminster went home and promptly opened up the altar rail to include others who had been baptized but not confirmed, whether Anglicans or not. Anglican writer and journalist Lyndon Grove said this was one of the most significant reforms that Somerville undertook, and his success with it in the Diocese of New Westminster helped to convince the House of Bishops to support it.[122]

At General Synod in 1975, Holy Baptism became the only essential rite of Christian initiation, and delegates also voted to ensure that no arbitrary age limit could be set in Canadian Anglican churches for first Communion. Many bishops returned home with a plan to have their own synods consider the issue before implementing it in their parishes. Some dioceses in the ecclesiastical province of British Columbia and Yukon chose to follow this route, and the 1976 minutes of the Provincial Synod show that there was no unanimity among the western bishops on how or when to implement the admission of children to Holy Communion. This synod held a long debate and eventually passed a resolution that allowed children to partake of communion at the discretion of the parish priest and their parents, after preparation and *with the proviso* that the issue be referred to the national House of Bishops and diocesan synods for further consideration.

The Diocese of New Westminster, thanks to Somerville, led the reform in 1973, not only in Canada but around the world. Scotland implemented the admission of children to Holy Communion second in 1978, New Zealand and South Africa in 1980, Australia approved it in 1981, and England waited until 1999, twenty-six years later. Following this success, Somerville cast his eyes on a larger reform . . .

It was a matter of justice

When Somerville was elected metropolitan in 1975, he became the archbishop responsible for the ecclesiastical province of British Columbia and Yukon and one of four senior bishops in Canada. This propelled him onto the national stage and put Somerville firmly in position to complete one more church reform that he had been working on since he became diocesan bishop. He grasped the opportunity with his customary tenacity, changing the Anglican Church of Canada irrevocably and influencing the worldwide Church too. The issue was a hot one — the ordination of women to the priesthood — and Somerville was "really for it."[123]

Bishop John Frame (Yukon) presents the new metropolitan of the Province of British Columbia and Yukon, Archbishop David Somerville, at Christ Church Cathedral. Vancouver, December 1975. (PDNW5-27)

Many credit David Somerville for achieving this massive and contentious change in Church practice. He was certainly the mover and shaker behind the proposal, and its enthusiastic champion, but he points out that he was actively supported by others, including Primate Ted Scott and Bishop John Bothwell of Niagara. He also happened to be in the right place at the right time — Somerville was the chair of the Committee on Ministry of General Synod when the issue solidified, and he felt that ordination of women was not so much a question of doctrine but of practice. He strongly believed it was also a question of *justice*. Many of his colleagues were surprised by the outspoken position he took. He was after all a male, unmarried Anglo-Catholic priest, and he came from a traditional background. However Somerville had listened to both sides of the debate carefully and had considered the issue from every angle. When he made up his mind in favour of the ordination of women, he did not waver.

While women had been ordained in Christian denominations in Canada and around the world for many years (since 1936 in the United Church of Canada), the global Anglican Communion still resisted having women priests in the early 1970s, and, in the eyes of the proponents of the idea, was woefully slow to embrace them. By the time Canada ordained its first women priests in late 1976, only two other national Anglican churches had done so too — those in Hong Kong (1971) and the United States (1974 uncanonically and 1976 officially, a couple of months before Canada). Although New Zealand had approved the reform in 1974, their first women priests were not ordained until 1977. The Church of England was one of the slowest to change in the Western world, and did not allow the ordination of women until 1992 — and then only after a colossal fight. By 1994, two-thirds of the Anglican Communion was ordaining women. The acceptance of female Anglican bishops took longer; they were first consecrated in 1989 in the United States, 1990 in New Zealand, 1994 in Canada, and not yet in England.

Men have held authority within Christianity since its beginnings. Men have also long dominated public life and the corporate world in the West, until losing their hold in the 1960s, when the postwar female baby boomers burst on the scene, refusing to be denied.

The position of women in society had been shifting since the 1920s, when the number of women in professional work began its inexorable rise — universities were accepting women in increasing numbers and went on doing so. For example, in 1920, 16 per cent of undergraduates were female; this rose to 35 per cent in 1968. By the turn of the millennium, women studying for degrees outnumbered men and often equalled men in medicine and law. But, although women were in the majority in Anglican congregations during the same decades, they were not part of Church leadership and could not even vote at General Synods until 1969. The Anglican Church of Canada was slower than society to recognize women's equality and to provide opportunities for them.

The introduction of oral contraception in 1964 proved to be the defining moment for women's march toward equality in society. "The Pill" gave women *choice* — for the first time women in all strata of society were able to control when and if they had children. Young women in the sixties and seventies eagerly grasped the opportunity of having a career *and* marriage and would not let go.

However, this new, exhilarating independence did not mean that society was in step. Acceptance of women as equals in society did not occur overnight as did the introduction of reproductive control — it lagged far, far behind and needed much pushing and shoving. Some would argue it still does, at least in a few resistant pockets.

The first Lambeth Conference* to raise the issue of women in the threefold order of ministry — diaconate, priesthood, episcopate — occurred in 1920. It resolved that the diaconate was the only order open to women but was not equivalent to the male order of deacon, which led to the priesthood. Ten years later, in 1930, Lambeth gingerly dipped its toes in the water on the issue of ordaining women to the priesthood after the Committee on the Ministry of the Church received two submissions from organizations supporting the idea. But the committee recommended that the "changing gender roles in society did not constitute sufficient grounds for changing the tradition of an all male priesthood," and the bishops hastily withdrew their toes. In between the two world wars, the episcopate could not imagine the concept.

The Second World War delayed the 1940 Lambeth conference to 1948, and, in the hiatus, Bishop Ronald Hall of the Diocese of Hong Kong and Macao, ordained a deaconess, Florence Li Tim Oi, to the priesthood in 1944 on an emergency basis in wartime without,

---

* The once-a-decade gathering of Anglican bishops from around the world, held in England.

consulting others in the Anglican Communion, especially Canterbury. Many in the hierarchy strongly disapproved of the bishop's action and called for his resignation after the war. Although her diocesan bishop urged Li to continue, she chose to stop serving as a priest, until resuming the position in 1979 when China embraced religious freedom and women's ordination became acceptable. Li's uncanonical ordination was not well known at the time, but may have served to consolidate the opinions of the world's bishops in 1948, when they reaffirmed their 1930 position on the issue. The ordination of women to the priesthood did not surface again on Lambeth's agenda until 1968, when the post-war period had changed everything and women were agitating vociferously for equal opportunities throughout society. Somerville did not attend this Lambeth gathering, but paid close attention to its proceedings.

At this conference a new generation of bishops debated the issue long and hard, using several reports from Lambeth's committees, most notably "Women and Holy Orders," released in 1966, which demanded the conference discuss the matter. This was the conference that opened the door for women who felt called to minister as priests by concluding that the ordination of women could be neither sanctioned nor forbidden, because there were no conclusive theological reasons for withholding it any longer. (Technically Lambeth could not "forbid" anything; it has no constitutional authority over the national churches in the Anglican Communion.) The conference resolved to open the diaconate to women, reversing its position taken in 1930, and this decision effectively opened up the threefold order of ministry to women. However, because it did not tackle the question of the admission of women to the other two orders, the priesthood or the episcopate, Lambeth left the issue open for national Churches to grapple with, which many did.

The bishops left England ready to study the issue at home and report their conclusions to the newly established Anglican Consultative Council (ACC) in time for their first meeting in 1971. The ACC collated the findings from around the world, added information from other denominations that did and did not ordain women, and circulated the package back for consideration by the whole Communion. At home, Canada took Lambeth's declaration as the green light, and, with the approval of the House of Bishops, began ordaining female deacons in 1969, before its next General Synod the same year. However, they hedged their bets by adding that opening up the diaconate to women was still not to be considered "a kind of internship to priesthood."[124] The primate also asked the Commission on Women to start discussing the matter. The door was opening wider, at least in Canada, and Somerville stepped through it, albeit carefully.

At the 1969 General Synod, Somerville watched as women in the Church rose up and lobbied loudly for the synodal vote and for equal opportunity, using the slogans "Women are part of the church, too" and "Let women speak for themselves." The noise and pressure was no accident, for it was the year that the Commission on Women delivered its report. [125] This body recommended change, major change, to eliminate the discrimination against women in the Canadian Church — for example, though hard to believe today, in nine dioceses it was still impossible for a woman to be elected as a churchwarden. When the vice-chair of the Commission on Women, Dorie Cuming, stood at the microphone and reported to the delegates on the issue of the ordination of women to the priesthood, she made the commission's position crystal clear: women should be admitted. She recommended that the primate, Howard Clark, initiate a study on the matter to establish the Canadian Church's position on the issue. Clark responded by convening a "Task Force on the Ordination of Women to the Priesthood" in 1970, comprised of both clergy and laity. The House of Bishops followed suit, striking a committee on "The Wider Ordained Ministry," on which three western bishops sat, including the Right Reverend Douglas Hambidge, Bishop of Caledonia, but not Somerville. He was the chair of the Committee on Ministry, which was also focusing on the issue. The 1969 General Synod marked the moment that the Canadian Anglican Church became willing to modernize the position of women in its " establishment," making it one of the earliest Anglican Provinces in the world to do so.

Somerville, like other ordained men in the Church, knew women who were called to the priesthood and whom the Church had excluded. One such woman was Elspeth Alley. In 1970, Somerville and Alley discussed the strong call to the priesthood that she had experienced at her confirmation when she was twelve years old. Knowing the futility of the situation as she reached adulthood, she had married and raised a family before she even thought of pursuing theological training. Alley's first attempt as a student in 1964 at the Anglican Theological College at the University of British Columbia was a failure. She lasted just one term, because of the hostility of male students: "I was not allowed to eat in the dining room or even to pass through with a tray. I ate my lunch in my car."[126] Somerville listened to Alley closely and sympathized with her tearful frustration, while encouraging her to try ATC again.

After Lambeth in 1968, the first meeting of the Anglican Consultative Council at Limuru, Kenya, in 1971 made a seminal decision. In a close vote, 24 to 22, the delegates agreed that any bishop with the permission of his synod could ordain women. The Bishop of Hong Kong and Macao went ahead almost immediately — his diocesan synod had already overwhelmingly approved the ordination of women in 1970, and he believed that his diocesan canons also protected his authority. A little more guarded, the new Canadian primate, Ted Scott, although he was a strong supporter, responded to the ACC decision with care, saying that in Canada the reform would need General Synod approval.

The primate's task force had not completed their deliberations by the General Synod of 1971, and, instead of tabling their report, recommended that Church House issue study guides to the dioceses and parishes, based on Lambeth Conference material from 1968 and other supporting documents. The depth of study on the ordination of women undertaken by the Canadian dioceses and parishes is not clear in archival documents or books on the topic. Some, but by no means all, dioceses brought resolutions on the matter to their synods for discussion, and many prepared reports on their positions for the upcoming General Synod in 1973, when it was to be discussed. The House of Bishops meanwhile, under the leadership of primate, Ted Scott, expanded the mandate of the "Wider Ordained Ministry" committee following the ACC statement that each national church could make its own decision on the ordination of women to the priesthood. This committee also considered the revival of the vocational diaconate for those not called to the priesthood, which also included women.

A non-General Synod year, 1972, saw the completion of the primate's task force, containing one majority report and one minority report.* Six of the seven members recommended that the Canadian Church accept the principle of ordaining women to the priesthood. Simplified, the majority report stated that Scripture did not expressly forbid the ordination of women, and that the exclusion of women at the altar had arisen from cultural and historical experience; it clearly supported the view that the greater scriptural teaching of liberation and justice should prevail. The report firmly stated that an all-male priesthood was a tradition only, and could be changed. The minority report argued that the ordination of women should be prohibited for Biblical, Christological (the maleness of Christ), ecumenical, and other reasons. The two reports were distributed throughout the Canadian Church in anticipation of the 1973 General Synod.

At Pentecost in 1972, Somerville ordained Alley to the diaconate after she successfully earned her theological degree. He told her he would ordain her to the priesthood as soon as he could. Since Somerville was already deeply involved in the issue on the national stage, he surmised he would be able to deliver on his promise. His participation in the discussions of the House of Bishops gave him a feel for how the issue would play out at the next General Synod, and this assisted him in his planning. Their meetings were not antagonistic, and some of those who were equivocating were convinced by "the force and direction of the debates."[127] Somerville regularly used the argument that a theology of sexuality that taught that only males could represent God was out of touch with the reality of the world. Bishops who remained opposed were in the minority, but had strong convictions. Somerville thought that was partly because they were threatened and did not want to work alongside women. He also recognized his colleagues' need for a conscience clause, if the resolution passed, that would accommodate those bishops who simply could not bring themselves to ordain women. Someone, and it may have been Somerville, expressed concern that no woman's voice had been heard

---

* Details of the two reports can be found in the book *Beyond the Walled Garden: Anglican Women and the Priesthood* by Wendy Fletcher-Marsh (artemis enterprises, 1995).

during the House of Bishops' deliberations. As Somerville was also the chair of the important Committee on Ministry for the national Church and guided that group's discussions, he was responsible for submitting their report for the General Synod of 1973, and it also was in favour of the ordination of women. However Somerville did not leave it there.

The 1973 General Synod took place in Regina, Saskatchewan, and turned out to be the crucial synod that led to reform of the Canadian priesthood. It was a blockbuster affair. Although Somerville did not move the historic resolution for tactical reasons, he was its acknowledged champion.

The Committee on Ministry presented the reports on the ordination of women to the floor of Synod before the motions were put. Somerville was in the forefront of this delivery, and afterwards delegates broke into small groups to study and discuss the contents of the reports. Somerville had wisely adopted a plan to minimize risk to the motion to accept the ordination of women in principle: he invited a well-respected member of the laity, Ms. Ruth Scott, who was the principal of the Anglican Women's Training College and a member of his committee, to propose the motion, and then he seconded it. This ensured that the order of laity voted first, then the bishops, with the clergy voting last. Discussion was lengthy and spirited on both sides of the matter, with several amendments being defeated that proposed referral of the issue to diocesan synods and/or parishes before a vote was taken at General Synod. These "delaying" amendments were defeated by the clergy, and, in so doing, they indicated a readiness to get on with it that surprised many. Those in favour of women joining the priesthood were elated at the way the situation was progressing, but eight bishops who opposed it did not participate in the debate or declare themselves — an action that had many wondering what they had up their sleeves.

The original resolution was amended (shown in italics) by all three orders to read: "That this General Synod accept the principle of the ordination of women to the priesthood, that this decision be communicated to the Anglican Consultative Council, and *that implementation not take place until the House of Bishops has worked out a pattern for the Canadian church that would include an educational process for the Church.*"[128]

This compromise resolution meant that the implementation of ordaining women to the priesthood had to wait until the House of Bishops had decided how to accomplish it. To be adopted, the resolution had to be carried in all three orders. As the laity had moved it, they voted first and approved it; then the bishops approved it; and, last of all, the clergy approved it, though by a smaller majority than the others. Somerville had expected and hoped that, once the clergy saw the laity's overwhelming support, many who were uncertain would change their minds and vote for the motion — and his strategy worked. But, despite the celebration of the historic vote, it was not over yet.

Although General Synod could not usually interfere with other dioceses' jurisdiction and authority, it could where matters of doctrine, discipline, and worship of the church were involved. As the ministry of women was included in those key areas, it looked as if the ordination of women might require a change in the ecclesiastical laws or canons of the Church; if so, the change would need a two-thirds majority in each of the three orders at two successive General Synods. This technicality could have delayed or even prevented the admission of women to the priesthood, but the church lawyers concluded the canons did not require amending. The women, who had experienced strong vocations and were watching the procedural wrangles closely, knew that it was now only a matter of time before they could stand at the altar and celebrate the Eucharist. Their hearts were full.

Somerville never planned that the Diocese of New Westminster should vote on the ordination of women. The issue was hashed out before the General Synod of 1973 at his monthly deanery meetings and in the individual parishes through formal discussion groups, led by the clergy. The next diocesan synod in New Westminster simply resolved to urge the House of Bishops to provide the Canadian Church, before the end of 1974, with the plans for implementing the ordination of women and for educating the church, as was agreed at the recent General Synod. Somerville continued to push the House of Bishops, to prevent them dragging their feet. He wanted the information as soon as possible, so that his diocese (and the church) could move steadily towards a clear, responsible, Biblical policy on this question and could actually begin ordaining women priests. After that the matter was not discussed again at a diocesan synod in New Westminster. In some other dioceses, however, there was "a major backlash . . . [and] the decision to ordain was slammed with highly intemperate language."[129]

Between the General Synods of 1973 and 1975, the House of Bishops discussed the ordination of women at every meeting except one. Tensions ran high, and the House was deeply divided. Early on in their deliberations, the primate, Ted Scott, seriously thought a rift was imminent with the eight bishops who did not declare themselves at the 1973 General Synod, but in retrospect, he decided that they were simply stalling for time. Without getting heated, Somerville kept up his argument that the ordination of women had nothing to do with theology and everything to do with gender; he continually insisted that it was a question of church practice and justice. The bishops' first declaration was to inform the Church that no immediate implementation would be forthcoming and sufficient time was to be allowed for a careful educational process. This resulted in a task-force report circulated to every diocese by the end of 1974 (as requested by the synod of New Westminster) and an agreement that individual bishops could choose how to handle the study within their own dioceses — as long as the work was concluded before the next General Synod in 1975. The study cautioned supportive dioceses not to jump the gun and follow the example of a U.S. bishop who had irregularly ordained eleven women in Philadelphia before the Episcopal Church of the United States had taken a national vote. The Canadian bishops, although each technically had the authority to ordain women at any time, did not want controversy. They desired to create a strong sense of respect for a decision of such magnitude when it was ultimately taken, so they wanted the issue decided by the national Church after education in the parishes, as well as in open debate and by secret ballot at the General Synod of 1975. The House also voiced their determination to remain connected with the whole Anglican Communion throughout the process, and hoped for support and involvement by all ecclesiastical authorities.

The House of Bishops was not able to reach unanimity in supporting the ordination of women in the 1970s; the divisions of opinion were too fiercely held. However, the bishops worked to ensure that no dissenting bishop would refuse to support a colleague who ordained women. They also voiced concern about the acceptance of women priests, but did not identify strategies to provide pastoral care to laity or clergy who were strongly opposed to the idea. The willingness to proceed improved in the House as the months progressed, but the eight bishops who had kept silent in the debate of 1973 continued to keep silent, and others remained reluctant to move forward. The House was unable to provide a deadline for proceeding. As those opposed were in the minority and a conscience clause was proposed to allow them the freedom not to ordain or hire women priests, Somerville was confident about the outcome at the key General Synod of 1975. However, he did insist women priests in Canada must hold equal authority and jurisdiction as their male counterparts and be fully accepted by them in dioceses that chose to ordain women.

At their meeting prior to the 1975 General Synod, the House of Bishops designed a plan to smooth the way for acceptance of the ordination of women in Canada, and Somerville kept the primate, Ted Scott, informed throughout the whole process. Scott was to open the issue, setting the tone and focus, and voting would be by secret ballot. The House also issued a "memorial," or memorandum,[130] for delegates, which asked for a simple reaffirmation of the principle approved in 1973. If it was ratified, it meant no further debate would occur. Then the way would be open to ensure no delays hampered the implementation of the ordination of women, a real anxiety of the supporting bishops.

Elspeth Alley never fought for ordination to the priesthood, believing that, if it was God's will, it would take place. She drew encouragement from Somerville, who said it was coming. Alley was neither an activist nor angry at the delays, for she put her trust in God and in Somerville, who was doing all he could. Other women found the wait almost unbearable, and felt the continuing pain of rejection and devaluation. But Alley did find the grassroots opposition between 1970 and 1975 distressing; she had been threatened by several male priests and ordinands and physically assaulted by one. She was also worried by the small group discussions in the parishes that demonstrated more negativity than support for the ordination of women.[131] The process ground on.

To help General Synod delegates prepare for the historic vote, everyone received packages of reports on the matter, and some of the laity and clergy had also previously participated in discussions in their own dioceses. Perhaps the most influential document was the memorandum from the House of Bishops, the majority of whom supported the motion. Somerville, as chair of the Committee on Ministry,[132] stressed the committee's concern about the decision on the ministry of women being delayed further, and also reminded everyone that "*all* ministries should be open to *all* qualified persons."

At the 1975 General Synod in Quebec City, the ordination of women was finally achieved, again largely due to Somerville. He helped draft the two resolutions that Ruth Scott moved and which he seconded. The first motion, as planned by the primate and the House of Bishops, called for Synod's reaffirmation of the principle of the ordination of women to the priesthood. The second asked Synod to affirm that it would be appropriate for women qualified for the priesthood to be ordained at the discretion of diocesan bishops acting within the normal procedures of their own jurisdictions and in consultation with the House of Bishops.

Both resolutions were carried at General Synod with surprisingly little fuss, though the mood was tense: the first motion earned 88 laity votes to 18, 75 clergy to 30, and 26 bishops to 8; the second motion received 95 laity votes to 9, 86 clergy to 19, and 27 bishops to 7. Next on the agenda came the conscience clause that Somerville knew had been essential to achieving a majority for the first two resolutions. He himself moved this resolution.

Most of the direct opposition to the ordination of women came from 10 per cent of Canadian clergy and emerged after the decision of General Synod. Two hundred male priests (eight of them bishops) from twenty-two of the thirty dioceses made a public protest by publishing a letter entitled *A Manifesto on the Ordination of Women to the Priesthood from Concerned Clergy of the Anglican Church of Canada* in the national Anglican newspaper attacking the pronouncement. Representatives of the group also addressed the House of Bishops after Synod. The response from clergy and laypersons who were offended by the *Manifesto* was fast and furious, and letters to the editor demonstrated that support for the ordination of women had actually predated the formal debates and studies of the Church. Although the issue was contentious, neither side had lobbied aggressively before the vote was taken. This was not the Canadian way, and it was especially not the Anglican way, at least in those days.

Somerville and other observers[133] put the historic achievement down to several factors playing out simultaneously in a period that was ripe for reform:

- pressure from the majority of the bishops and the primate, Ted Scott, who believed in it and who knew how to work the system;[134]
- firm and vocal leadership from a respected bishop (Somerville);
- the support of most of the laity;
- women who kept asking "What are we waiting for?" and pressing for action;
- the example of the Episcopal Church of the United States next door;
- the limited and poorly organized opposition to the ordination of women in Canada;
- the fact that the Anglican church in Canada was relatively small and General Synod participants numbered in the hundreds, not thousands; and,
- the canons did not need amendment.

Although the two Canadian ecclesiastical provinces of Canada and Ontario, which existed before the first General Synod of 1893, participated in the voting in 1975, they reserved the right to also vote on the issue themselves before taking action. Whether individual dioceses supported or rejected the ordination of women depended largely on the position taken by their bishops. But having said that, most of the laity and clergy welcomed the change, with many feeling deeply that the priestly ministry would be enhanced by women who brought complementary gifts to the role. With 66 per cent of the House of Laity having supported the ordination of women in 1973 and over 80 per cent in 1975, it came as no surprise that several parishes promptly requested ordination for their female deacons, who were serving as priests in all ways except celebrating the Eucharist. They had to wait a just bit longer.

Meanwhile the executive of the Province of British Columbia and Yukon met in a Roman Catholic retreat house in Vancouver for another historic vote. They elected Somerville to replace the retiring archbishop and metropolitan of the ecclesiastical province, and the new archbishop took delight in saying that he was the first Anglican archbishop to be elected in a Roman Catholic convent. Somerville was installed at Christ Church Cathedral on December 9, 1975. The primate also appointed him to be his representative to the Council of the Anglican Centre in Rome, an annual responsibility, which Somerville relished.

Despite the approval of the ordination of women at the 1975 General Synod, the House of Bishops still had the right to implement it cautiously. They did not hurry as they wrestled with the implications and consulted other Anglican provinces in the world Communion. In a long-winded but sensitive resolution that covered all viewpoints, the House of Bishops eventually announced that bishops could start ordaining women after November 1, 1976, and they would inform other churches in the Communion of their decision. Author Wendy Fletcher-Marsh noted in her book[135] that, if other churches' feedback had been overwhelmingly negative, the first ordinations would have been postponed or even cancelled. However, Primate Ted Scott, who strongly supported the implementation, lobbied other primates who fiercely opposed the ordination of women and convinced them to respect Canada's right to make this decision. In so doing, Scott initiated the "agreement to disagree" within the world Church when Canada took the initiative ahead of many others.

The bishops also formulated guidelines for the first ordinations. Somerville insisted the House make very clear decisions about the selection and training of female ordinands and the type of support they would get in their ministries when they met opposition. The outcome of his insistence was that women were to be chosen and trained exactly the same as male priests, with the issue of support and how it would be provided being left to dioceses to decide. The Canadian bishops chose St. Andrew's Day, November 30, 1976, for a synchronous ordination across the country. The House, above all, wanted the services to be as "normal" as possible, using the same order of service as always and including male ordinands too. Although the occasion would be special for the women being ordained, it was to be business as usual.

Then all that remained was for the primate to invite the bishops to let him know who they would be ordaining on November 30, and only four dioceses responded with names. The bishops of New Westminster, Cariboo, Niagara, and Huron got ready to make ecclesiastical history in Canada.

Somerville was elated to be in the position of acting on his long-held belief in equality and justice for women within the Canadian Anglican Church. In Christ Church Cathedral in Vancouver at 8 p.m., he joyfully delivered his promise to Elspeth Alley and ordained Virginia Briant and Michael Deck at the same service.

As in Holy Matrimony, the ordination service provides an opportunity for anyone to say that the service should not proceed due to "an impediment." Somerville prepared himself ahead of time for the possibility of an objection to the ordination of Alley and Briant. He was wise to do so, and he admitted to a *frisson* of nervousness when he reached the critical words. No sooner had he felt it, than the Reverend James Penrice marched up the chancel steps in front of the congregation of over a thousand. Keeping his face composed, Somerville waited. Penrice was shaking so much he was unable to unroll his script, and Somerville took it from him, opened it up, and held it while Penrice read out his objection. The bishop then said calmly, "Thank you for your objection. I recognize your right to do so, but we are proceeding according to the direction of General Synod and the House of Bishops, so the service will go on." Penrice retrieved his script and walked down the long aisle of the cathedral, under the congregation's gaze, and out the door. The congregation, and no doubt the ordinands, relaxed. Somerville continued.

The western dioceses, often perceived to be more progressive than those in the east, did not exhibit this tendency over the ordination of women. The Diocese of New Westminster passed a resolution in 1974 urging the House of Bishops to supply information on the topic, and never discussed it or voted on it again, because Somerville knew that the synod would "only get in a great tangle."[136] Instead, the voice of his diocese spoke at deanery meetings and in parish discussion groups. According to Somerville, the diocese accepted the pioneer women priests well, although some older male priests were not comfortable, and twelve signed the *Manifesto*. In the Diocese of Caledonia (northern British Columbia), Bishop Douglas Hambidge declared himself early as a supporter, but never addressed the issue in his charges to synod. The delegates who had been at General Synod the year before, raised it for discussion at Caledonia's 1974 synod. Not one priest in this diocese signed the *Manifesto*, but five of thirty-four clergy opposed the diocesan motion approving the ordination of women in 1975. Hambidge ordained the first woman priest in Caledonia in January 1977.

In Yukon the bishop did not support the moves towards ordaining women, and in his charge to the twentieth synod made this abundantly clear. No women ministered as priests in Yukon until 1983, when the dissenting bishop no longer served the northern diocese.

The Diocese of British Columbia (Vancouver Island) also seemed lacking in enthusiasm — at its synod in April 1975, the matter was discussed in an educational way but never voted on. However twenty-four clergy signed the *Manifesto*, and no women were ordained in Victoria until 1987, eleven years after the first Canadian ordinations. The Diocese of Cariboo, whose bishop supported the ordination of women, affirmed the proposal at its synod of 1974, and never discussed it again. The next event in Cariboo was the ordination of Patricia Reed on November 30, 1976, notable because the Canadian primate, Ted Scott, preached. Three priests in Cariboo signed the *Manifesto*. The Diocese of Kootenay, Scott's previous see, first raised the issue seven months after the first women had been ordained in Canada. The matter was never discussed or voted on in their synods, and only one member of the clergy signed the *Manifesto*. However, it took another seven years before Kootenay ordained a woman.

The records show that in dioceses where the bishops opposed the issue, female ordinations remained on hold until the bishops retired and/or were replaced by those with a more supportive attitude. Within fifteen years all Canadian dioceses ordained women to the priesthood. The conscience clause, so essential to the success of the 1973 and 1975 resolutions, eventually became obsolete and was rescinded in 1986.

By 1992, 51 per cent of the Anglican Communion had female priests in fourteen national churches, four of which were in Africa, and Canada was second only to the United States in numbers. Five hundred women priests have been ordained in Canada since November 1976. Now, at the beginning of the twenty-first century, women at the altar celebrating the Eucharist and serving parishes in North America are commonplace and unremarkable.

Next on the Church's agenda was the admission of women to the episcopate, and Somerville did not participate in this obvious next step; he was off the national stage and enjoying retirement. The Anglican Church of Canada met this milestone in 1994, when Victoria Matthews was consecrated suffragan bishop of Toronto. The Church of England took much longer to come to grips with women priests and eventually "swallow[ed] the ordination of women but are [still] choking over women bishops," according to Somerville.[137] The Church of England still does not recognize women bishops ordained elsewhere in the Anglican Communion or the priests of either gender that these female bishops have ordained.

The only Lambeth Conference that Somerville attended was held in 1978, after Canada started ordaining women, and he did not enjoy it much. The oppressive "old boy" network tended to exclude new bishops; the way the conference was conducted was poor; and Somerville came down with food poisoning. The highlight for him was meeting Archbishop Desmond Tutu and discovering they agreed on many matters. Another very contentious debate on the ordination of women took place at this Lambeth Conference, with many bishops still steadfastly opposed, even though Hong Kong, Canada, the United States, and New Zealand had all proceeded to do so. This Lambeth acknowledged the legal right of each Church to make its own decision on the ordination of women, with a vote of 316 for, 37 against, and 17 abstentions. And it was here that the Communion first decided to live together in disagreement, and this position was to hold until the issues of the ordination of gays and lesbians and same-sex unions disturbed the *status quo*.

For some current perspective on the ordination of women, the *Ottawa Citizen*[138] reported in August 2004 that more women were being ordained as Christian ministers and priests than men. Fully two-thirds of all United Church ministers ordained in the previous eight years had been women and, in 2004, there were only seventeen men in a cohort of forty-nine. Anglican, Evangelical Lutheran, and Presbyterian churches show similar statistics: Presbyterians had 40 per cent female ministers (with the first ordination of a woman in 1962); Anglican female priests comprised 20 per cent, but more were being ordained; Lutherans employed 27 per cent women pastors, but trends indicated this figure too would rise to 50 per cent by 2008. The newspaper also noted that, as a rule, women experience the call of the Holy Spirit to ordination later than their male peers, between the ages of about thirty-five to fifty. The priesthood is often a second career for women, and they bring much worldly experience to their ministries.

In contrast, the evangelical denominations have been slower to accept women as ministers — the first female pastor of a Christian Reform Church was ordained in 1995, and other churches are still debating the issue. One of these denominations that has not followed the majority is the Pentecostal Assemblies of Canada, which has been ordaining women for decades. To date, the Eastern Orthodox churches and the Roman Catholic Church do not ordain women and are unlikely to change their practice, though not all their female adherents support this stand.

So once more, Somerville had sung a new song. Along with the Right Reverend John Bothwell, Bishop of Niagara, he led the charge for the ordination of women to the priesthood in Canada. The challenges to the ordination of women in Canada arose mostly in the House of Bishops, where Somerville was in a perfect position to exercise leadership. He did so in his typical non-anxious manner, honouring everyone's position, but always pressing forward with tenacity and determination, while the primate endeavoured to attain a consensus. Somerville's indefatigable efforts meant that Canada became one of the first national Anglican churches in the world to ordain women to the priesthood, led only by the Episcopal Church of the United States a few weeks before Canada.

"It was the best thing I've ever done"

Somerville, never one to shy away from controversial ventures, took up a new cause right at the end of his episcopate, although this one was conducted out of the limelight. He quietly set the diocese on its long walk towards equality rights for gays and lesbians, which would be taken up by the present diocesan bishop, Michael Ingham.

One day in 1980, a gay friend of Somerville's from St. Mark's in Vancouver approached the bishop and proposed establishing a chapter of Integrity, the organization of Anglican gays and lesbians. His reason for approaching Somerville was that, if Integrity got off the ground, the members would need a sympathetic church in which to hold their meetings, which always began with a Eucharist. In 1980 many frowned upon the whole idea of homosexuals in church taking Holy Communion, reading the lections, and administering the chalice. But Somerville didn't, and he gladly offered the fledgling group the cathedral in which to meet. Integrity Vancouver became a viable organization due to his liberality and enabled gays and lesbians, many of whom had not come out in those days, to participate safely in a regular Eucharist with their partners. However, when the cathedral's wardens found out about Somerville's action, they were upset and made Integrity unwelcome, much to the bishop's dismay. Integrity left, and began to meet and worship elsewhere, eventually finding a comfortable reception at St. Paul's in the West End of Vancouver, where the members still meet regularly.

Somerville retired, as he promised, at the end of 1980, after being a bishop and archbishop for over ten years. However he immediately joined the Vancouver School of Theology for three years as its Anglican chaplain. Since his previous appointment in the 1960s, ATC had merged with the United Church's Union College in 1971 to form VST. The school had changed, and Somerville preferred the more modern version. He discovered a more mature student body, which of course included women. Participation and interaction pervaded the teaching and learning styles, something the retired archbishop had encouraged, and it pleased him. For the second time, Somerville found he enjoyed university life and taught Anglican Studies. While he modelled his love of the Church, his students loved him and his lectures. Lynn McNaughton, the current

Archbishop David Somerville's formal retirement photo, taken as he handed over the diocese to the Right Rev. Douglas Hambidge, former bishop of Caledonia, 1980. (DNW10-1)

Anglican chaplain of VST, admired the way Somerville distilled forty years of Church experience for students in the 1980s: "We learned, not about God, but about 'knowing' God."[139] She clearly remembers Somerville's first sermon to the students, in which he said "Our job is to make the invisible, visible."[140] He was still producing memorable sound bites.

Somerville left VST in 1984 and continued to surprise even in his second retirement — in 1985, at sixty-nine, he got married. With much pleasure, the Canadian primate and his old friend from ATC days, Ted Scott, performed the ceremony uniting Frances Best with David Somerville in Toronto. Today friends of the couple cannot think of one without the other, and say the pair is delightful to watch together. Somerville and his wife are indeed close. They enjoy lively discussions on myriad topics and take pleasure in an active joint social and spiritual life.

Somerville with Frances Best in Qualicum Beach before they married.
(Somerville collection)

Frances and her first husband, Canon Jim Best, became the only family Somerville had after his mother died. When he needed rest and relaxation from a stressful episcopate, he would escape to spend a few days with them in Qualicum on Vancouver Island and replenish his batteries; when he needed companionship on several overseas vacations, the Bests went along too. "It seemed perfectly natural, after the Canon died, for Fran and me to continue to be together,"[141] Somerville said, looking back on the decision. Also he believes that marrying Frances was "the best thing I've ever done,"[142] because her presence in his life has created a supremely happy and fulfilled retirement for him. Somerville has continued to indulge in his lifelong hobbies of botany, music (today he loves CDs), and literature, enjoying the additional time retirement has allowed him to spend on his interests, and he has also been able to spend more time with friends, old and new. As he was always in demand to preach, lead retreats, and do Sunday duty when clergy were on holiday, Frances commented that his "retirement did not seem at all like a life of leisure."[143] One of those requests brought Somerville full circle: in 1989 the bishop of Cariboo asked him to preach at the seventy-fifth anniversary of the incorporation of the diocese. The service took place in the Ashcroft church where Somerville's parents had been married and he had been baptized.

Retrospectively, Somerville's clerical colleagues agree that he possesses the four key qualities of a great leader and bishop: self-differentiation, vision, perseverance in the face of obstacles, and a non-anxious presence. Throughout the strident opposition to reforms that he initiated and those he actively supported, the inevitable delays, and some personal attacks, Somerville managed to remain serene. Ingham says that the sacramental foundation to Somerville's life and the fact that he always started and ended his days in prayer have allowed the former bishop to withstand the slings and arrows that came his way.[144] Bishop Jim Cruickshank adds that Somerville's ability to think clearly, to listen to those with opposing views, to formulate his position, and then to articulate a clear stance were at the root of his successful episcopate and the reason he was so universally respected in the Canadian Church. Somerville always worked quietly, without fuss or confrontation. Many others have remarked on how much his clergy liked him throughout his time as bishop of New Westminster, even when they did not fully agree with his reforms. Somerville had the gift of making even the newest, youngest priests in the diocese feel like equals and colleagues, which inspired their constant loyalty and unwavering support.

When asked in 2000 for a sense of the future for the Church, Somerville returned to one of his longstanding predictions of forty years before, commenting that he thought the Christian Church was becoming increasingly irrelevant to many in society who, at the same time, were exhibiting a great hunger for things spiritual. He discussed his previous expectation that the Church would have no income, nowhere in which to hold services, and no friends in high places.[145] In his quiet but measured tones, the former archbishop advised, "I've got an idea that God is going to give us a strong push out of real estate" and "into a closer relationship with the people outside the walls." Wistfully, he concluded, "I'm only sorry I won't be here to take part in it!"[146]

The present diocesan bishop, Michael Ingham remembers Somerville's thoughtful encouragement of him when he was a young rector in his first parish in the diocese: "He didn't tell me what to do, but rather asked penetrating questions about what I *had* done!"[147] Somerville's gentle, wise humour made Ingham rethink some of his actions and consider different approaches to parish challenges. Ingham also observed that Somerville, after he shed the burdens of his episcopate, developed "great . . . dignity and mellowness, which probably isn't possible while in office."[148] Today Ingham and Somerville have lunch together a few times every year, and, when they meet, the current bishop says the former bishop debates circles round him: "He tires me out intellectually! . . . Somerville is reading quantum physics

Archbishop David Somerville (L) and Bishop Michael Ingham meet at synod, May 2005. (Janet Morris)

and he's up to date with the latest Buddhist and New Testament scholarship."[149] At ninety, books remain Somerville's constant companions, and thinking his lifeblood.

Somerville is openly moved and tickled with delight by the attention and honours lavished upon him. "I have three buildings [named for me]* . . . and I'm going to do what the English sovereign does, do a progress around the diocese and stay for a week in each place!"

The Most Reverend David Somerville at the dedication of Somerville House, April 2005. (Bruce Jeffrey)

---

* The buildings include a residence at VST, one at Camp Artaban, and one near to St. James', which is used for social outreach programs.

He considers that he is unusually fortunate to be ninety, commenting, "It's wonderful to have lived long enough to hear this [praise]. For most people, it's at the funeral that people get up and say nice things. I am really quite overwhelmed and overcome." Simply put, his colleagues and friends think Somerville deserves every one of his accolades.

Somerville's courageous actions throughout his episcopate provided a model of careful autonomy for national churches in the Anglican Communion, despite loud demands from Canterbury, Lambeth, and primates to delay the ordination of women and do nothing in case it offended other ecclesiastical provinces. Without him and others like him, the reform might never have happened. Somerville contributed much to the Anglican Church of Canada, the Province of British Columbia and Yukon, and the Diocese of New Westminster in the twentieth century, and arguably to the wider Communion — as Ingham says, "the Gospel acquires authenticity through its incarnation in a person like him."[150]

Somerville, the man and priest, is the legend; his work, the legacy.

David Somerville at home in retirement, 2005. (Julie H. Ferguson)

PART THREE

"Little Big Man"

**The Most Reverend Douglas W. Hambidge,
Seventh Bishop of Caledonia, 1969–1980
Seventh Bishop and Fourth Archbishop of
New Westminster, 1980–1993
Eighth Metropolitan of British Columbia
and Yukon, 1981–1993**

Sharply contrasting with the bishop before him and the bishop after him, Douglas Hambidge was more of a "low" churchman, a term he prefers to avoid. By the time he met the more "high-church," Somerville at his consecration in Prince Rupert, both had come to understand that the Church "was a bit bigger"[151] than either of them, and the terms were irrelevant. They worked as bishops side by side for many years, until Hambidge took over from Somerville in the Diocese of New Westminster. They came to know each other well. But differences aside, Hambidge had a similar start in life to his predecessor and successor. He too had come from humble beginnings.

Tough and wiry, Hambidge is a short man, standing about five foot five. He has finely sculpted features, surmounted by a high forehead, and thin, wide lips that frequently broaden into an engaging smile. His pale blue-grey eyes constantly twinkle with interest, which hints at his determination to find out more about everything. Before time thinned it and turned it silver, he had black hair. The mitre gave him height during his twenty-four-year episcopate — not that his compact frame ever bothered him, for he was always comfortable in his own skin. Strong, and with good hand-eye coordination, he was mechanically inclined and played a good game of squash. Hambidge has a quick, dry wit and can amuse with a phrase — in short he sees the funny side of things, and it makes him an excellent storyteller and facilitator. His modesty is evident within a few minutes of conversation, and so is his attitude to service. He is a skilled listener, who asks open-ended questions that elicit answers. Hambidge never presumes anything about anybody, and, because of it, learns about people quickly, looking for what lies beneath their exteriors. Now seventy-eight, he is still full of energy, bustling around the diocese and beyond, enjoying the demand for his workshops and sermons and serving as the Chancellor of the Vancouver School of Theology.

"If you're a Hambidge, you go to church!"

Douglas Hambidge was born in 1927 in Fulham, an area of London close to Chelsea, to a father who was a labourer and a mother who had been in domestic service before she married. He was the youngest child of four, with three sisters ahead of him, who lived in a very ordinary home. Douglas's family was always involved with the church — his father had been a warden for years and his sisters were frequently volunteering for something. "If you're a Hambidge, you go to church,"[152] his mother used to say. There was no argument, ever, and Douglas grew to like it. As most English kids do, he took instruction and was confirmed at fourteen, remembering that the service struck him as rather dull.

Douglas Hambidge, aged sixteen, in London
during the war. (Hambidge collection)

Douglas joined the church's youth group, run by an excellent
vicar, Canon Gilbert Williams, who had trained in Toronto and served
most of his ministry in western Canada. Douglas heard a lot from
Williams about Canada and soon made up his mind to visit the country. One evening, a couple of years later, the priest asked the teenagers
what they would do if they suddenly came into a lot of money. The
sixteen-year-old surprised Williams, and himself even more, when he
blurted out that he would train for ordination. Afterwards the priest
asked him, "Were you serious?"

Douglas replied, "Well, not really. I don't have the money."[153] He
went home and told his parents what had happened. Initially they
did not encourage their son's vocation, because they were afraid to
raise his hopes for what they thought was an unlikely path for him to

follow. Once they realized his determination, however, both quickly became fully supportive. His father died soon afterwards.

Like Somerville and most young men who have experienced an early calling, Douglas was encouraged to pursue it by an understanding priest. However, the London Blitz interrupted his high-school education and he did not matriculate (graduate), which was to delay his goal. His school closed, and Douglas was assigned to a machine shop, working twelve hours a day for the war effort. He experienced the dislocation of a great city hit by air raids almost every night. However Douglas never gave up on his matriculation and took correspondence courses. He would stagger home from an exhausting day and study as the bombs rained down. Just before peace was declared, Douglas was called up. The army did not take his plea that he needed to finish his matriculation as sufficient reason to defer his service, so he ended up in boot camp a few days after his eighteenth birthday in 1945.

Fortunately, he missed the European war and spent three relatively happy years in the Royal Army Service Corps, rising through the ranks to become a non-commissioned officer. The RASC was responsible for supplying everything the army needed, and, when required, transported troops from one area to another. The RASC taught Hambidge to ride motorcycles, drive trucks and ambulances, and later to be a mechanic, all which proved invaluable later in his chosen career when he found himself in northern Canada. Hambidge served for two years in the Middle East at a fascinating time; he was posted to Palestine in 1947, while the British Mandate (government) was still in effect but drawing to a close. The army experienced some hazardous and bloody moments, as Jews and Arabs fought each other over territory, having only their hatred of the British in common. The establishment of the state of Israel on May 14, 1948, saw the British forces chased from Jerusalem with gunfire, and Hambidge remembers escorting a convoy of trucks through a hail of bullets. Trucks that were hit were abandoned, but Hambidge got through. When the company reached Port Said, he was demobilized, but not until the army tried to entice him to stay in with a promotion if he signed on for another five years. He was mildly tempted but refused, saying, "No. I know what I have to do."[154]

Hambidge in the British army in Italy, 1946.
(Hambidge collection)

Hambidge's vocation, instead of weakening, strengthened while
he was in the forces, and month by month he became more convinced
that he should be a priest. Back in London, as he still had not matric-
ulated, he scouted around for a place to complete his education.
Hambidge found that the London Bible College offered matriculation courses, as well as theological studies. Once he had finished the
British equivalent of Grade 12, he transferred in 1949 to the London
College of Divinity, part of London University, financed by a substantial ex-servicemen's grant from the government that solved his
inability to pay the tuition fees.

The college was in Lingfield, Surrey, a delightful old village not far
south of London. Students spent every Sunday and one evening a
week doing parish work to gain experience. Hambidge was twenty-

five when he graduated in 1953. He was immediately ordained a deacon and assigned to St. Mark's, Dalston, a parish of twenty-five thousand in the Borough of Hackney. Rough and tough, the neighbourhood was in the heart of London, a little northeast of its centre, and a world away from the more sedate Fulham of his childhood. Hambidge quickly discovered that his service in the army, at the lower end of the scheme of things, had prepared him well for St. Mark's. His chief responsibility was with the youth group and, as a fringe benefit, he was instructed to join the badminton club. Hambidge also led a Bible study for the young people after church on Sunday evenings, as well as open-air evangelistic services of witness on Saturday evenings.

Hambidge graduates from the London School of Divinity, 1953. Principal Donald Coggan, a future Archbishop of Canterbury, congratulates him. (Hambidge collection)

Nothing fazed the young deacon. He had been exposed to the best and worst of characters and behaviour in the army — dreadful swearing, dirty jokes, and exhibitions of poor conduct. This exposure left him with a good understanding of humankind. "I was aware of what ordinary people were like, because I was one of them. . . . I found I could speak to people as a fellow traveller rather than as someone who knows all the answers."[155] Hambidge believes that his army service made a huge difference to his future in ordained ministry.

Hambidge was ordained priest in the fall of 1954 and spent two more years at St. Mark's. The ordination ceremony took place at St. Paul's Cathedral, the spiritual heart of London, which has seen so many of the nation's foremost thanksgivings, weddings, and funerals. The magnificent building, designed by Christopher Wren and consecrated in 1697, had miraculously survived the Blitz unscathed, while everything around it was flattened. Although an ordination is always very meaningful, Hambidge remembers his more for those who attended it — his mother and his three sisters and their husbands were filled with pride and gave him their wholehearted support. The priest, Gilbert Williams, who encouraged his vocation and his desire to see Canada was waiting for him after the service on the steps of the cathedral. "He, more than anyone else in the world, enabled me and carried me. . . . We kept in touch until he died,"[156] recalled Hambidge.

Hambidge met Denise, the love of his life, during his curacy, and they married towards the end of his time at St. Mark's. The couple had decided that, if they were to experience Canada, they had better do it immediately and as immigrants. Canon Williams wrote to several Canadian bishops on Hambidge's behalf, which resulted in an offer from the Diocese of Caledonia. The young couple planned to work there for only a few years, fully expecting to return to London and their families afterwards.

"I felt I was a failure"

Sent to the one-point parish of All Saints' in the diocese of Caledonia, the Hambidges moved in 1956 to Cassiar, in far northwestern British Columbia. The mining town lay just south of the border with Yukon, and about three hundred kilometres east of Skagway, Alaska. Four years before they arrived it had been a tent town, accommodating the 250 miners and construction workers who built the town and asbestos mine. Situated in stunning, but remote, mountainous terrain, Cassiar was a typical company town that also offered spectacular summer and winter recreation for all residents. However Hambidge and Denise had never hiked, hunted, or curled in their lives. Nor had they ever lived in a small town, with its goldfish-bowl existence. The winters were unlike any they had lived through, with many feet of snow, deep cold, and long, dark days. The newly married couple could not have been more out of their depth. Coming from the huge city of London and a parish of twenty-five thousand, they experienced culture shock that was beyond description.

The energetic Hambidge didn't have enough to do in Cassiar, for his congregation numbered only twenty-one. Also, what he did do was laughed at. He behaved as if he were a parish priest in a big English city. "I didn't know anything else. . . . They were two bad years."[157] In the 1950s, Cassiar residents were a hard-drinking, unsophisticated lot, who had nothing in common with the young priest and his wife, although Hambidge did understand them. The couple had no car (he borrowed the doctor's when he had to), they missed the culture offered in London, and they had to manage with only the necessities of life. Denise was homesick, which was not helped by letters from her mother that told her how much she was missed. Hambidge quickly learned that he could connect with his entire congregation every evening at the local curling rink, so he learned to curl. He met aboriginal people for the first time in his life in Cassiar — they lived in a tent on the fringe of town, but did not attend the church. Hambidge and his wife visited them regularly, and he would hold a service for them. The young Londoners endured, but lived for the day they could return to England.

After two miserable years, the time came to depart in 1958, and, at the last minute, the bishop offered Hambidge the four-point parish of St. James's in Smithers, left vacant when the incumbent was killed in a highway accident. Hambidge accepted it, and the couple deferred their long-awaited return to London. But God had a hand in it, and staying in Canada was the best decision they could have made. Smithers, in British Columbia's lovely Bulkley Valley, turned out to be their homecoming and the place where Hambidge says he discovered what ministry was all about. Further south than Cassiar, the town of several thousand lies between Prince Rupert and Prince George, and is also nestled among stunning mountains, lakes, and rivers; Smithers is the gateway to some of British Columbia's most outstanding wilderness areas. Outdoor activities and the winters were already familiar to the Hambidges, but, by now, they were kitted out to cope with the cold and snow. Smithers also had more cultural activities to interest them and its warm rural hospitality provided them with an active social life and friends. The Hambidges settled in and, much to their surprise, found they liked the community. Hambidge was kept busy with four congregations strung out along fifty miles of the Yellowhead Highway, and Denise gave birth to their first two children, Caryl and Stephen, there.

The four congregations that made up his parish included Smithers, Telkwa, Quick, and Houston further to the southeast towards Prince George. This meant that Hambidge drove well over a hundred miles every Sunday — he had his own car by now — and delivered four sermons at five services. The parishioners were young and active, and he got to know most of them well, driving miles to visit them in their own homes and rarely leaving without eating a meal with them. There were Bible studies, Sunday schools, meetings, youth groups, and parish gatherings for him to attend. Babies were "being born like crazy"[158] in the late 1950s, and Hambidge baptized most of them. The rectory was home to the Smithers youth group: "Crowds of kids" remembered the former rector with delight. "We had a great time."[159] They played games, read the Bible, and simply enjoyed being together. When the Hambidges' daughter, Caryl, was born, the youth played "Pass the Baby (Parcel)" with her. Hambidge was run off his feet in Smithers, but happy.

With very little money and two small children, it was hard for the Hambidges to go out much; even an evening at the movies had to be saved for and planned. He played badminton to stay fit when he could. On the road, Hambidge would read a little, but at home he devoted himself to the family. They always liked to travel, and went on long camping trips for their summer holidays.

Hambidge had limited contact with First Nations peoples in the Smithers area. However, he began to get to know the Gitksan of Kitwanga, Gitwangak, and Kispiox when his bishop asked him to take a funeral in the parish of Kitwanga. The funeral did not go well, due to Hambidge's ignorance of Native ways, and the weather was foul. As the coffin was lowered, the grave's sides collapsed from the incessant rain and half the village fell in after it. Afterwards, the village elders complained about Hambidge to his bishop, who gave him a few pointers about ministering to First

Nations peoples. His number-one recommendation: do not work by your clock. Hambidge took the advice to heart, and began to engage with and learn from the Gitksan. Later, when Hambidge left for another parish, the village of Kitwanga would present him with a Native print as a thank-you gift and inscribed at the bottom in their language was their nickname for him, "We Gyet," which means "Little Big Man." Despite his inauspicious debut, he had been accepted.

The far-flung parish centred on Smithers was not without its challenges. The smaller congregations needed to establish a sense of identity, as they often felt they were the "poor relations who got what was left over from the ministry in Smithers." Hambidge wanted them to have more than just a Sunday service from him. He spent much time convincing them that they were fully entitled to their share of his time, and drew diagrams to give them an idea of the proportion they were receiving. Hambidge also joined the Royal Canadian Legion as chaplain, and used it as an avenue to reach those who were not Anglicans, but he found the most effective route through which to reach out was the local radio station. Like Somerville, he became a regular broadcaster, and soon everyone knew him, churchgoers or not.

When the new radio station, CFBV, came to town, they asked Hambidge if he would like a spot with which to do what he liked. He jumped at the opportunity, and soon he was broadcasting every evening just before 7 p.m. Hambidge broadcast live, rarely pretaping his programs, because he preferred the immediacy it provided. He made his spot a sort of "Thought for the Day" and often told enthralling stories about the pioneers of the region that instantly connected with his listeners. He quickly became popular. His slightly clipped English accent gave him away all over his parish, and he was recognized in the gas station, the grocery store, everywhere. The citizens enjoyed and were interested in his stories and ideas, so they tuned in regularly. The community rapidly absorbed Hambidge as one of their own.

After six tiring years in Smithers, and having lost their craving to return to England, Hambidge asked his newly elected bishop, Eric Munn, for a one-point parish. Canada was now truly "home" for the Hambidges, and he and Denise became Canadian citizens.

In 1964, he gladly accepted the offer of the parish of St. Martin's in Fort St. John.

Fort St. John, on the Alaska Highway, is a resource town in the heart of Peace River country in northeastern British Columbia. High-grade oil and natural gas had been discovered there in the early 1950s, and the Hambidges found themselves in a rapidly growing, modern city, a five-hundred-kilometre drive northeast of Prince George. Set east of the Rockies, on the prairies, Fort St. John feels as if it is in Alberta rather than British Columbia, and its citizens relate more to Edmonton than Vancouver. Residents enjoy endless daylight in the summer and spectacular displays of the *aurora borealis* in the winter. Wildlife abounds.

Although Fort St. John started out as a one-point parish, after several years it became a twelve-point. Priests kept leaving and the bishop kept asking Hambidge to look after more and more congregations. Eventually, he was responsible for Fort Nelson 250 miles north and Bear Lake 250 miles south, with others almost as far-flung in between. Congregations numbered four or five at Cecil Lake on a good Sunday, twenty at Taylor, maybe thirty at Fort Nelson, all of which had their own tiny churches. None could be combined and, of course, Hambidge could not visit them every week, but he did establish a regular schedule. In winter, services had to be held in someone's home, as the log churches had no heating. Hambidge always delivered a good service, even if only two turned up, and he took teaching the faith just as seriously. To reach Fort Nelson every other Sunday, he left Fort St. John right after the morning worship and drove furiously all day, arriving in time to take an evening service. Then he spent the next day visiting the parishioners, the shut-ins, and the sick. The next Sunday, Hambidge repeated the drive, but to the south: "I used to burn a car out in three years. They were quickly beaten up — most of the roads were gravel. The Alaska Highway was better in the winter, because all the potholes were full of ice."[160] Hambidge was not the least bit concerned about driving in all weather and conditions — in this his army experience came in handy. He knew, with his ability as a mechanic, he could fix most breakdowns. Recently, however, he admitted that he pushed the limits occasionally and had a few tricky moments.

Meanwhile, his family was growing up, and he tried to spend as much time at home as he could. He and Denise had their third and last child, Graham, in 1968 while in Fort St. John. His huge parish and family demands meant Hambidge had little time for leisure.

In 1965 he was appointed Canon of St. Andrew's Cathedral in Prince Rupert. Hambidge was also able to continue his radio ministry in Fort St. John, first doing a daily devotional spot called "Strength for the Day" and a thirty-minute "Sunday Profile." He quickly became a well-known radio personality in the Peace district as well, and added open-line programs and round-table discussions. Much to his delight, his prime-time, open-line show topped the ratings of the Alberta premier Ernest Manning, who also had a Bible program. Hambidge used his skills of theological reflection to tackle any topic of local interest. Still broadcasting live when he could, he had to tape his Sunday show. The head of the station gave Hambidge a key, and he used to slip in late on Saturday night and record, leaving the tape in a box for the next day. People who lived out in the bush told Hambidge that his "Sunday Profiles" programs were "the only church we've got and we gather round on a Sunday morning to listen to you."[161] Those who came home from the oilfields on Sundays to be with their families also listened to him as they drove. Everyone from miles around knew Hambidge, and he was excited with the reach of his radio ministry, as well as proud of the results.

Two years after his last child, Graham, was born, Hambidge's bishop of five years died unexpectedly. As Eric Munn had become a close friend and a source of much encouragement, Hambidge felt the loss keenly. He was now forty-two and an experienced priest who loved ministering in the towns and villages of northern British Columbia. In March 1969, Hambidge attended the electoral synod that would choose Munn's successor. He filled his station wagon with clergy who did not want to drive, and they headed south to Caledonia's see city of Prince Rupert. On the long journey, the car got a flat tire and Hambidge changed it expertly while his colleagues watched. Next day the synod started at 9 a.m., and an hour later it was over. Hambidge was bishop.

"It's a lovely parish . . . 150 miles from the nearest water tap."

The Londoner who had started off ill at ease in the north was now the bishop of Caledonia, leading a vast northern diocese that was sparsely populated and comprised a high percentage of First Nations peoples. When the result was announced, Hambidge remembers, "I just couldn't believe it. I was really speechless."[162] When asked by Godfrey Gower, the archbishop, if he accepted the election, Hambidge could only squeak out an inaudible "Yes!" He had imagined happily serving as a parish priest all his life, and had no desire for episcopal office. Neither had he sought it. The election result simply stunned him.

Denise already knew when her husband phoned later to tell her the news; a parishioner had heard it on the radio, along with the rest of Fort St. John, and called her. The radio station had interrupted regular programming to announce it: "Another first for CKNL — Canon Hambidge has been elected bishop!" On the long drive home to Fort St. John, the car got another flat tire. This time the clergy changed it, and Hambidge watched in thoughtful silence. His reflections on the trip were profound, and he realized that the Church had spoken clearly and God's call had been loud. Hambidge did not argue with it and

Hambidge with his family on the day of his consecration in Caledonia, 1969.
L to R: Caryl, Denise, Graham (on his mother's knee), the new bishop, Stephen.
(Hambidge collection)

had reached a measure of acceptance by the time he arrived home. Denise had also thought about it, and knew their lives had changed forever. She started packing for the move to Prince Rupert.

The new bishop of Caledonia was young for the mitre, and admitted that he felt inadequate for the task. He knew only parts of the diocese and some of the clergy well. Now he was responsible for over ten thousand Anglicans, fewer parishioners than his first parish in London, but spread over a formidable 536,128 square kilometres. His diocese was the whole northern half of British Columbia, stretching from the Queen Charlotte Islands in the west to the Alberta border in the east, and from the Yukon border in the north, south nearly to Prince George. This vastness made Caledonia the second-largest diocese in area in Canada, but its division into four regional deaneries eased the burden. Hambidge may have been unsure of the ways and needs of the aboriginals that made up 50 per cent of his flock, but one factor was to help Hambidge starting out. He had watched and admired how his predecessor, Bishop Munn, had done the job, and he began by following his model of close association with the clergy and laity.

Archbishop of New Westminster, Godfrey Gower, consecrated Hambidge in the auditorium of Prince Rupert high school on Sunday, May 11, 1969, assisted by his co-adjutor, Bishop David Somerville, the bishop of Yukon, John Frame, who preached the sermon, and the assistant bishop of Cariboo, Tom Greenwood. People arrived from all over the diocese to attend, often travelling many, many miles, and packed the hall till it was overflowing. The Nisga'a, the Haida, the Tsimshian, and the Gitksan arrived to play for the consecration, and the service was from the old prayer book, ordered with no input from the incoming bishop.

Hambidge remembers little of the ceremony and, at the time, did not recognize the significance of the First Nations involvement. He was still pinching himself and wondering how he got there from his modest beginnings. After the service, when a CBC reporter asked him what his vision was for Caledonia, Hambidge replied, "I don't have one. I'm going to find out."[163] That attitude turned out to be the essence of his long episcopate — his vision or strategy was not the issue, the diocese's was. "God speaks to the church, not only to bishops," he said.[164]

Archbishop Godfrey Gower, metropolitan, presents Hambidge
to the diocese of Caledonia after his consecration in Prince Rupert,
May 11, 1969. (Hambidge collection)

The new bishop's installation* took place in St. Andrew's
Cathedral on the following Thursday. It was a smaller affair, as everyone who attended his consecration had returned home. Then
Hambidge's learning and work commenced. His synod office was not
promising; it was one room in the basement of the bishop's house. He
had only one member of staff: Eileen James, the secretary-treasurer of

---

* In the late 1960s, installations were usually performed separately from the consecration.

the diocese, who also acted as his secretary. He used to carry a small tape recorder in his car and learned to dictate letters while driving. "I hate it when you come home," Eileen used to say as he dropped the tape on her desk, often containing fifty letters. Hambidge soon realized he was going to be a "working" bishop; there would not be much delegation of tasks for him, although he gave away what he could of the day-to-day administration. Hambidge chaired his first meeting the day after his installation, and visited the radio station in Prince Rupert, expecting to be welcomed with open arms. Their refusal to allow him to broadcast was a disappointment. Then Hambidge undertook his first tour of his diocese.

Despite the fact that he made it in a car, it was an expedition reminiscent of George Hills's progresses around British Columbia. The journey through sparsely inhabited wilderness was long — no confirmations had been done for a year and he had to catch up with those — and filled with new places, people, and experiences. The benefit of the confirmation backlog meant that Hambidge quickly got to know his flock of clergy and parishioners. A few years before, the northern parishes strung along the Alaska Highway had been absorbed into the Diocese of Yukon, so Hambidge started out with over forty congregations and seventeen clergy, smaller in numbers than New Westminster but much larger in territory. The bishop would burn out as many cars as he did while a parish priest.

Hambidge quickly discovered a strong sense of community in the diocese. The parishes cared about each other, despite the distances between them. He also began to get to know the First Nations' Anglicans who made up almost 50 per cent of the parishioners. Many were Nisga'a in the Nass Valley, who lived in the three villages of New Aiyansh (population: 1,200), Greenville (800), and Kincolith (400), and Hambidge found they were "passionately committed to their church."[165] Caledonia also took in the Queen Charlotte Islands (Haida Gwai) of the Haida nation, as well as the Tsimshian and Gitksan peoples.

Whenever he visited Fort St. John, Hambidge hit the airwaves again. The manager of the station, Mel Stephenson, would call the bishop and say, "Come in and do an interview!" and they would sit around the microphone and chat about whatever took Hambidge's fancy. The bishop loved it. The first time Hambidge showed up as a bishop, the manager put on a record. It was "Deep Purple" and Hambidge retorted, "You're playing my song!"[166]

Caledonia was an assisted diocese, which relied on the national church for sufficient money to operate. When these funds were reduced by a huge $20,000 the year before Hambidge took over the diocese, the loss influenced everything. With only three parishes self-supporting before the cuts, the bishop saw himself in a pioneering, rescuing role. Hambidge immediately focused on guiding the diocese to form a vision for its future and to build a strategy to accomplish it. He spent three or four days at each parish, always participating in the community's life, taking a Bible study or visiting the sick, as well as facilitating their strategic planning. He talked with the parish council and held evening gatherings for everyone, during which he discovered their needs and ideas. Countless times around the diocese, he asked the question, "What do you believe God wants us to do? What do you believe God wants you to do as a parish?"[167] From the beginning, Hambidge insisted that he did not own the diocesan vision and ferreted it out of others by initiating discussions about stewardship, parish responsibility, parish requirements, and the type of clergy they wanted. Then he listened. At the beginning of the 1970s, his flock discerned that they must have more self-supporting parishes. Some achieved that vision and others had to be pushed into it. By 1978, half the parishes had succeeded, and their assessments doubled in eight years, reducing Caledonia's dependence on the national church and stirring a spirit of confidence. Hambidge also instituted a common stipend for clergy that meant everyone was paid the same salary, housing allowance, etc. Those with more responsibility, like regional deans, received a "responsibility allowance," and those in very remote areas were paid an "isolation allowance" to compensate for their higher cost of living.

Another articulated requirement was for less turnover in clergy — the average priest's stay in a parish, when Hambidge arrived in the north in 1959, was only eighteen months, because of the isolation, the high cost of living, and dismal stipends.* Given that it took about five years to build up a parish and Hambidge could not increase the

---

* The cost of living in the north was 30 per cent higher than Vancouver, and the stipends 50 per cent lower. The bishop received a lower salary than the average parish priest living in Vancouver.

pay in a financially strapped diocese, he implemented an incentive. He warned prospective priests that, if they opted to leave in less than five years, they would have to pay back the money spent in relocating them to Caledonia. The strategy helped, and the bishop had less trouble finding priests for remote parishes than he expected: "I found that people responded to a challenge."[168] Hambidge never hid the negatives by saying, "Oh! It's a lovely parish. You'll enjoy it out there — 150 miles from the nearest water tap!"[169] Rather, he told priests that Caledonia was tough and the pay was lousy, but that they would enjoy a strong sense of community. Fewer vacancies occurred during his tenure. Hambidge was very proud of the fruits of this labour. He found it exciting, worthwhile, and was very satisfied when growth took place. A by-product of the intense effort was the solid relationships that developed. Hambidge made lots of friends, many of whom he is still in touch with today.

Another source of pride for Hambidge was the awakening of the diocese to social-justice issues during his time. The first revolved around liquor stores, a seemingly odd focus for a religious body. At that time aboriginals were not allowed into liquor stores to buy alcohol and had to get their supplies from bootleggers. Hambidge's first synod as a priest in Caledonia decided that this was a justice issue, not a liquor issue, and asked the bishop to lobby the government. He did so, saying that Caledonia did not think that life should be spent drinking, but it was an injustice that one race of people were not allowed into liquor stores.

The matter of the ordination of women took longer for the rural diocese to work through, and Hambidge did not rush things, although he supported the reform from the outset. In 1974, delegates who had been at General Synod the year before raised it for discussion. Caledonia listened to the minority who objected and allowed them to object. "We spent a lot of time on it. We talked about it a lot and we prayed a lot. We talked about it some more and said, 'No, we're not going to just rush off and leave some people behind,' and gradually we saw, as a diocese, that we could move without forcing anybody to do anything. Nobody was being compelled. But we said, 'Before all else, it's a justice issue.'"[170] No priests in Caledonia signed the *Manifesto* opposing General Synod's decision to go ahead with the reform, but five of thirty-four clergy opposed the Caledonian motion that approved the ordination of women in 1974. By the time Somerville ordained two women in Vancouver in November 1976, Caledonia was ready too. On January 9, 1977, Hambidge ordained the first woman, Dorothy Daly, in a warm and intimate ceremony in the small Chetwynd church in the Peace district.

Hambidge also guided Caledonia through the upheavals of liturgical reform. He encouraged the experimental liturgies that led to the *BAS*, the move to pull altars forward and have priests facing their congregations, and more modern music. He had to prevent one of his more eager priests writing a new liturgy every week, and insisted that he only try the approved alternative liturgies. He supported his clergy in embracing the changes, but he found they needed to be done incrementally. The greatest acceptance occurred when the clergy listened to the opinions of those in the pews and did not thrust reform upon them. Change evolved more slowly in the rural outposts of Caledonia than in urban parishes, but it did happen.

Bishops have more than diocesan responsibilities. They are members of the national and provincial Houses of Bishops, deliberating on many subjects, they often sit on committees of the national Church, and sometimes they contribute to studies and commissions that the primate establishes. Hambidge was no exception, but initially he did not enjoy the regular meetings of the House of Bishops. In the 1970s, he found the thirty-odd bishops were separated into have and have-not dioceses — those dioceses that were self-supporting and the nine that were "assisted" by the national church. "We [the assisted dioceses] were treated like poor relations . . . and were not expected to engage in debate."[171] They were often called the "welfare bishops," and Hambidge was so offended by the attitude of the "big boys" towards them that he asked the primate if he could resign from the House.

But everything changed when Ted Scott became primate. At the meetings, Scott set up an in-house bar, so the bishops could socialize together in the evenings, and David Somerville, when he became metropolitan in 1975, laid down standards of behaviour with which the Canadian bishops were expected to comply. Another result of the new leadership was training for new bishops, which turned out so well that the "older" bishops took the week-long workshops too. Together they studied conflict resolution, time management, burn-out, and other relevant topics, just as Somerville had done in the 1960s. Hambidge discovered quickly that unshared episcopal stress is real and hazardous, especially for bishops who undertake too much. Later, in New Westminster, he learned to lean on his archdeacons and discuss the most stressful issues with them, as well as play squash — hard. Hambidge also always took regular vacations, blocking them out in his diary the previous September in black felt pen so he could not erase them.

Early in his episcopate in Caledonia, the Canadian House of Bishops asked the bishop of Yukon, John Frame, and Hambidge to take part in the study "The Wider Ordained Ministry," and to provide recommendations to the Anglican Church of Canada. The request stemmed from Lambeth 1968's decision to permit women into the diaconate, which subsequently opened the way to the ordination of women to the priesthood. Frame and Hambidge looked at the issue broadly and included an inquiry into the recovery of the vocational diaconate in their study process.

In the late 1960s, all deacons in the Canadian Anglican church were male priests-in-waiting. The diaconate was considered a transition period, usually of about a year, that all priests went through after theological training and before being ordained to the priesthood. Hambidge and Frame discovered that there were a number of priests who had actually been called to the diaconate, not to the priesthood, and some laity who were called to be permanent deacons. From there, the two bishops set about devising a way that would allow individuals to serve the Church of God as deacons. Although not a new idea, the ministry of the vocational diaconate had fallen into disuse in much of the Anglican Communion. Vocational deacons, often employed outside the church in regular jobs, serve as a bridge between church and community, and help to support and nurture church members in their ministries.

Frame and Hambidge looked at how best to re-establish this ministry. They consulted widely, and slowly developed a course of action to make it happen. They did not rush the process; in fact, the first vocational deacons were not ordained in New Westminster until June 1995,* after Hambidge retired. The two bishops had to consider everything: discerning the calls, selection, training, titles, and even clerical collars. Hambidge had to reassure some clergy who were afraid that unpaid vocational deacons might take over their roles. He also steered the resolution re-establishing the diaconate in New Westminster at the 1986 synod when he was metropolitan. Nowadays many parishes have one or more deacons, both male and female, who work in their own careers and model servanthood to their parishes in myriad ways, bringing new perspectives and gifts to the clergy teams. Hambidge is very proud of his part in the process that returned the vocational diaconate, and remembers, with a smile, that he and Frame were at opposite poles when it came to the ordination of women: "We were close friends but had different theologies. [Frame] never budged in his opposition to women in the priesthood."[172]

Wal'aks Im Kran Dadils

Unaware of the significance of it, Hambidge was adopted by the Nisga'a into their Raven family at the reception after his consecration. For the Nisga'a, this gathering was considered a "feast" and, traditionally, at such events they announce adoptions and names. Hambidge watched and listened as the hereditary chiefs of the Eagle, the Raven, the Killer Whale, and the Wolf clans gave speeches in Nisga'a and then together shouted out, "Wal'aks Im Kran Dadils" at the end. The priest from New Aiyansh, John Blyth, explained to the new bishop what was happening, and told him that he had been identified as a chief or leader and named "Wal'aks." Hambidge also received paddles, a sweater, all kinds of things as gifts, but the name was the most important of all. After the speeches and gift-giving, Hambidge was presented to the head of the Raven clan, Phyllis MacMillan: "This is the woman who's adopted you. She's your mother."[173] Hambidge spoke and thanked her, but admitted later, "I frankly thought it was just a nice way of welcoming a new bishop, and I really didn't expect to hear another word about it."[174]

---

* Bruce Morris, Marilyn Hames, and Margery Sager.

Hambidge in 1993 with his adoptive Nisga'a parents —
Patrick (L) and Phyllis (R) MacMillan. (Hambidge collection)

The significance of naming in Nisga'a tradition is similar to that of many ancient cultures. Every recipient of a Nisga'a name *belongs* to the Nisga'a and is expected to live up to the meaning of their new name. Hambidge's name, Wal'aks, translated into "the bearer of the living water," and had been carefully chosen for him from the Nisga'a treasure house of names. Adopting a person into the family also helps the Nisga'a get around the unease they feel when dealing with strangers. As soon as Hambidge deduced what was going on, the new bishop realized Wal'aks was a powerful name and came with responsibilities. "It challenged my whole ministry," he said in retrospect.[175]

Two weeks after his adoption, Phyllis phoned Hambidge and said, "Wal'aks, there's a wedding in Greenville and you have to be there."

"Do you want me to take the service?" asked Hambidge.

"No!"

"Oh! You want me to preach?"

"No! You're family," said his mother, as she bade him goodbye.

Then there was the matter of visiting. The first time Hambidge dropped by to see his mother, he knocked on her door. No answer. He knocked again and then again. Eventually Phyllis opened the door and asked, "What are you knocking for? You're a member of the family. I won't answer the door again if you knock. You walk in!" Soon after that visit he was with one of his "aunties," and she asked him if he would like a cup of coffee. "Yes! I'd love a cup of coffee," replied Hambidge.

"Well, get it then!" she said.

"I didn't know I was allowed to," murmured the chastened bishop, who was still operating as a visitor with British manners.

As the trust between Hambidge and Nisga'a grew, his mother asked if he would perform the marriage of one of her "sisters." He happily agreed and, instead of receiving a fee, was given a beautiful red and black Nisga'a blanket. Initially Hambidge thought it would make a unique wall-hanging and then realized it could be made into a stunning cope. Knowing that he must ask permission to do so, he approached his mother. "Would anybody be offended if I wore it for the wedding?" he asked.

"No, I don't think anyone would mind," Phyllis replied with a straight face.

Nisga'a blankets are the equivalent of identity cards. Hambidge's has a border of triangles which signify he is a chief. On the back is a raven in a nest, which demonstrated that he was a new Raven. Around that is a circle, signifying the moon. This symbol honours Denise, Hambidge's wife, whose Nisga'a name means "daughter of the moon."

Hambidge wearing his Nisga'a blanket as a cope and showing the symbol of a raven in a nest surrounded by a moon. (Hambidge collection)

The wedding day arrived and Hambidge proudly donned his new cope, red and black, with its magnificent button embroidery. He entered the church to await the bride and was quite unprepared for the reaction — the people in the pews began weeping, men included. Hambidge was unaware then that the blankets had been banned by the government and church for about seventy years, along with the Nisga'a ceremonial regalia and totem poles. His conversion of the blanket into a cope to wear in church was overwhelmingly symbolic for the Nisga'a, and a first for the Anglican Church of Canada.

Hambidge's decision to convert the Nisga'a blanket into a cope also signified the major turning point in his relationship with the Nisga'a. It demonstrated to his adoptive family that he had accepted their values and supported them wholeheartedly. Wearing his blanket cope was also a profound moment for Hambidge. At that moment he felt, deep inside, that he truly was an elder of the Nisga'a nation, a son of his Raven mother. Their problems had become his. He said, "I couldn't accept the gifts and the privilege without the responsibility."[176] As the Nisga'a began to talk to him more freely, Hambidge heard about their land-claim issues. Soon they were directing him to get involved as a spiritual chief of theirs, not as a bishop of the Anglican Church. He took their lead.

Hambidge wearing his Nisga'a mitre
with three ermine tails and the symbol
of his adoptive family, a raven.
(PSA, uncatalogued)

After the wedding, more and more Nisga'a brought out their long-hidden blankets to wear, talking sticks and totems reappeared, and the men again made traditional headdresses for special occasions. Then Hambidge's Nisga'a mother realized that he needed a mitre to go with his cope. She directed that it be made as befitted a chief. As chief's headdresses always had three ermine tails, the new mitre was to have them. When Hambidge heard about this, he explained to Phyllis that a bishop's headdress must have only two. "You're going to have three," she retorted. Hambidge did not argue, and so his striking Nisga'a mitre has three ermine tails.

Bit by bit, it began to dawn on Hambidge that the ceremony after his consecration meant something far more than he had anticipated. Adoption really was adoption! He really was a member of the Raven family. He might be a bishop, but he was Nisga'a too — a Nisga'a chief with a servant role. Hambidge was a part of the movement to conduct worship services in the Nisga'a language, which also led to the devising of a written form of what had always been an oral tradition.

In 1972, Hambidge responded to his new responsibilities and arranged to hold the first ever synod in New Aiyansh, the main Nisga'a village; he also invited the primate, Ted Scott. Scott's attendance was significant, because it signalled the Canadian Church was beginning to appreciate that the relationship between the Nisga'a and the Church was different than first supposed. The primate said, "The Indians are bringing that to which they belong to God."[177] The elders got very excited over the honour of hosting synod and decided to paint the village for the occasion, taxing each family $5 per head to pay for it. The bishop also got a note: "Please send your $5." New totems were erected for the occasion, and blessed in the Nisga'a way by a chief and in the Christian way by their bishop.

The synod feast was spectacular — the dishes were traditional and bountiful, and the entertainment was the like of which no synod had ever seen. In full ceremonial regalia, some brought out for the first time in decades, seventy Nisga'a danced and sang, shining with pride, before Hambidge and Scott. It was only the second time the Nisga'a had performed the celebration since the laws banning such events had been repealed in 1951. The whole evening rang with a joyous and authentic outpouring of Nisga'a spirituality to their Christian

God, which moved everyone who was lucky enough to be present. Late, late into the night, the Nisga'a adopted the primate, as they had Hambidge, and gave him a very special blanket, which had taken much thought and work to produce. Scott, as the spiritual leader of all Canadian Anglicans, was not adopted into a family but into the whole Nisga'a nation. His blanket was embroidered with the symbols of all four clans, and his new name, *Gott Lisims*, meant "the heart of the nation." The chiefs told him that he was expected to uphold the spirit of the Nisga'a nation. Scott was overwhelmed with emotion and found it hard to speak. A while later, he managed to say that only one other moment in his life had meant as much, and that was when he became primate. Scott went on to support the Nisga'a cause in every way he could.

The Most Reverend Ted Scott, primate of Canada, at the historic synod of the diocese of Caledonia in New Aiyansh in April 1972. He is about to receive his Nisga'a name of "Gott Lisims" and his blanket. Hambidge is behind Scott on the left. (DNW13-2)

After that mind-expanding experience, Hambidge continued to sit quietly and listen to his Nisga'a family and others. He learned of their deep conviction that they *were* the church, the Body of Christ. He discovered more about their passion for the Nass River Valley, about eighty kilometres north of Prince Rupert, where they had lived and thrived for over ten thousand years. He absorbed their worries about the politics of the land settlement they were facing, and experienced their belief that it would eventually be solved. Most of all, Hambidge allowed the Nisga'a to guide him and never told them what he thought they should do.

Hambidge learned early that the Nisga'a spoke for themselves — always. He would attend their meetings with non-Natives simply to add his voice as a Nisga'a if asked. The bishop uses as an example the later struggle they had with AMAX of Canada Ltd. AMAX was mining molybdenum in Alice Arm and, allowed by federal government permits, dumping the heavy-metal tailings into the Nisga'a fishing grounds, poisoning halibut, salmon, and King crabs. After a year of futile efforts with Ottawa, the Nisga'a contacted Hambidge saying, "We think you should come along with us to the meeting with the Canadian president of AMAX." He did so, sporting his purple shirt and clerical collar, and surprised the president when he told him that he was not the spokesperson. The session began with introductions around the table.

"My name is _____ and I am a lay reader in the Anglican Church."

"My name is _____ and I am a warden in the Anglican Church."

"My name is Douglas Hambidge and I am a bishop in the Anglican Church."

"My name is _____ and I am on the parish council of St. Andrew's."

When the president announced that the business of the day would begin, Hambidge interjected quietly, "Well, before we get down to business, it's our custom in the Nass villages, whatever the business is, to begin with prayer. It's a bit embarrassing to start the business without a prayer. It's not our way of doing things." So the lay readers prayed and discomfited the president. Indeed, the whole meeting confused him, and, while he acknowledged that he understood what the Nisga'a were asking for, he drew Hambidge aside afterwards and asked some questions. The president did not know how to respond to their invitation to attend the Nisga'a Tribal Council. Hambidge told him he had to attend and had to attend the whole three-day event. "Go and sit there for three days and just listen," Hambidge advised. To give him credit, the president did, but it was not enough to convince his company to change their mining practices.

In the end a larger concerted effort was required to stop AMAX's dumping of tailings, and the Nisga'a mobilized the Anglican Church at the beginning of the 1980s. The Nisga'a and the church organized several large protests and demonstrations in Vancouver (attended by the primate and Hambidge, fully vested in their blankets, and Somerville in his more pedestrian cope), at which the elders spoke eloquently and demanded a public inquiry into the affair. In Caledonia, the Nisga'a collected over one hundred thousand signatures on a petition. When government action was not forthcoming, nineteen Canadian bishops contacted the prime minister, Pierre Trudeau, calling for change. Finally General Synod authorized the purchase of four AMAX shares, and the Anglican Church of Canada attended a shareholders' meeting in New York, where it pushed through a resolution for a moratorium on dumping until a public inquiry was held. Afterwards AMAX's Canadian president contacted Hambidge personally to tell him that AMAX was changing its policies in Alice Arm. The Nisga'a had won back their right for clean fishing grounds, but they had yet to restore their self-determination. That effort would take longer.

For a corporate president or a government official to listen to a First Nation as AMAX's did was the exception. Bureaucrats from the department of Indian Affairs would often arrive in the Nass by float plane, address the Nisga'a on the dock, and take off again, seldom walking around the village. Some would visit the village but would announce information to the residents and not stay long enough to listen to their response. Hambidge used to stay for three or four days at a time, always with his ears pricked. During Hambidge's time, each Nisga'a village had a resident priest, who, in the early days, was non-Native, but later was aboriginal, called by the community. Hambidge relied on the priests to warn him if he was about to do something contrary to the Nisga'a ways.

There are six thousand Nisga'a, twenty-five hundred of whom live in their beloved Nass Valley in four villages. Their ancestral lands are achingly beautiful. They lie between rugged mountains along the 380 kilometres of the Nass River, from its glacial source to its estuary on the Pacific Ocean. It is a valley of stunning alpine landscapes, clean air, and ancient forests. Winters bring deep snow. The Nass watershed has provided the Nisga'a with their home, food, medicine, building materials, and fuel since the last Ice Age. Formerly salmon were their currency and allowed past generations of Nisga'a to trade deep into the interior and up and down the B.C. coast. The abundant oolichans, small fish rich in oil, caught and preserved in their thousands, were the river's resource that prevented starvation at the end of long, hard winter seasons. The Nisga'a never had a treaty with the colonists. This land was their land.

Christ Church in Kincolith, in the fall. (Elizabeth Sillett)

Then in the late 1800s, the colonists and missionaries arrived on the West Coast, and the Nisga'a way of life began to change. They were culled by European diseases, they were herded into postage-stamp reserves in the 1860s, and later the children were torn from their families and taken to residential schools. In the name of "assimilation," the church and governments forbade them to speak their language or to practise their traditional spirituality and culture. Regalia, totems, and potlatches were banned. With no land or identity left, the Indians translated the word "assimilation" into "cultural genocide" — a term that Hambidge adopted too, and uses frequently.

It took the Nisga'a nation 130 years to regain their aboriginal rights, and they began their quest during George Hills's episcopate. In the 1870s, just after British Columbia joined Confederation and the federal government became responsible for Indian affairs, the Nisga'a journeyed to Victoria to make their case for their beloved Naas Valley with the young B.C. government. They were supported in their quest by several Christian denominations who sought justice for them. On arrival, the Nisga'a delegation was refused entrance to the lieutenant-governor's office. They never had a chance to talk to Joseph Trutch (a member of Bishop Hills's cathedral congregation), who had been appointed as the first lieutenant-governor of British Columbia in 1871. Trutch, who had been instrumental in creating the Indian reserves in the mid-1860s, had little time for and no understanding of the indigenous people of British Columbia.

By contrast, Hills, the first bishop of British Columbia, understood what their land meant to the Nisga'a and suffered the loss with them as the heaviest burden they had to bear. He spoke of it during his first return to England in 1863: "and thus a barbed arrow was driven into their breast, and not removed while the white man was there."[178] Hills, a century before Hambidge, would have had no hesitation in publicly opposing the B.C. and federal governments' policies and incurring the displeasure of many of Victoria's leaders, because he was not a bishop who sought popularity. However, at the time of the Nisga'a visit to Victoria, Hills was not much involved with their cause, being more preoccupied with his disobedient dean.

In the first treaty of modern times, in 2000, the Nisga'a would earn the right to self-government, joining Canada and British Columbia as full citizens and removing the stigma of being "beggars in their own lands."[179] The Nisga'a had achieved their independence without violence or civil disobedience, using the courts and politics of non-Natives, as well as employing super-human patience. However it was a difficult journey and they needed advocates to help them. Hills and Hambidge were two; Thomas Berger, QC, was another.

How come it's not ours?

Hambidge's first exposure to aboriginal land claims took place at a meeting of the Canadian House of Bishops in the early 1970s. Here he heard about the James Bay Project, where Quebec Hydro was about to flood Indian land without consulting the First Nations who lived there. Sparked by this, Hambidge started actively investigating the history of land claims in Caledonia. By digging deep into the archives of his diocese, he discovered that his predecessor, the first bishop of Caledonia, William Ridley, had urged the first synod in 1879 to support the Natives in a just settlement of their land claims. Ridley was referring primarily to the Nisga'a struggle that had occasioned their visit to Victoria in the mid-1870s. His concern was not seriously taken up until many generations and ninety years later when "Little Big Man" Hambidge came along. It was through his efforts in the 1970s, and those of his successor, John Hannen, that the church began to gain insight into its part in the destruction of First Nations livelihoods and cultures.

Early in his episcopate, Hambidge learned that the Nisga'a view of land was quite different from his non-Native understanding of it. First Nations people do not see land as private property that can be bought and sold, but rather as given in trust by the Creator and held communally for the good of all. They say, "Of course, the land is yours, but it's mine as well."[180] Their land cannot be owned in the sense that a buyer pays for it and receives title to it, while the vendor pockets the money. Furthermore, the bishop discovered the Nisga'a had never signed a treaty with the non-Natives during the European colonization, which was common in British Columbia. This was both a blessing and a curse.

Without a treaty or title deeds in another's possession, without any money changing hands, and without losing the land in battle, the Nisga'a asked the bishop, "How come the land is *not* ours?" Hambidge could not answer them. He posed the same question repeatedly to federal and provincial politicians and bureaucrats, but never got a satisfactory answer from them either. "It's unanswerable," he finally realized, but the question lay at the heart of the Nisga'a court cases about their aboriginal rights. Judges had great difficulty establishing how or why the ancestral lands belonged to the Nisga'a, because there was no evidence to settle it to the satisfaction of non-Native courts. Neither could the judges show the land belonged to anyone else. Decades passed as the process ground on with no resolution.*

As Hambidge began to get more involved in the land-claim issue, the Nisga'a frequently asked him to attend meetings with them. Often in the background, but a significant presence nonetheless, he lent his support to his people, as a Nisga'a first and a bishop second. However he did mobilize Caledonia's 100th synod, reminding the members that Bishop Ridley raised the issue at the first synod, and saying, "It's a justice issue and we can't just sit on the sidelines. This is our issue as a diocese."[181]

From there, the diocese became active in contacting governments and their representatives. When negotiations stalled and a non-Native parishioner suggested blockading a road into the Nass, the Nisga'a said, "Don't you dare! Keep out! We'll tell you what to do."[182] Confrontation was never their way of solving disputes. However the Nisga'a and the Caledonian synod did launch one joint rally when their land claim was before the courts and the government was still logging in the disputed territory. It took place on the steps of the legislature in Victoria, and Hambidge addressed the gathering. The demonstration was quiet and non-violent, conducted with typical Nisga'a respect for all.

Hambidge encouraged the priests in the villages, who were also adopted Nisga'a sons, to attend the three-day Nisga'a Tribal Council meetings. He always went to them, sitting quietly and never speaking, though he never quite got the hang of the circuitous way matters were discussed and the way proceedings could go late into the

---

* For more details, visit The Nisga'a Treaty at http://www.kermode.net/ nisgaa/speeches/

Hambidge's cope and mitre in this photo were a gift from his
clergy in 1979 on the occasion of the hundredth synod of
Caledonia and the tenth anniversary of Hambidge's consecration.
(Hambidge collection)

night. His overriding impression of these meetings was the patient, respectful way everyone listened and heard everyone else. "I wanted people to know that I didn't turn up only when I was invited to say something; that I was there because I wanted to be there." [183] His was a powerful message, which the Nisga'a have never forgotten.

Two years before Hambidge became the bishop of Caledonia, the Nisga'a had reluctantly given up on the stalled negotiation process and had asked Thomas Berger, OC, QC,* to sue the B.C. government to obtain recognition of their aboriginal title to their

---

* Later Mr. Justice Thomas Berger of the Supreme Court of British Columbia, who headed the Mackenzie Valley Pipeline inquiry.

land, which British Columbia claimed as Crown land. They had decided to use the courts, because it was the non-Native way of doing things, raised most of their own considerable legal fees. The Church covered the shortfall.

The Nisga'a lost the case in the B.C. Supreme Court, but appealed in the Supreme Court of Canada, where the judges ruled, in a split decision, that aboriginal title existed before Confederation and had never been extinguished. The Nisga'a flew immediately to Ottawa to meet with the prime minister, Pierre Trudeau, who promptly reversed his long-held position that aboriginal title did not exist. Trudeau promised to review the federal policy and pledged action. The ruling had taken six years, but it changed federal policy forever and opened the door to modern land-claim negotiation based on trust, respect, and the rule of law. Hambidge celebrated with his Nisga'a flock, but at that point none of them expected resolution to take another twenty-five years.

The Nisga'a's ordeal was far from over. The British Columbia government refused to join the negotiations, claiming that land settlements were solely a federal matter. When the feds would not sit down without the B.C. delegation, a stalemate resulted that lasted years. "We were so frustrated that at times we could weep," the Nisga'a leaders said.[184] Both the Caledonian and the provincial British Columbia and Yukon synods resolved to press the B.C. government for action, and promised to provide the Nisga'a with moral and spiritual support. A temporary resolution of the stalemate occurred when the Nisga'a MLA, Frank Calder, crossed the floor of the legislature in Victoria and joined the Social Credit Party, which won the next election in 1975. Soon after that, the B.C. government agreed to meet with the federal government and the Nisga'a Tribal Council in New Aiyansh to begin formal negotiations.

When the Nisga'a asked Hambidge to attend the first historic negotiation meeting with the federal and B.C. governments in 1976, he was very honoured. They directed him to collect a federal and a B.C. minister from Terrace airport, to conduct the opening worship as one of their chiefs, and then to listen. In the hall, the government representatives sat on one side, with the Nisga'a Tribal Council opposite; the elders were in a place of honour on a raised platform. The entire event was solemn and dignified and began with the peace ceremony — the sprinkling of eagle down among all the participants. Hambidge, wearing his Nisga'a cope and mitre, opened the proceedings with prayer. Then he heard the president of the Nisga'a Tribal Council tell Judd Buchanan, the Minister of Indian Affairs, and the B.C. Labour minister Allan Williams, "Our elders must be sitting up in their graves with the excitement of this day....We are going to share what we have, not only with B.C., but with all of Canada. But we are going to share our natural wealth with honour."[185] Chief Joseph Gosnell laid out the Nisga'a position: he asked for complete and unrestricted rights on their own land with no government intervention, compensation for resources taken in the past without their consent, and full Canadian citizenship for their people. Everyone was so filled with anticipation, they could not believe it when nothing happened afterwards. No more negotiations took place until the 1990s, fifteen years later.

Some Indian Affairs ministers were better than others, including Jean Chrétien when he was part of Trudeau's government. He at least made an attempt to spend time in the villages. But Chrétien showed his ignorance when he once asked a chief, "How much do you want for the land?" The chief responded, "How much do you want for your mother?"[186] Other ministers who sat at the negotiation table had no clue at all, and did not appear to engage. All of them struggled to understand the Nisga'a's concept of land, and few comprehended that, for the Nisga'a, their land is a part of them, impossible to separate, entrusted to them by God, and not for sale. Occasionally the Nisga'a asked Hambidge to speak, and he did.

Hambidge, frustrated and in the hopes of kick-starting the process again, launched a letter-writing campaign of considerable proportions. When the government of British Columbia disappeared from the scene after the meeting in 1976, the bishop repeatedly nagged the bureaucrats in charge to return to the table. He also wrote letters to federal ministers, demanding that they halt all forms of development or resource exploitation in the Naas Valley before the land settlement was concluded. Any injustice, and Hambidge put pen to paper; he never let up. When Jack Davis, the then-federal minister of Fisheries was cancelling Native salmon licences, Hambidge wrote to him complaining of the effects of his actions on the Nisga'a, and copied the letter to the newspapers. When the minister's staff failed to show their boss the letter, Davis saw it for the first time in print and overreacted. His secretary called Hambidge. "How dare you write a letter like that to the newspapers and not send it to the minister!" he yelled down the phone. Hambidge explained that he had, and offered to send a copy of his original letter to Davis, but the minister chose to respond on a radio talk show. Davis announced, "The bishop seems to think that God put these salmon in the rivers. Let me tell the bishop that it was the federal government."[187] After that it was a free-for-all in Caledonia! All the newspapers and radio stations picked up the story, and soon everyone was howling with laughter. Hambidge's effort paid off. The federal department backed off and the Nisga'a kept their salmon licences.

In 1982, the Constitution Act formally recognized and protected aboriginal rights for all time, an act that was binding on the provinces, as well as the federal government. However, it was not until 1991 that representatives of the B.C. government rejoined the Nisga'a treaty negotiations, fifteen years after the first historic meeting together in New Aiyansh. By this time Hambidge was no longer in Caledonia, and had become an archbishop in New Westminster, but he was still a Nisga'a. He followed the process closely, and the tribal council continued to call on him when needed.

There were no residential schools in Caledonia. Nisga'a children were sent to St. Michael's School in Alert Bay on Vancouver Island, and a few went to St. George's in Lytton for their education. A significant number attended schools in the Lower Mainland of British Columbia and were boarded with local families for ten months of the year. Hambidge's Nisga'a mother had attended St. Michael's when it was led by a man who was years ahead of his time: certainly, he taught the aboriginal students non-Native ways, but never at the expense of their culture. He was an active Anglican and a committed Christian, who also believed in teaching them leadership. The leaders, who were instrumental in achieving the Nisga'a Treaty, firmly believe they could not have done it without their leadership training from St. Michael's. So the Nisga'a, by and large, escaped the abuse in residential schools, and the Diocese of Caledonia was not involved in the lawsuits that derived from it.

Why has God never called an Indian?

Only in the five years prior to Hambidge's consecration had the Diocese of Caledonia begun to embrace the aboriginals' religious needs with any vigour. His predecessor, Bishop Munn, realized that sending priests to Indian villages on Sundays only was not enough, and he sent them to live in the communities. When coupled with the marked increase in the time Hambidge spent with them, it made all the difference. Hambidge insisted the First Nations participated in synods, and he asked them how they wanted to approach various issues, giving them the opportunity to do so in their own way. The villagers soon began to feel part of the diocese and no longer its poor relations. Next on Hambidge's agenda was the question of ordained ministry for aboriginals.

Hambidge had wondered for a while why no aboriginal had been ordained in the past, and he and the priests in the villages started querying the First Nations about it: "Let's talk about why God has never called an Indian," he asked countless times.[188] It took many village discussions and a long time for them to begin to respond and say, "Maybe God is calling." Eventually the Nisga'a started to hear God, and then slowly they told Hambidge what they had heard. After that, the first name surfaced from a community, and the process became easier. The Haida on the Queen Charlotte Islands had a slightly different reaction from the Nisga'a to the possibility of one of their own being called. They asked Hambidge, "Don't you think we deserve a white man?"[189] In the end, Hambidge ordained seven aboriginals, six through to the priesthood and one to the diaconate, all of whom were called by their communities. The first of three Nisga'a ordinations took place in New Aiyansh in April 1976. Eventually Hambidge also ordained one priest and two deacons in Old Masset, and one deacon in Kitkatla.

The village always made the decision about who was called, not the individual. This tradition of the community raising up candidates as servants of the community dates back to the early church, and parallels Nisga'a spirituality. Hambidge did not always agree with the village's choice, but he was proven wrong in every instance. He recollects two particular individuals that he was reluctant to ordain. The first, on being told by the elders and Hambidge that the village had

SING A NEW SONG

chosen him to be their deacon, said, "I don't want to be." An elder retorted, "It's none of your business."[190] Hambidge later ordained the young man as tears streamed down his face, but the community had spoken and their choice proved sound. The second candidate, who worried the bishop, was usually more drunk than sober. "He's quite unsuitable," said Hambidge, but the elders were adamant, "No, no. We know him." The call from his community instantly turned the man around, he sobered up, and Hambidge ordained him to a successful ministry.

Hambidge developed a unique program of training for those called by their communities. The indigenous candidates for ordained ministry were all educated locally in Caledonia. Sending them to a non-Native theological college was inappropriate for those from an oral culture, and was also financially unfeasible. Through a program coordinated by Hambidge's wife, Denise, the students studied in their own villages with the guidance of local tutors, using an American program designed for the Navajo nation. They did not take written exams. Later the ordinands attended a three-week residential program in Port Edward organized by the New Aiyansh parish priest, John Blyth, in which Hambidge, priests, and elders from the villages taught. Their focus was relating the Native culture to the Anglican faith, and both the teachers and the taught learned vast amounts about Christianity, Anglicanism, and Native spiritual tradition. The participants found it exhausting too, but no one wanted to stop at the conclusion of the three weeks. At the end of the first program, the elders and the Church agreed that the candidates were ready to be ordained deacons. Everyone wore their blankets.

Hambidge assumed he would be ordaining the new deacons to the priesthood the following year, but the Native communities told him that they would let him know. One village did not call him back for five years, until they felt the time was right. The response to Hambidge's indigenous ministry was not all positive. Some theologians were concerned that the training was insufficient and lowered the standard of the clergy, because the Native priests did not have degrees. However, the bishop did not waver in his conviction that the aboriginal ordinands were just as well educated for their role as were non-Native priests and deacons. When the Vancouver School of Theology visited and checked out the program, they

Hereditary Nisga'a chief Eli Gosnel teaching the "Christianity and
Native Spirituality" unit at the first training program in Port Edward, 1972.
The cedar ring is a symbol of eternity and God. Nisga'a chiefs wear the rings to
acknowledge the presence of the Great Spirit with the chief.

Discussing the spiritual significance of Nisga'a blankets.
(Photos: PSA, uncatalogued)

An ordination in New Aiyansh in the mid-1970s after the Nisga'a blankets began to be worn. L to R: Hubert MacMillan (priest), John Blyth (archdeacon), Hambidge, Herbert Morven (deacon), Rod Robinson (lay reader and later priest). (PSA, uncatalogued)

quickly discovered that the Caledonian students were as good as any of their students who had taken written exams and earned degrees. The aboriginal ordinands demonstrated their learning in other ways. Calls are still heard and acted upon in the villages today, and the most recent ordinations took place in early 2005.

The process that Hambidge and others conceived and implemented has grown into a world-renowned extension program at VST, managed by the first tutor from Caledonia. Aboriginal students can now earn a master's degree in divinity that incorporates the traditional spirituality and culture of First Nations. In fact, VST has received invitations to expand into Hawaii, which did not materialize, and into Indonesia and Thailand. However, without Hambidge's vision (and that of others) and his constant encouragement of VST, there would not be a Native Ministries Program today.

It's a big city and I've become a country boy

After eleven years in the episcopate, Hambidge had worked out his own understanding of the role of a bishop. Instead of sitting at the top of a pyramid, he saw a bishop at the hub of a wheel, with the spokes radiating outwards to the rim. Each part of the wheel was interdependent, and Hambidge visualized a good bishop as holding the various ministries together. By now he considered himself a consultative bishop; his most well-used phrase was, "Let's talk about where God is leading us." But he was not indecisive, consulting everything to death. He reflected after hearing others, and then made up his mind. Neither did Hambidge see himself as superior to anyone, and he never stood on ceremony. He worked hard, sometimes too hard. Others described him in the 1970s as "an energetic, unpretentious, and good-humoured Englishman . . . noted for his often hilarious one-liners and his appalling tendency to drive the precarious roads of his diocese as if he were the only person within miles."[191]

After Hambidge had been in northern British Columbia for nearly twenty-five years, and bishop of Caledonia for over a decade, he began to wonder if he should consider moving on. In previous years, when approached to allow his name to stand for election in another diocese, he had always refused. In 1980, concerned that he was getting a bit too comfortable, Hambidge reluctantly let three individuals nominate him for New Westminster. He was more than a little scared of Vancouver and kept worrying that he had made a mistake: "It's a big city and I've become a country boy."[192] Eventually Hambidge realized that he had to let God and the church provide the answer and not him, so he let his name stand, despite his misgivings. With eighteen candidates on the slate, he considered he was a very long shot indeed, because he was unknown in the diocese of New Westminster. Everyone agreed with him.

Late in the day of the election in June, Somerville placed a phone call to his fellow bishop, who was in Ontario preparing for General Synod. "We've just elected you. . . . Will you accept?" he asked. For Hambidge, it was Prince Rupert in 1969 all over again. "Yes!" he squeaked back, "I guess I will." Hambidge had no idea who had voted for him, and still doesn't.

Hambidge arrived in the big city in September 1980, and, as co-adjutor bishop of New Westminster, settled into a synod office that was more suited to the job, unlike his basement room in Prince Rupert. Having been a bishop as long as Somerville, Hambidge did not need training, but he did need to familiarize himself with an urban diocese, four times larger in numbers than Caledonia, if not in area. New Westminster had eighty parishes and a great many outreach programs, because it was able to support them financially. Hambidge discovered the diocese could also afford a communications officer to handle public relations and publicity, a luxury he had never known in Caledonia, and one he had to get used to employing. Hambidge started his learning process by attending policy meetings, listening to various program leaders, visiting parishes, and getting to know the office staff. Synod staff remember that the bishop-elect talked a lot about Caledonia. When they complained to him about it, Hambidge explained to them that he was grieving a loss, "It was like walking away from a family."[193] He knew his adjustment would take a while, and he was patient. He also realized that he would not be able to serve an urban diocese such as New Westminster in the same way as he had Caledonia. They bore no comparison to each other whatsoever.

This multi-ethnic diocese stretches from north of Kingcome Inlet on the mainland of British Columbia down to the United States border, taking in the land west of the Coast Mountains to the shores of the Pacific Ocean, including Whistler and the towns of the Sunshine Coast. Hope, at the head of the Fraser Valley, is the most easterly city. The communities contain populations from many faith traditions, who have been brought to the West Coast of Canada through surges of immigration after the Second World War. The mixture of both rural and urban parishes includes one of the largest parishes in Canada: St. John's Shaughnessy, in upscale Vancouver. Greater Vancouver has a vibrant cosmopolitan flavour, a growing population heading towards two million, with large numbers of Canadians whose origins stem from Asia, India, and Europe, as well as tens of thousands of First Nations people.

Hambidge soon learned that the control in the diocese and the synod office resided in two individuals, neither of whom were the current bishop or the bishop-elect, which mildly concerned him. This finding led to the most important activity he undertook during the turnover: he decided to go out and spend time in the ten deaneries, taking the pulse of the diocese.

With his characteristic vigour, Hambidge set ten twelve-hour meetings in the span of twenty days, at which he met each regional dean alone in the morning, the dean and clergy in the afternoon, and the dean, the clergy, and the laity in the evening. "It was very intense. I took all the notes. I didn't want anyone else interpreting what I was hearing,"[194] remembered Hambidge. He facilitated the meetings, so that they were open and honest. Hambidge gave everyone permission and opportunity to voice their views of the diocese, its current priorities, and what they thought they should be, and the problems they were encountering. Lastly, and very importantly, he encouraged the deaneries to describe the relationships they had with the synod office and its staff. At the conclusion of the twenty days, Hambidge was fatigued but had a clear picture of — and a strong feel for — his new diocese. He had his detailed notes transcribed and circulated to each deanery, the Diocesan Council, and the synod office staff.

The minutes of the meetings caused some waves, especially in synod office. Hambidge moved quickly to increase its level of customer service and to ensure a welcome for the parishes and clergy that approached it for assistance. He also worked to broaden the authority, so that the deaneries shared the episcopal ministry, rather than the office governing the whole diocese.

On November 30, 1980, Somerville installed Hambidge as the seventh bishop at Christ Church Cathedral in front of 1,400 people. The bishop was now fifty-three. The ceremony began with Hambidge knocking at the door of the cathedral and saying, "I, Douglas, whom God has ordained to be a shepherd and servant . . . come to you desiring to be recognized, invested, and installed." The service was a blend of ancient and modern liturgies, with a new musical setting that included bells and bongo drums. Hambidge reaffirmed his promises, and Somerville duly invested him with "all the temporal and spiritual rights and responsibilities that pertain to that office." The new bishop of the diocese received gifts symbolizing his new role: a pastoral staff that had belonged to the first bishop of New Westminster, Acton Sillitoe, the pectoral cross of Adam de Pencier, bishop from 1910 to 1940, and his episcopal ring engraved with the

Hambidge is installed as bishop of New Westminster in
November 1980. (DNW10-2a)

diocesan crest, amongst other gifts. In his address, he charged the
diocese "to strengthen, to confront, to change the face of society."[195]

An outcome of Hambidge's series of meetings with the deaneries and one of his first decisions as the bishop of New Westminster
was to appoint four regional archdeacons. Inserted between the
parish clergy and the bishop, they acted as bishop's assistants, who
worked outside the synod office as conduits, keeping Hambidge
informed of parish life, identifying potential difficulties within parishes, and supplying pastoral care for the clergy. Each archdeacon still
had his or her own parish, as well as providing this support system for
the parishes of two or three deaneries. Hambidge expected his
archdeacons to do a lot of listening — he instructed them to listen
closely to both the clergy and the laity in their areas of responsibility.
The archdeacons had little authority but, through them, the bishop
kept abreast of was happening on a day-to-day basis. Hambidge also
met formally with his archdeacons three times a year in two-day sessions at the abbey in Mission. He found he could delegate at last —
something he had always firmly believed in doing — and was able to
extend his reach deep into the diocese without rushing around doing
everything himself. The other benefit of the new arrangement was for
the clergy, who found it difficult to confide in a bishop who was also

their boss. Somerville had done this differently — he took on the connection with the parish clergy himself.

Hambidge had already learned that a bishop had to be visible to give an element of unity to the diocese. He wanted to be, "not a distant person, but someone who is in the middle of things."[196] Instead of doing all the parish visiting, as Somerville had, Hambidge made himself visible in new ways. He focused on the sense of community in the diocese, just as he had in Caledonia. He kept parishes informed about the activities of their neighbouring parishes, and he encouraged them to undertake projects jointly, hoping they would grow closer instead of operating independently. Combining his visibility with the parish collaboration, Hambidge arranged diocesan events to bring everyone together. He conducted deanery Bible studies, usually in Lent, and instituted annual Servers' Conferences, Churchwardens' Days, and Church Secretaries' Conferences, providing leadership for each event himself. They were held at different locations every year and always opened with a Eucharist to celebrate the participants' contributions to the church. Hambidge was on a mission to enlighten the laity about their own ministries in the church. He always started the discussion process with an invitation to the eighty-odd attendees: "Let's talk about the ministry of wardens/servers/secretaries."[197] In an era when most Anglicans thought ministry meant being ordained, Hambidge delivered a new spin on an old concept — baptismal ministry. Most conference participants had not considered serving at the altar or typing to be "ministries," and lively discussions ensued. The bishop also made sure he celebrated these ministries at every parish event he attended, and soon parishioners got the idea and began to see themselves as key ministers in the Body of Christ, as the Nisga'a had always instinctively understood. Eventually the different groups even wrote handbooks about their ministries and made useful connections in other parishes that helped them provide better service. Hambidge, still excited by the topic in retirement, enlarged on it recently: "I'm absolutely convinced that all of us are called to a ministry. Let's all enjoy it!"[198]

Like Somerville before him, Hambidge supported Integrity Vancouver by presiding at one of their monthly Eucharists each year, never dreaming that within a few years the diocese would have taken up the gay-lesbian cause as its own.

Hambidge became metropolitan of the Province of British Columbia and Yukon a year after he became bishop of New Westminster. When the provincial House of Bishops elected him in November 1981, he was not as surprised as he had been when he was elected as bishop of Caledonia and New Westminster. By then, Hambidge was the senior bishop in the province, and had been acting metropolitan for a few months. Hambidge explained the responsibility: "The metropolitan has no authority in another diocese. He can't even visit without an invitation. It's more a supportive ministry than authoritative."[199] However, if a group of clergy or laity are having problems with their diocesan bishop, they can seek advice and assistance from the metropolitan. If that happens in a formal way, in writing, the canons state that the metropolitan must get involved and investigate. Then s/he has authority. If the issue is serious, the metropolitan must call a court of inquiry. Hambidge had to intervene like this only once, and found it distressing. Metropolitans are the five senior bishops in Canada, one of whom is the primate, and are given the title of Archbishop. They carry significant weight in the provincial and national Houses of Bishops and often are well known at the international level. As metropolitan of the province of British Columbia and Yukon, Hambidge had six dioceses under his care in the 1980s and met regularly with the primate and four other metropolitans before each meeting of the national House of Bishops.

The street is our diocese, no less than the interiors of our churches[200]

Hambidge brought his knowledge and concern for indigenous peoples with him to New Westminster, but it was a very different scenario in Vancouver. Although Natives were present in their thousands, a much larger number than in all of Caledonia, Anglican aboriginals were a scattered minority in the diocese and difficult to identify. Many had migrated from their rural reserves to large cities during the 1950s and 1960s, and more were arriving with hope in their hearts in the 1980s. All were out of their natural environments, and many suffered — some struggling with chemical dependencies and some entering the sex trade. Most had abandoned their Anglican roots when they left home. Hambidge was able to see beyond the drunks and drug addicts of skid row, but many in the parishes could not. The only remaining Indian village in the Diocese of New Westminster was Kingcome Inlet, north of Powell River, a very remote location, accessible only by float plane or boat. While many in the diocese thought the focus should be on Kingcome, Hambidge strongly disagreed and urged New Westminster to take up its responsibilities towards the large numbers of urban aboriginals as well.

Kingcome, in the 1980s, was a shadow of the community it had been when it became part of the Diocese of New Westminster in 1927. With a population of less than a hundred, and a split between two rival families, it was suffering financial difficulties when Hambidge took over from Somerville. The village had wanted a resident priest ever since the Reverend Eric Powell left in the 1950s, but it was, by now, too small to justify one, and the tiny church of St. George's was in poor repair. Several alternatives had been tried in the intervening years. In the 1970s, during Somerville's tenure, the diocese sent a theological student each summer to the village. In the 1980s, Hambidge sent the priest from Alert Bay to Kingcome one week each month, and later the Vancouver Cree priest, John Jeffries, spent a few days there each month. The first two alternatives failed, because the students were ignorant of aboriginal societies and the Alert Bay priest's time was constantly eroded by the pressures of his own parish. The latter solution worked best, because Jeffries was aboriginal, albeit from the Prairies, but it ended when he resigned in 1986. Hambidge was convinced that, to have any measure of success at Kingcome, it needed to be made a specialist ministry. He also knew that, unless Kingcome was ready to receive such a ministry, for which they could claim ownership, success would not be forthcoming. Because the village was in disarray, the leaders were unable to decide exactly what they wanted, and Hambidge put the matter on hold waiting for a solution to come from the villagers. As a result, Kingcome continued with an irregular ministry.

Throughout his episcopate, Hambidge used to visit Kingcome annually for a week just before Christmas, and he enjoyed it. He was never surprised or discomfited when services started later than scheduled, or not at all if the village was busy with something else — his experience in Caledonia had taught him that. The *Book of Common Prayer* was used in Kingcome, which Hambidge thought was of limited value to the villagers. He favoured the Qu'Appelle liturgy that the Nisga'a had adapted. As always, however, Hambidge allowed the village to direct him and never moved to initiate anything without discussion with the elders. However, he was disappointed to be told not to wear his Nisga'a cope when he presided there. Hambidge could never change their belief that they deserved the best, and that the best was "white." He was also saddened, though not surprised, that Kingcome was aware of belonging to the bishop, not to the diocese.

In 1984, Jeffries, the Cree priest, and his wife started the Longhouse Council of Native Ministry in Vancouver in concert with a United Church minister in the hopes of reaching the urban aboriginals. This project was funded by the diocese and the United Church. When Jeffries resigned two years later, the diocesan council was unconvinced of its value and withdrew funding from the Longhouse, leaving the United Church to continue alone. With that decision, the urban requirements for Native ministry clearly needed further work and another approach. Hambidge made huge efforts to provide it for aboriginals in Vancouver and to educate the non-Natives into their responsibilities towards the First Nations people, but it was a struggle. He was aware that the predominately non-Native parishes did not welcome aboriginal Anglicans into their midst, and, because of it, most Natives stopped attending worship. This made it difficult to locate indigenous Anglicans in the huge city, for they were not members of parishes. In the mid-1980s, Hambidge did gather a small group of Anglican aboriginals in St. Paul's Church in the West End, and he listened to what they wanted. At the end of the day, they told the archbishop that they would get back to him, but they never did. Hambidge reminded them once, but nothing came of it. He bided his time, and eventually St. James' became the gathering place for First Nations Anglicans in Vancouver. The rector of St. James', David Retter, who had been one of the priests in the Nisga'a villages during Hambidge's Caledonian episcopate and an adopted Nisga'a, made them welcome.

The Diocese of New Westminster, and the whole church, has been through three distinct periods in its 126 years, according to author Roberta Bagshaw.[201] These have affected its relationship and ministries with indigenous people. The first began when Hills was the bishop of British Columbia (Vancouver Island) and ran from 1879 to 1895. This was a time of pioneering and missionary work, which was focused on turning indigenous people into non-Native Anglicans. The second ran from 1895 to 1950, its "Imperial" period, when the diocese busily upheld its British heritage for floods of immigrants from the "old country," and focused little on the First Nations. And lastly, from 1951 to the present has been a period of questioning that legacy (Hambidge was one of the first to do so), experimenting with new ministries, and encouraging the involvement of non-Natives in First Nations issues. The real movement towards a directed aboriginal ministry occurred after the recommendations of the Hendry Report were approved at the 1969 diocesan synod, and continued during Somerville's episcopate. Jeffries's appointment and the implementation of the Longhouse Council was a direct result of this resolution, and so was Project North.* Later, in 1994, the diocese resolved to attempt to establish a self-determining aboriginal community within the Anglican Church in New Westminster. In 1997 they employed a part-time coordinator of Aboriginal Ministry. Sherry Small, the present coordinator, is a Nisga'a and one of Hambidge's cousins.

At the end of his episcopate, Hambidge was frustrated and saddened by what he saw as slow progress in this area of urban aboriginal ministry. The only result of his determined efforts towards a ministry aimed at First Nations was at St. James' in the Downtown Eastside. Hambidge observed only limited improvement in attitudes and understanding of non-Natives towards aboriginals. However, he did recognize why. The majority of members of the diocese had little or no contact with First Nations people, and therefore a limited imperative to develop programs.

---

* Project North, founded in 1977, was an interdenominational pressure group that responded to economic development and environmental concerns that had an impact on First Nations lands.

Life on the international stage

During his last six years as Archbishop of New Westminster, Hambidge took on his first international role. He had the honour to serve as the episcopal representative for Canada on the international Anglican Consultative Council from 1987 to 1993. This body is one of the four "instruments of unity" in the world's Anglican Communion, which include the Archbishop of Canterbury, Lambeth Conferences, and the Primates' Meetings. It is the only instrument that has the laity among its voting membership, and, for this reason, it is considered of vital importance to the well-being of the Anglican Communion. The council facilitates the work of the churches of the Anglican Communion, is a repository of and the central exchange for information for its members, and helps to coordinate social action worldwide. One of its most important roles is to develop common policies with respect to the global mission of the Church. The council meets every three years in different places around the world. In 1990, Hambidge was elected to the Anglican Consultative Council's Standing Committee (or executive) and to the Finance Committee.

Archbishop Hambidge meets Pope John Paul II during his visit to Abbotsford in September 1984. (DNW13-9)

Members of the council learn about the Anglican Church from a broader perspective than they can achieve sitting in their own dioceses, and they often see the needs of the world in a more urgent light. During Hambidge's time, the Anglican Consultative Council developed a way to assess provinces' effectiveness in mission; they studied theological education; and they revised the membership of the council so it was fairer to the smaller provinces. Hambidge also met Nelson Mandela, which was a highlight of his time on the council.

A beacon of hope

Hambidge was still bringing his considerable influence to bear on the Nisga'a negotiations for their land settlement, even though he was no long bishop of Caledonia. In 1985, along with the other major Christian denominations of British Columbia, the Diocese of New Westminster met with the B.C. attorney general to press the sluggish government to negotiate in good faith with the First Nations towards just settlements of aboriginal rights and titles. New Westminster, with Hambidge's encouragement, also worked to bring business and labour leaders together with the First Nations to discuss development possibilities after treaties were signed. In 1989, the Aboriginal Rights Coalition (previously Project North) published a pamphlet explaining aboriginal land rights for all Christians in British Columbia, and organized a two-day workshop connecting hunger with land use.

Hambidge's charge to synod that year reminded the diocese that there were forty-two thousand First Nations people living in and around Vancouver, 70 per cent of whom were Anglicans, and New Westminster had done little to find out why they were not in the pews. In 1992, Hambidge wrote to the Nisga'a and the two levels of government, encouraging them to come to a just decision in their negotiations, which had finally restarted the year before. In 1993, the Chrétien Liberals and Harcourt's B.C. New Democrats at last did something positive together and created the B.C. Treaty Commission, which formalized the negotiation process and led eventually to the Nisga'a settlement and the signing of the treaty.

In the end the Nisga'a relinquished over 90 per cent of their ancestral land in the negotiations. They now control fewer than two thousand of the original twenty-five thousand square kilometres, in which they have entitlements to forestry, fishery, and wildlife resources. But they also negotiated the re-establishment of their legal system, institutions, and cosmology, and they will begin paying income and sales taxes as their experience in self-government consolidates.

Once the treaty was finally negotiated and approved-in-principle in New Aiyansh in March 1996, it had to be ratified by the B.C. legislature and the House of Commons. Big-business interests, the B.C. Liberals, and the federal Reform Party opposed the treaty every step of the way. The B.C. Liberals even launched a legal challenge that was quashed in the B.C. Supreme Court. Misinformation and myths cluttered the press and the airwaves.

The Nisga'a asked Hambidge, in retirement, to make a presentation to the B.C. Select Standing Committee on Aboriginal Affairs, which was gathering public opinion about the treaty, and Hambidge delivered the presentation in 1996, when the committee held hearings in Campbell River. He addressed the fears of the non-Native population in his address, and debunked the myths that had sprung up about the proposed treaty. He showed how much of their ancestral lands the Nisga'a were relinquishing. Most of all Hambidge gave a clear picture of the essence of the Nisga'a and how important it was, to Native and non-Native alike, for them to control their destiny as equal Canadians after more than a century of misplaced paternalism.

Chief Joseph Gosnell of the Nisga'a addressed the B.C. legislature in a moving speech just before the house debated ratification of the hard-won treaty. Fortunately, the Liberals were in opposition, or it might have been defeated. In Ottawa the bill passed with 80 per cent of Liberals, Progressive Conservatives, New Democrats, and Bloc Quebecois MPs supporting it.

With Royal Assent, the treaty passed into Canadian law on April 13, 2000. A beaming Gosnell stood on the steps of the Senate chamber, surrounded by other Nisga'a leaders, and joyfully called the treaty "a beacon of hope for aboriginal people around the world."[202] On May 10, the Nisga'a at last stepped out of the Indian Act and became fully fledged Canadians and self-governing once more, within and protected by Canadian law. It had taken 130 years, and many remarked on the Nisga'a patience, prudence, and peaceful persistence. Now they faced the challenge of converting to a market economy in a sophisticated technological age after years of dependency.

Hambidge missed the celebrations in the Nass Valley that marked the Nisga'a's momentous success — his invitation arrived a week late — and he did not presume to simply show-up. He had attended and preached at a smaller celebration in Victoria at St. John the Divine Church (the iron church consecrated by Bishop Hills in 1860), which took place after the ratification in the provincial legislature. Joseph Gosnell, the president of the Nisga'a Tribal Council, who had been a leader in the negotiations, spoke about Hambidge's part in their success and gave him a gift in appreciation for all he had done. The Nisga'a remain intensely aware and proud of what Hambidge contributed and, when they see him, remind him and others of it. They also do not let him forget that he is Nisga'a, and still needs to live up to his name of Wal'aks. Hambidge is unlikely to forget.

The success the Nisga'a achieved has had a global impact. Aboriginal groups from all parts of the world visit New Aiyansh to discover how they did it and to find out what self-government is like after more than a century of oppression. The aborigines of Australia are still talking with them. Nisga'a leaders have given presentations to large international conferences, and eloquently told the story of their long journey. They are also credited with defusing some of the more violent approaches that a few First Nations favoured to achieve aboriginal rights. The advice Chief Gosnell still provides to the groups that visit to discuss land claims is simply, "If it takes ten thousand years . . ."[203]

Although attitudes are slowly changing in Canada, political and individual opposition to aboriginal land claims remains prevalent. Non-Natives still do not grasp the Native concept of land ownership and are afraid that, if First Nations are given more land, they will expel those living and working on it. "Nothing could be further from Native thinking than that,"[204] says Hambidge, repeating what has become a mantra of his: "They don't own the land. They say, 'It is entrusted to us [by God, the Great Spirit], and we're stewards of the land.' When a white man asks . . . if he can build a house on their land, they say, 'Of course.'"[205]

Let's see what God is calling us to do

Hambidge believed in making a clean and immediate break from the parishes and dioceses he worked in when he left, either for a new appointment or for retirement. So, the day after he retired as archbishop of New Westminster in 1993, he and Denise got on a plane for Africa to avoid the temptation of hanging around too long. Hambidge had accepted a volunteer position as principal of St. Mark's Theological College in Dar es Salaam in Tanzania, a small college for Anglicans and Moravians, and he served there for two years. He recalls, "I taught four lessons four days a week, and managed the administration of the school in the rest of the time. For those two years I was also the assistant bishop of Dar es Salaam, which took me to various parishes for confirmations on Sundays."[206] Hambidge lectured in English on the Old Testament, preaching, liturgy and worship, and English as a foreign language. During his time in Tanzania, he also served as the theological-education consultant to the House of Bishops there.

When he returned to life in Canada, the retired archbishop was asked if he would be one of the facilitators of a recently begun training program for new bishops run by the Council of Anglican Provinces in Africa. It takes place in a different location in June each year, and Hambidge went to Uganda (2001), Malawi (2002), and Tanzania (2004). There was no school in 2005, and Hambidge said, "I doubt if I'll go again, as medical insurance and fares are prohibitive — and I am getting older!"[207] Currently he serves as Chancellor at the Vancouver School of Theology.

The style of Hambidge's episcopate was very different from that of Somerville's, who had been elected by the greatest majority in the history of New Westminster. Hambidge was less laid back, more blunt. He delegated different tasks and favoured a more traditional diocesan structure and organization. His dry British wit was not always understood. The sudden contrast was difficult for some; not everyone adjusted to his style of running New Westminster. However, he also brought an inexhaustible supply of energy, a focus on parishes and parishioners that made them feel a part of a diocese, as well as his

Hambidge after returning from Africa. (Note his ebony
pectoral cross from Tanzania.) (Hambidge collection)

Chancellor of the Vancouver School of Theology, 2005. (Hambidge collection)

extraordinary ability to dig underneath the surface to discover the truth. Hambidge gets people talking and then he listens — his listening skills are legendary. He also never presumes. He is a man who believes he is no different from his flock, journeying the same road, and meeting the same obstacles. He asks questions first and takes action second.

When asked about his major challenges as bishop and archbishop, Hambidge retrospectively identified his major ministry as the development of a community of faith in each diocese. He found it easier to do in Caledonia, although the distances were greater than in Vancouver, because people and parishes depended on each other more in the north. New Westminster posed greater difficulties. Here the parishes were more likely to compete and hide their weaknesses rather than seek each other out, and Hambidge found southern British Columbians were entirely more isolated and self-sufficient. His second challenge was to develop an episcopal ministry that could build a community in which participants could live with their differences — where they could "fight and love each other at the same time."[208] Thirdly, Hambidge spoke about his focus on facilitating parishes and individuals so they could discover their God-given ministries. In retrospect, he felt that he had not completed this in New Westminster when he retired, but thought that progress had been made.

In a footnote to his thoughts on challenge, Hambidge also viewed his formation of partnerships with New Zealand's Diocese of Wellington and the Diocese of Northern Argentina as important in countering the risk of too much diocesan introspection. He chose one partner to be like and one to be unlike New Westminster, in order to bring new perspectives and new approaches to ministry into the diocese.

One challenge Hambidge did not mention in 2005, but was evident during his long service as a bishop, was the time he was apart from his family. As his children were growing, so were his responsibilities. He was away from home over 50 per cent of the time, whether travelling nationally or within his dioceses. Now Denise has her husband at home most of the time, and, when he travels, she can join him.

Observers of Hambidge's long episcopate identify two highlights, one of which is different from his perspective. The first is his blend of ministry and community, and the second, of course, is his profound attachment and service to the Nisga'a.

Many, including the current bishop of New Westminster, remember Hambidge's deep sense of ministry as one major gift he brought to his episcopates. Early on, Hambidge understood ministry as belonging to the whole church, not just to the clergy, and this principle guided all he achieved in Caledonia and New Westminster. He combined his concept of ministry with the development of community in Caledonia and brought the package south to help bring New Westminster's disparate collection of congregations together. He always attempted to get his dioceses to operate like families, and resisted imposing his vision or decisions on them. Hambidge facilitated both clergy and laity to discuss and discover their direction together, while he listened for the will of the diocese or parish to emerge. He taught his second diocese how to work more cooperatively and to share responsibilities, sometimes in the face of resistant individualism. Hambidge would say, "What I lack, you complement in me, and together we're complete."[209]

In the face of some opposition, Hambidge remedied the lack of indigenous priests and deacons in Caledonia, which had ordained only one aboriginal in a century. He vigorously pursued and developed a training program that honoured the oral tradition, for First Nations individuals who were called by their communities, and it became world-renowned.

Hambidge also played a major role in re-establishing the vocational diaconate. He is much respected for his work in demystifying baptismal ministry for the laity. Today, almost every parishioner knows what it means and can identify at least one of the ways they minister, inside and/or outside the church. His favorite line, "Let's see what God is calling us to do," will not be forgotten in Caledonia or New Westminster for a long, long time; it may even become part of the diocesan vernacular. Hambidge would be pleased with that.

Although he left Caledonia in 1980, a quarter of a century ago, the Nisga'a still revere Hambidge and talk about his unrelenting support of their cause as if it happened yesterday. His natural humility leads him to downplay or omit much of what he has done and to say that the Nisga'a achieved their treaty themselves. To some extent that is true, but one has to wonder what would have happened if

Hambidge had not been there as a constant presence and catalyst. The Nisga'a say that Hambidge's part in their struggle for justice in their land settlement was critical, and they are deeply proud of what he did for them. But his ministry with the Nisga'a did much more. It educated the Church into acceptance of traditional Native spirituality as part of their expression of Christianity, allowing First Nations to replace British church ornaments with their own art and artifacts; he established the indigenous ministry; he taught non-Natives about First Nations and returned the Nisga'a's identity in the eyes of every Canadian; and, by holding the historic 1972 synod of Caledonia in New Aiyansh, Hambidge restored the Nisga'a heritage.

"When the Nisga'a people continued to struggle for justice on this land, only the Anglican Church stood by us in our hour of need. We will never forget this. As long as the river flows, as long as this land shall last..."

Chief James Gosnel,
president of the Nisga'a Tribal Council, 1976

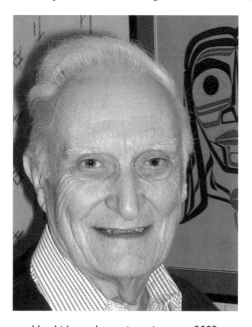

Hambidge at home in retirement, 2005.

PART FOUR

"We Must Overcome Our Loss of Nerve"[210]

The Right Reverend Michael C. Ingham
Eighth Bishop of New Westminster, 1994–

Sometimes on Sunday mornings the current bishop of New Westminster imagines the first bishop of British Columbia sitting in the passenger seat of his car as he drives to one of his many parishes to preside at their services. He likes to tell George Hills about the changes that have taken place in the last century and a half since his predecessor stepped off the ship in Esquimalt. Michael Ingham shows the first bishop new buildings, talks about society today, describes the economy, and explains about cars and airplanes and how easy it would be to make his journeys in the second millennium. He acknowledges Hills's accurate prediction that the West would become great. The current bishop also admits to a strong connection with Hills, and finds his imaginary presence comforting. Ingham thinks they have much in common, considering the difficulties they have both faced, and that Hills would relate to the challenges he lives with on a daily basis.

Who is Michael Ingham, the man the Canadian press portrays as having shaken and stirred the Anglican Communion worldwide? Why is he vilified by some and loved by others?

Ingham is a complicated package: ordinary, yet extraordinary; liberal, yet conservative; progressive, yet traditional; sensitive, yet tough; compassionate, yet no pushover; intellectual, yet down-to-earth; practical, yet romantic; servant, yet leader; and spiritual, yet worldly. This paradoxical nature has blended well in Ingham's case and has fused into a well-integrated, multi-faceted personality that flashes fire on occasion but mostly glows from within.

Larger than life, Ingham has an imposing presence, especially when fully vested for special occasions. A friend actually gasped when she saw him the first time in his mitre and cope. Tall and well built, he has large hands on which he wears a gold wedding band and his huge episcopal amethyst, both of which he treasures. Ingham has an unruly mop of curly hair that was once red and is now grey, and a photogenic smile. He wears glasses, but in conversation he takes them off and fiddles with them as he talks. Even seated, his energy intrudes — he is constantly moving, often changing position, leaning forward to make a point, reaching for a cup of tea. Ingham speaks with care, weighing each word. His voice is deep, well-modulated, and firm, with no trace of a Yorkshire accent. He is articulate, which displays his love of language and his incisive mind, and he talks freely once he is comfortable. His warmth is there, but not always visible to a stranger. Ingham has learned to keep his face neutral, which encourages others to open up to him, for he is an excellent listener. His wit bubbles up too, and he can laugh uproariously when something tickles his funny bone. Most often he laughs at himself.

Ingham's journey has been long, sometimes trying, and always fascinating. From humble origins like both Somerville and Hambidge, he now is as comfortable with politicians and royalty as he is with the poorest of the poor in Bangalore; though, after getting to know him, one quickly determines that Ingham would probably prefer to be working in India or on a university campus.

His favourite delinquent

Ingham's first memory of God and the Church of England was attending confirmation classes when he was fourteen, although he had been baptized in a Wesleyan chapel as an infant. As his parents had never taken him to church or practised any faith in the family home, to see Michael in his local parish church would have been startling enough, but to see him as a confirmand was astonishing, especially to his peers. Even so, this early paradox, in a life of paradoxes, marked the start of his journey in faith.

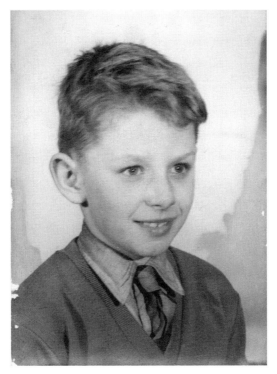

Michael Ingham aged eight. (Ingham collection)

An only child born in Yorkshire, England, in August 1949, Ingham came from solid British stock. His father had served in the British army in the Second World War and was a truck driver who had moved into management by the time his son went to univer-sity. His mother was a medical secretary working full-time and caring for her family and their home in Bradford. Neither went to church, although Dorothy had been brought up a Methodist and Herbert a Moravian Christian. When Herbert's regiment liberated the concentration camp at Bergen-Belsen, he lost whatever faith he might have had in one afternoon, and became a lifelong atheist. So on Sundays the young Michael played soccer and other games with his friends instead of going to church. At least he did until a local parish volunteer went around the neighbourhood asking parents if they wanted their teenagers to attend confirmation classes. Michael's parents had no objections, and so along he went one night a week for instruction and to the Sunday service: "I remember nothing . . . but the petrifying boredom . . . [and] moralizing sermons of no intellectual content."[211] The curate's classes must have been equally mind-numbing, because the boys spent their time ribbing him mercilessly and misbehaving.

Nothing and no one prepared the young Yorkshire lad for what happened at his actual confirmation. (Today he carefully warns those being confirmed himself before the service.) When the Bishop of Blackburn laid his hands on Michael's head, the teenager felt an electrifying jolt of extraordinary power that left him "absolutely uncomprehending." He remembered that, when he returned to his seat, "I could see all the colours in the church . . . the brass rails shining, I could smell the flowers. All my senses were heightened . . . I was acutely aware . . . and I felt like I was walking on air." [212] Michael's mom noticed his odd reaction and asked, "Are you all right?" The boy replied, "I don't think so." Today the bishop explains, "Of course, now I know that [the jolt] was the Holy Spirit. It was the first of a series of privileged experiences of the Holy Spirit and its power that I have had in my life,"[213] but in 1963 he had no vocabulary to express it to his mother.

The following Sunday, when his friends called to collect him for soccer, Michael declined, saying, "I'm going to church." And he did — alone. When he continued to go to church, his peers were very puzzled and decided he'd "got religion." He had.

After his confirmation, events led Michael to meet individuals who carried him forward on his faith journey. Without them he probably would have remained an ordinary, faithful member of the laity. When his cousin invited him to play snooker with other boys at Church House, the diocesan office a hundred yards from his grammar school in downtown Bradford, Michael accepted. There he met John Teasdale, the diocesan secretary, who became his first confidant and a strong formative influence. Michael was initially drawn to this group of boys because of their intellects, and later he started attending the Anglo-Catholic parish of St. Columba with them. "I loved the elegance of the liturgy. I loved the fact that it stimulated all of my senses and was not simply a Word-centred form. But most of all [I loved it there] because I was not an oddity — fifteen and without my parents!"[214] Michael relished the intelligent preaching, which stirred his thinking and made him look at the world in a new way. After every Sunday Eucharist, the adults and young people would sit around and discuss current events, world politics, church issues, and faith. The schoolboy was entranced, feeling welcomed and valued for himself. Michael never forgot it: "I learned there was a sacramentality and depth that is firmly rooted in Jesus Christ but totally open to the world."[215]

Teasdale eventually explained to Michael what had happened at his confirmation and, assisted by the high-church environment he was now in, the young man began to understand the experience. "I learned how the mystery of God can enfold you . . . and transform you. The utter transcendence that poured from the walls of [St. Columba] drew aside a veil between this world and a greater world . . . allowed me to see myself as a part of a much larger reality . . . connected to the saints. When you're fifteen, it puts some direction in life."[216] Teasdale also predicted that Michael was going to be a priest, but the teen just laughed it off.

By this time, Michael was embarking on a program of rigorous self-improvement, although he would not have described it that way. He subscribed to *The Times*, the famous London newspaper, and had to use a dictionary to understand what he was reading. He started going to orchestral concerts. And he had his first exposure to grand opera when he went to a performance of *La Bohème* in Leeds: "I was destroyed by the singing, totally emotionally slaughtered by the music and Puccini's dramatic close."[217] When his friend broke in with, "Let's go for a pint!" Michael was still lost in the tragedy of broken-hearted love. At that moment he knew he was an incurable romantic. He was adventurous too, and remained committed to sports. After his confirmation, he toured Europe on a bicycle with two friends: "I was a fierce cyclist. . . . I had racing bikes, touring bikes, and regular bikes."[218]

Teasdale continued to mentor Michael as he approached the end of high school, encouraging and reminding him that he had a good mind and that God was calling him. With his parents' approval he applied for and was accepted by Leeds University to study theology, but he still wasn't convinced of his choice, thinking that journalism might suit him better. In the July between high school and university, Teasdale took Michael's group of young people to Paris, where Michael met an attractive young woman who was at Edinburgh University. It was a brief summer romance, but he came home and immediately applied to, and was accepted by, New College, the University of Edinburgh's Faculty of Divinity.

Life at university was not as he expected. The keen student couldn't understand a word of the first two theological lectures he attended, and the girl he had met in Paris turned out to be engaged to someone else. So the young man switched to the arts faculty and there found his feet. He would end up earning a master's degree in Politics and Moral Philosophy in three years, which was possible in Edinburgh. But it was the city itself, not his university studies, that presented another critical fork in Ingham's journey.

Edinburgh introduced Ingham to another defining influence in his life. Old St. Paul's, another Anglo-Catholic church, drew the university student, and he began attending regularly. There he met its rector, Richard Holloway,* who would go on to become the Bishop of Edinburgh and later Primus of the Scottish Episcopal Church and is still today considered to be one of the most brilliant and powerful minds in the Anglican Communion. Holloway's sermons captivated Ingham; they were stimulating and preached Christianity as a system of thought. "I had lucked in again. I always thought God had intervened wonderfully in Paris," Ingham observed later. [219]

---

* Richard Holloway was rector of Old St Paul's from 1968 to 1980. He became Bishop of Edinburgh in 1986 and the Primus of the Scottish EpiscopalChurch in 1992, retiring in 2000. Holloway has served on various eminent commissions, including the Commission for Human Fertility and Embryology, and has written over twenty books. For more details, visit www.westarinstitute.org/Fellows/Holloway/holloway.html.

As Ingham adjusted to leaving home and family, he discovered the whole tradition of Christian intellectual thought — Augustine, Aquinas, Wesley, etc. — and devoured it. He studied systems of thought and politics, as well as the coherence of alternative systems of ideas, constantly measuring Christianity against them. In short, Ingham learned how to think, how to question methodically, how to develop a position, and how to argue cogently on either side of an issue.

While his mind was searching for flaws in the Christian argument, his soul was being nurtured in the deep sacramental devotionalism of Old St. Paul's. Holloway, then a conservative with a passion for social causes, stretched, challenged, and pushed Ingham to his intellectual limits. "I came alive in those days," recalls the current bishop of New Westminster, "and started taking all my friends, including my girlfriends, [to Holloway] on Friday nights to debate around his kitchen table. He would wipe the floor with us! We had some knock 'em down, drag 'em out arguments about sexuality in those days too."[220] Ingham also began serving regularly at Old St. Paul's at the early Wednesday mass and on Sundays. "It was feeding me in non-verbal ways,"[221] he remembers.

On earning his M.A. in politics and moral philosophy at twenty, Ingham was ready to pursue theology, so he reapplied to New College, Edinburgh, and, at the same time, decided to explore his growing vocation to the priesthood. He studied for his second degree in systematic theology at university while living in Coates Hall, the seminary of the Scottish Episcopal Church. Ingham found it an uneasy mix of lifestyles, but one that delivered yet another mentor into his life.

Alistair Haggart* was the highly intellectual principal of the seminary and a liberal theologian, whose positions were often diametrically opposed to those of the then-conservative Holloway. So Ingham lived between the two poles of conservative and liberal theology, debating with Holloway at Old St. Paul's and Haggart at Coates Hall.

---

* Alistair Haggart became the Bishop of Edinburgh, 1975-1986, and Primus of the Scottish Episcopal Church, 1986-1992, preceding Holloway. Both men, as primus, had enormous influence and anchored the centre left of the Anglican Communion during a time of increasing conservatism.

Ingham (R) with Alistair Haggart (centre) when he was Primus of the Scottish Episcopal Church and visiting Vancouver in 1979. They are with the dean of Christ Church Cathedral, Rev. Canon Herbert O'Driscoll (L) who always provided a listening ear for Ingham. (DNW5-D.23)

The young man also began exploring interfaith issues for the first time and reading ever more widely. But Ingham, like others, resisted the old-fashioned constraints of the seminary, and played devious practical jokes on the principal in the hopes of improving the students' lot. Haggart nicknamed him his "favourite delinquent," a term of affection rather than of criticism. Ingham had begun to push the envelope, albeit in a lighthearted way.

Systematic theology differs from dogmatic theology, because it looks at Christianity as a system of thought that can be compared with other systems, such as Marxism, Humanism, Existentialism, Nihilism, etc., rather than examining the teachings of Christianity and how they support each other. Ingham found himself in debate, not with other Christians, but with the works of Jean-Paul Sartre and Albert Camus, and the movies of Ingmar Bergman. His challenge was to defend the faith from the sciences and the social sciences, during a time when the cultural and popular thinking on religion concluded that it made no sense, because it was not verifiable through the scientific method.

Ingham performed brilliantly at the faculty of divinity, earning a first-class honours degree, and came top of his year.

Although Ingham could have been ordained then and there, he had not reached a definite conclusion concerning his possible vocation. He had come to believe that philosophy raised questions that only theology could answer, and he definitely felt a tug, a summons to the ordained life. It was an inner imperative, but he chose not to take the plunge at that point in his life. At only twenty-three, he realized, "I was not emotionally ready."[222] In fact, Ingham was starting to wonder if he had a different kind of vocation, one similar to the academic ministry that he saw exemplified by Holloway and Haggart. So he chose to do postgraduate work, selecting Harvard's offer over Oxford's.

His choice of Harvard stemmed from experiences he had enjoyed during the summers at university, which had opened him up to other cultures and societies. Through an organization called the British Universities' North America Club, a certain number of students worked in each other's countries on temporary work visas, and Ingham had signed up. He spent the summer of 1971 in Connecticut on a construction site. At the end of the job, he bought a $99 Greyhound bus pass and toured the United States and Canada from end to end, spreading his wings and observing how North Americans lived. Ingham fell for the way of life: "[The society] was everything that Britain was not. It was a meritocracy and not an aristocracy. If you had ability you were not held back . . . it didn't matter what your father did."[223] So Harvard became the obvious choice for a Yorkshire lad who enjoyed the United States and, like George Hills, had neither the correct "old school tie" nor the "breeding" for a successful career in the church in the United Kingdom.

The summer of 1972 found Ingham studying Judaism at the Hebrew University in Jerusalem, a choice of his own, encouraged by Haggart. He lived in residence and worshipped at St. George's Cathedral, a small Christian community. Ingham arrived in Tel Aviv airport on a Friday evening, the Jewish Sabbath. There was no taxi to be had, so the lanky student heaved his baggage onto the top of an old Arab bus and settled in for the trip to Jerusalem, surrounded by chickens and goats. Hours later and ravenous, he eventually found his room at the university and committed the first *faux pas* of his visit by cooking up a breakfast of eggs and ground beef in the dorm kitchen while his fellow students were at a prayer meeting. When they returned they were horrified: Ingham had defiled their kitchen by mixing meat and dairy products in the same pan. Covered with shame, he washed everything and replaced the food, but it was not until later that he fully understood the gravity of his mistake. Eventually Ingham, the only Christian in the group, redeemed himself and made friends.

Ingham studied the history and philosophy of Judaism, Jewish philosophers, and Jewish theology. His orthodox professors treated Ingham well, because he was biblically literate and many of the Reformed Jewish students were not. Ingham also learned much about the internal pluralism of the Jewish faith and Jewish communities around the world, discovering that they rival Christian diversity. Along with the other students, Ingham went on field trips, visited kibbutzim, and was immersed in Jewish culture for months. His student friends taught him what it was like to be seen as a persecutor of the Jews: they blamed the Holocaust on Christian Europe, and viewed Ingham as a representative of the tradition that had done great damage to the Jewish people. Although his father had raised similar questions, Ingham had never personally engaged with the issue until then, and found the Jews' perspective sobering.

While Ingham was in Jerusalem, the massacre of Israelis took place at the Munich Olympics, and he witnessed Israel switching to a war footing in the blink of an eye. Ingham felt the nation's intense anxiety; he encountered tanks in the streets; he could not leave the country because the airports and seaports were closed; and in class he sat next to fellow students who were carrying machine guns. It was eye-opening and frightening, and the young man was deeply affected by it all.

Before Ingham left for Harvard in the United States in the fall of 1973, he went to India for the summer with twenty-five other university students, because Holloway nominated him to lead the group under the sponsorship of the English Speaking Union. It was an experience of total immersion: in Bombay, the students lived with Indian families and had jobs in the city. Ingham worked at the YMCA and roomed with orthodox Hindus, exploring their faith while he was there and proclaiming Christianity perhaps a little too enthusiastically. The family with whom he stayed was as keen to share their experience of the truth as he had been with them. Ingham also met with followers of Gandhi and became a supporter of non-violent resistance, learning only later that Gandhi had been influenced by Jesus' Sermon on the Mount. For the first time in his life he was exposed to desperate, grinding poverty, the results of little or no health care and sanitation, and the effects life without hope had on people. The experience made him rethink his outlook.

Ingham's encounters with Judaism and Hinduism never left him. He was beginning to realize that there was "a whole way of doing Christian theology that actually took into account the largeness of God instead of the narrowness of the Christian way."[224] The visits to Jerusalem and Bombay provided Ingham with a new line of spiritual thought and inquiry that he pursued avidly in the years to come and which later resulted in his book *Mansions of the Spirit*. The maturing adult was evolving into a progressive, liberal thinker.

But back at Harvard Ingham studied contemporary American theology and was surprised to find himself debating from a conservative perspective throughout his time there. In the 1970s, arriving as a self-acknowledged liberal from the more conservative Edinburgh Faculty of Divinity and able to argue from almost any point of view, Ingham discovered that Harvard's excessive liberalism was too shallow for his taste. He became known as "the great conservative" — a novel experience. He nurtured his faith by worshipping with the Cowley Fathers at the nearby Society of St. John the Evangelist and often ate supper with them afterwards, enjoying their wisdom. Again, the juxtaposition of a deep sacramental life with a stimulating intellectual world fed Ingham's well-being.

Harvard ended Ingham's academic career. After eight years he had had enough of the "intellectual incest and scholars feeding off each other"[225] and wanted to do something "real" for a while. He wrote to Haggart, who was now the Bishop of Edinburgh, and told him that he was ready to be ordained. In 1974, Haggart found a parish in Inverness for Ingham, but it did not excite him. He simply could not imagine exchanging vibrant Boston for rural Scotland. His break came through the Cowley Fathers, who suggested that Ingham see if there was an opening in the United States by asking the Dean of the Episcopal Divinity School in Cambridge, Massachusetts. Dr. Harvey Guthrie recommended throwing the net wider by including Canada, and he wrote to bishops in both countries on Ingham's behalf. Canada strongly attracted Ingham, because he had been following the Anglican Church of Canada's struggle towards the ordination of women to the priesthood, and admired the social-justice agenda of the charismatic and intellectual Pierre Elliott Trudeau. Six weeks later, Ingham received a call from the rector of St. John the Evangelist in Ottawa, who was urgently seeking a curate. He flew up in February to take a look.

Ingham with the Bishop of Ottawa, the Right Rev. William Robinson, who had just ordained him to the priesthood, December 8, 1974. (Ingham collection)

Ingham discovered a large, urban parish with an educated congregation and was attracted to it from the start. However, getting appointed was not so easy. A lengthy correspondence ensued between the bishops of Ottawa and Edinburgh, in which Haggart complained that they had invested a lot of money in training Ingham and wanted him back. In the end the bishop of Edinburgh traded Ingham for money to the Bishop of Ottawa — though Ingham never discovered how much. He was ordained deacon at Christ Church Cathedral in Ottawa on August 6, 1974, and priest on December 8. Ingham intended to obtain two or three years of parish experience and then return to university to teach, either in Scotland or the United States. God had other plans.

I had found a bishop I wanted to work for

Primarily an academic, twenty-five years old, in a new country and a new city, in a new role, and knowing no one, Ingham found the adjustment to priesthood and the "real" world difficult. No one teaches new priests "to be ordained," and Ingham "discovered, as every newly ordained person does, that ordination is not a coat that you can put on and take off . . . it means you have to reorder your life in fairly substantial ways."[226] But in one respect he was fortunate: the parish suited him. Creative in ministry, innovative theologically, and on the leading edge of contemporary liturgies, it was full of bright young parishioners, wonderful music, and excellent lay participation. Ingham's rector asked him to start a youth group from scratch, and the new curate ended up with thirty keen teens who met at his house every Sunday night. He took them on canoe trips and to movies, and quickly learned they were asking different questions from those he had asked around Holloway's kitchen table in Edinburgh. Ingham tackled it well, however, and some of those teens still keep in touch with him as adults and visit him when they are in Vancouver.

Ingham admits to being very lonely during this period. He was single and didn't want to be. He was acutely aware of appropriate conduct, and did not ask girls out from within the parish, but girls outside the church shied away from him because he was ordained. The rector pushed Ingham hard, and, missing the intellectual stimuli of a university campus, the young curate did not feel at home in the church immediately.

After a year he went to his bishop and told him that he had made a mistake, but the bishop advised staying and gaining as much as he could from the experience. Ingham acknowledged his counsel, went back to St. John's, and slogged onward. Early in his time in Ottawa, he had met another British priest, John Baycroft, with whom he could talk, discuss ideas, and exchange books. Their friendship kept Ingham alive intellectually and eased this period of culture shock and loneliness. A year later, Ingham again asked his bishop to liberate him, and he countered by offering Ingham a parish northwest of Ottawa. Driving to take a look, Ingham was perturbed when the radio stations faded out. Needless to say, he declined that suggestion.

Soon after this proposal, Ingham was tempted by an offer from Montreal Cathedral. At the same time, Herbert O'Driscoll, the former rector of St. John's Ottawa, who was now dean of Christ Church Cathedral in Vancouver, invited him out to tea. Ingham told him he was looking for a new job and got the satisfying reply from O'Driscoll: "I'll speak to David Somerville for you, if you like." Two days after the Montreal offer, Somerville phoned Ingham and said: "I have a parish out here that nobody wants. Would you like to look at it?"[227] Ingham flew out almost immediately, telling himself that, however bad the parish was, he was going to accept it. Vancouver had attracted him in 1971 during his continental Greyhound tour, and when his plane flew into Vancouver airport, he experienced "such a sense of coming home . . . my soul relaxed."[228] Meeting Archbishop David Somerville clinched it for him — "I had found a bishop I wanted to work for," recalled Ingham.

But not much else in him relaxed. The parish of Christ the King in Burnaby took some getting used to in 1976, and demanded all of Ingham's skills and patience. It was the one in which Somerville had had to intervene when the rector failed to separate the sexes in the church hall a couple of years before. Christ the King was different in the extreme, filled with "alternative Christians" and so "New Age" in style that it seriously discomfited Ingham. His predecessor had a ponytail and did not wear vestments but donned an orange caftan every Sunday. Occasionally the pews were piled on the lawn, and the congregation reclined on cushions on the church floor. The Bibles had been replaced by copies of *The Joy of Sex*, Sunday school was passé, and the parishioners had not heard a sermon in the traditional sense for years. On his first Sunday, when Ingham wore his clerical collar and vestments and preached from the Biblical texts of the day, he was met with bewilderment and anxiety. His non-traditional, blue-collar flock thought he was taking them backwards, and Ingham realized that, for all his so-called

Ingham soon after he became rector of Christ the King in Burnaby, B.C., September 1976. (The Ven. R. Harrison)

theological liberalism, "I was actually quite traditional liturgically. I couldn't connect with their customs that seemed to me to be flaky."[229] Lessons were learned on both sides.

The entire church leadership resigned within his first two weeks, not because of Ingham, but because they were burned out from trying to keep the parish going without a priest for the previous year and a half. Within four weeks, Ingham had restored Sunday school, banished the books on sex and replaced them with prayer books, preached from a freshly dusted-off pulpit, and instituted a Bible-study group that no one attended. His reforms were not popular, and he increasingly felt a failure as the months wore on. Bishop Somerville understood what he was going through. "David was marvellous, absolutely marvellous,"[230] recalls Ingham, and the bishop kept him going with wise advice and practical encouragement. So did Herbie O'Driscoll. When the situation became intolerable and loneliness overwhelmed him, Ingham would drive out to Lighthouse Park in West Vancouver and sit on the rocks and let the ocean deliver its healing touch.

Eventually, both the congregation and Ingham came round, each making concessions to the other, listening, and rubbing along. Though he was still unmarried, one of Ingham's successes in the parish was his discussion group on marriage: "tons of people attended and we had bags of fun."[231] When the time came for Ingham to leave four years later and he stood in the pulpit to tell his parishioners of his departure, he was moved to tears: "I realized I had come to love them all."[232] At the church door after his last Eucharist, a woman told him, "You came here as a distant intellectual and we have taught you the common touch."[233] Ingham agreed humbly, aware that he was still learning how to weave both together. The parishioners of Christ the King had started the process for him.

In 1980, Ingham faced another fork in his journey — the most difficult yet. The Bishop of Edinburgh phoned him to let him know that a parish had become available. It was a perfect match for him — the university parish of Edinburgh. It had a huge church beside Edinburgh Castle just off the High Street, with a vast eighteenth-century apartment overlooking the Princes Street Gardens as the rectory. Ingham flew back to meet with the parish and the search committee. Upon his return to British Columbia, he had a difficult two weeks waiting for the phone to ring.

When it did, and the bishop offered him the appointment, the agonizing really began. Ingham had never been so aware that the choice he faced was pivotal. Although he was sensing a call to move on from his parish in Burnaby, he was nagged by an inner voice saying, "Don't go back."[234] Ingham listened to the voice and again sought out O'Driscoll to talk over his dilemma. The dean helped him realize that Canada had become his home and was the best place to be, although it was presently lacking a parish that suited the young priest. With considerable anxiety, Ingham refused the offer in Edinburgh. "To have [decided] that from a place where I was not happy and felt a failure was extraordinary; the hand of God perhaps,"[235] Ingham concluded.

Two weeks after he made his fateful choice, the West Vancouver parish of St. Francis in the Wood dropped into his lap. Ingham sometimes thinks, even today, that "God wanted to know if I was big enough to make a decision of such difficulty"[236] before presenting the real option. St. Francis in the Wood is an exquisite church in a perfect location. The church nestles in tall evergreens overlooking Tiddly Cove next door to Lighthouse Park, where Ingham used to seek solace. It has a traditional lych gate, a beautiful memorial garden, and provides spiritual refreshment to a well-heeled, predominately business community, close to Vancouver. The parish and Ingham took to each other at first sight. The congregation was filled with cultured, educated parishioners who were spiritually mature, and he had the intellect to match. "It was the making of me as a priest and the happiest ten years of my life,"[237]Ingham recalls, and, while there, he finally accepted that "From the moment of confirmation . . . my life had been laid out for me."[238] Soon after Ingham joined St. Francis, Douglas Hambidge was elected to replace Somerville.

Ingham had to shed his bias against big business. Living in Ottawa had stimulated his interest in international affairs, and he was seriously involved with world development at both the national and diocesan level, both of which had led to a developing prejudice against capitalism. At St. Francis he was exposed to a highly creative business community, which could and did take risks. "They know how to put wheels under ideas and make them work. I had tons of ideas . . . but what I learned at St. Francis was that [the parishioners] took me seriously and said, 'Okay, this is how you do it.' I just had to provide the leadership of vision and then get out of the way."[239] Ingham was frequently surprised at the both the ingenuity and generosity of St. Francis's congregation. The parishioners converted his prejudice towards the business community to a recognition of its value.

Then Ingham found Gwen. His years of being a lonely single were dissolved in an instant when they met in the fall of 1980 at a cathedral breakfast in Whitehorse, Yukon. Ingham, the city boy, was visiting as the Diocese of New Westminster's representative for Yukon's episcopal election. Gwen's sophistication and intense femininity, coupled with her intellect, took his breath away, and, while getting to know her, he learned she had lived in Dease Lake, B.C., in a rustic cabin, alone but for a ferocious German shepherd. Gwen had hauled her own water, split her own firewood, and lived without electricity. The

Priests are not exempt from taking marriage-preparation classes – Ingham and Gwen together at St. Clement's, North Vancouver, February 1982.
(DNW5-D.44)

disconnect intrigued him, and he pursued her. Ingham soon discovered Gwen was a Vancouver-born high-school teacher, working in Whitehorse, who played the organ for Haynes Junction's church and was a deeply committed Christian.

By the time Ingham left Whitehorse, after a very short stay, he and Gwen had agreed to keep in touch. They wrote to each other, ran up large phone bills, and met occasionally. Within two years, in June 1982, they were married, and later would have two daughters — Cara-Jayne in 1989 and Robyn in 1992.

Ingham and Gwen on their wedding day in June 1982. (Ingham collection)

I had to learn to be more thick-skinned

Computers intrigued Ingham from the beginning and led to his first foray into writing and publishing. Gwen gave him a small, primitive machine from Radio Shack for Christmas 1984, with the condition that he must write a book. Ingham set about the task with a will and devoted much thought to what the book should be about. As he had received an advance copy of the new *Book of Alternate Services* in page proofs, he thought he might be able to write a book explaining the differences between it and the *Book of Common Prayer*. Ingham hoped he might beat the scholars to publication, and this incentive kick-started the project. Knowing that to succeed he had to tackle the subject from an original angle and with a format accessible to everyone, he chose to identify themes within the different liturgical rites of the church and link them. The approach had never been done before: "I decided to treat the liturgies collectively as expressions of consistent and coherent themes, rather than as distinct and individual rites, which is how liturgical scholars tend to approach the subject."[240] He chose themes that included women and men, spirituality, mission, and evangelism, and even liturgical experts thought it was a superb idea. Ingham offered a critical comparison of the *BAS* and the *BCP* rites; though always from a position of healthy respect for the older tradition, he explored a way forward that would help congregations understand the *BAS* using modern scholarship. Much to Ingham's astonishment, no competitors to his book emerged. It turned out to be the only book of its type published on the *BAS*, and is in its third printing.

When *Rites for a New Age* (Anglican Book Centre, 1986) appeared, Ingham was quite unprepared for the reaction to it. Many immediately saw it as controversial and threatening. The book was trashed in the *Anglican Free Press*, a conservative publication from the Maritimes, where they clung to the *BCP*. Some reviews were savage. And the knives came out. Soon the first-time author, who thought he had written *Rites* well, was bleeding from head to foot. Ingham commented, "I have always listened to criticism and never shut myself away from it. . . . I have never required anybody to agree with me . . . but I had to learn to be more thick-skinned."[241] This experience was the first time Ingham found himself in the crosshairs of a targeted attack and, although he didn't know it at the time, the conservatives' reaction to *Rites* was preparing him for worse to come.

I learned something new every day

Rites for a New Age was partly responsible for Ingham's next posting. Michael Peers had been primate of the Anglican Church of Canada for two years when he decided to reorganize his office structure by adding a Principal Secretary.* Peers wanted someone who was ordained, who could relate well to other clergy and bishops, and who could write well. Primates give countless speeches around the world; they have to compose papers for conferences; they write articles for publication; and, of course, they preach at major events at home and overseas. The job of a primate is so overwhelming, without having to research and create all this written material, that many in the Communion have help. Peers had reached the point where he needed assistance, and his eyes fell upon Ingham in 1989.

The two men did not know each other well, but had met regularly at General Synods and at the National Program Committee of which Ingham was the chair. Ingham had always admired Peers — he appreciated his extraordinary intellect and vision, as well as his generosity of spirit. Peers liked Ingham's writing skills and thought his national committee experience would be an asset to the new position he was creating.

The job entailed travelling extensively with Peers within Canada and around the world. The pair met and worked with other primates and their entourages. Together they attended General Synods, and Ingham learned the life and work of other dioceses, gaining a deep understanding of the cultural differences inside and outside Canada. He researched and wrote many of the primate's speeches, sermons, papers, and other statements, in part or completely. Ingham attended every meeting of the Canadian House of Bishops as recording secretary. The job was hectic, demanding, and ever-changing.

To Ingham the work was fascinating, and he says he learned something new every day of the four years he was Peers's principal secretary. The transition from the West Vancouver parish to Church House in Toronto was not difficult, for Ingham's work on national

---

* The Principal Secretary is not second in command to the primate but an aide-de-camp.

committees meant he already knew the staff there and had established relationships. One of the bonuses of his new job was having weekends off; it was the only time in his married life that he and Gwen were able to go to church and sit next to each other in the pew. Ingham also enjoyed the novelty of receiving the liturgy, instead of always presiding.

Ingham became comfortable in both the rarified atmosphere of Lambeth Palace in London, where he often stayed, and in tiny churches of remote parishes in the Arctic. He met and became friends with Archbishop Desmond Tutu and the Dalai Lama. He got to know the other principal secretaries, many of whom subsequently became bishops and archbishops around the world. He visited every continent. Ingham heard all the influential primates speak and debate at major gatherings and absorbed the issues that demanded the attention of the Anglican Communion. In short he was at the heart of it all — and it was heady stuff.

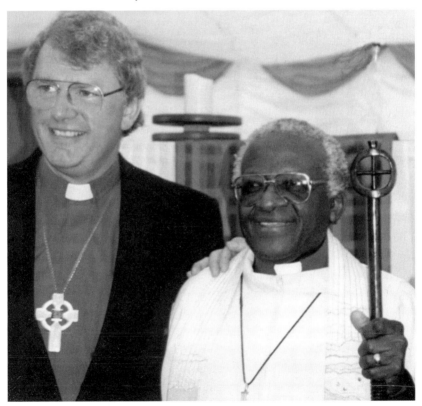

Ingham with his friend Archbishop Desmond Tutu in 1995. (Ingham collection)

Even so, after four years Ingham was getting restless, despite the many advantages his job brought. He was unable to speak or to vote at General Synods, and he found it frustrating: "they were debating issues I cared passionately about but I could take no part."[242] He could not participate in the synods of the Diocese of Toronto, as he did not belong, nor in the Diocese of New Westminster, where he could have voted, since he was not there. Ingham also missed parish ministry and was afraid his pastoral skills were getting rusty. He disliked the thought that he might be becoming a bureaucrat. When they were in Australia, Ingham discussed his dilemma with Peers in a sidewalk café over an ice cream. The primate listened carefully and understood instinctively. He agreed with Ingham and made it clear that he would be pleased to let his secretary go as soon as the right appointment presented itself.

It did so when the rector of Christ Church Cathedral in Vancouver, the Very Reverend Jim Cruickshank, left to become Bishop of Cariboo. Ingham was invited to submit his name for the vacancy, and Peers advised him to do so. Archbishop Douglas Hambidge appointed Ingham both rector of the cathedral and dean of the diocese in early 1993. Ingham moved back to the West Coast with his family to take up what turned out to be a short appointment.

His time with Peers had demystified many aspects of the national and worldwide church for Ingham, not the least of which concerned bishops: they were no longer the exalted beings that he had once thought they were. Ingham discovered that they all had foibles and idiosyncrasies, just like normal people, and that they could and did make errors of judgement. He also learned how bishops work together nationally and internationally, despite their differences, and watched with admiration as Peers built relationships that avoided polarization in a diverging communion. Ingham came to appreciate more of the wonderful diversity of Anglicanism, which is so imperilled today, and honed his diplomatic skills, which he felt did not come naturally to him.

But the single most important outcome of his time as principal secretary was exposure. Ingham got to know every bishop and every diocese in Canada, most of the primates in the world, and many of the other nations' bishops. He developed relationships with them and long-lasting friendships with a few, as well as experiencing some of their different cultures. But what is much more fundamental — they got to know Ingham.

I may try to push the boundaries

Michael Peers preached at Ingham's induction as dean and rector of Christ Church Cathedral in early 1993, which was quickly followed by Archbishop Hambidge's resignation. That decision had a significant impact on Ingham's job. Not only did he have the parish to serve, he had to assume the episcopal responsibilities of the outgoing bishop as commissary of the diocese — though not those of ordination and confirmation. Ingham worried that he neglected the cathedral congregation, as his work for the diocese at the synod office consumed a great deal of his time.

All too soon for Ingham, the flurry of preparations inherent in the election of a new bishop swept the Diocese of New Westminster. The first task of the episcopal search/nominations committee was to write the diocesan profile, and they spent time discerning the requirements for the episcopate in the remaining years of the 1990s and into the new millennium. Once this visioning process concluded, they wrote the diocesan profile — a document that described the state of the diocese, predicted the issues to be faced, and defined the qualities of an ideal bishop. Presciently it said, "the new bishop will lead the diocese through a period of dramatic change on many fronts."[243] Three key issues identified were the changing demographics of the diocese, the different family models emerging in Canada, and questions surrounding human sexuality. The committee described the new bishop they sought as being "a person of prayer and discerning faith; [someone who] recognizes his/her own strengths and weaknesses, with an ability to care for others."[244]

Eighteen candidates were nominated, including a couple of diocesan bishops and, at the last moment, the Very Reverend Michael Ingham, who also agreed to let his name stand. The nominees' ages ranged from forty to sixty-three, with most in their forties. Some were Canadian born and bred and a few came from the

United States and the United Kingdom. They came from cities and towns from coast to coast. Candidates represented both genders, the full spectrum of Anglican beliefs, and most had impressive educations. All prepared curricula vitae and written responses to the diocesan profile. They also answered probing questions about their vision, their passion, their pastoral approach, their spirituality, and the strengths and weaknesses they would bring to the episcopate if elected. The committee circulated these and videotaped interviews of the nominees to the electoral synod delegates for consideration. Reading the candidates' responses to the profile and their thoughtful answers to the questions provides intimate glimpses into their priorities, leadership styles, and their spiritual lives.

Some of nominees wrote in generalities that did not provide clear direction, and a few seemed to write in code, using Biblical references throughout their submissions. Still others wrote superbly, well enough for publication, but only two pinpointed what was really needed. Ingham was one.

His response to the profile was written in a clear, conversational style, rather than a scholarly one, and tackled head-on the challenges facing the diocese. He identified the changing demographic expected through immigration and its anticipated impact on the church, saying the diocese must integrate immigrants better, and he provided a choice of solutions. He brought up human sexuality, amongst several issues gaining ground, and said that the diocese must deal with it openly, sensitively, and honestly; he displayed his determination to face these controversial issues "constructively and without acrimony."[245] He believed then, and still does, that "healthy Christians have the ability to listen, and a willingness to work together."[246] Ingham also visualized improvements in education to support lay ministries and to expose biases, education that would deepen the understanding of complex issues and reach beyond stereotypes of ethnicity and sexual orientation. He addressed the issue of expensive parish structures that diminished the ability to continue ministry and mission and implied that perhaps some churches could be "without walls." Ingham described a future episcopal style that needed to be consultative and collaborative: "We need a bishop with the gifts of courage, integrity, and humour."[247]

Ingham's answers to the questions posed also make fascinating reading; they were revealing and focused continually on inclusivity and caring:

> *My vision and hope for the church is that it will become an inclusive community, where every person is welcomed . . . and where the gifts of each one are recognized and called upon. Where the church now excludes, I would seek to include. By this I mean, people from non-Anglo cultures, people with disabilities, people of different sexual orientation, and people who in all kinds of ways haven't got it . . . together.*[248]

He also mentioned his desire to build understanding of, and a dialogue with, other faith communities, one of his passions. Ingham showed his willingness to wade into political issues, such as health care and poverty, from a social-justice standpoint by developing relationships with decision-makers. One major concern of his was the pastoral care of the clergy and their families, who often suffered burnout and sometimes even depression. Ingham also wrote, "I would be a defender of Anglican tradition and at the same time try to press its boundaries forward."[249]

During the videotaped interviews, all candidates responded to a series of set questions, as well as a few questions that differed from candidate to candidate. Ingham remembers that he was asked for his position on gay and lesbian rights. He said, "that the church could no longer hide from difficult issues and . . . needed a way of addressing them, a way of approaching them, a way of thinking about them that was neither confrontational nor deliberately provocative and was neither dishonest nor fearful."[250]

As far as he was concerned, Ingham made it clear that he would need time to nurture himself and his growing family. In fact, he went as far as to tell the electoral synod delegates that "sometimes I would be unavailable — just having fun."[251] He concluded his writing by assuring everyone that he would seek another position after ten years or so, for everybody's sake including his own.

On September 25, 1993, the special electoral synod made up of 390 clergy and laity convened at St Catherine's, North Vancouver.

Ingham attended, and remembers it as "a frightful day."[252] After the opening Eucharist, the candidates withdrew into a private room between the balloting, so they did not have to mingle with the delegates; Ingham read a book to take his mind off the events in the main hall. The laity and the clergy sit separately at an electoral synod because they vote separately. One newcomer to the diocese, a priest, remembers that the atmosphere amongst the clergy was intense throughout the day, and the tension in the air built palpably as the votes progressed. She was also aware that, when Ingham emerged to vote, he appeared composed. Ingham said that the candidates felt like fish in a barrel and sympathized with each other.

Only three real contenders emerged on the first ballot, and, once the remaining fifteen withdrew, the third ballot left only two of three seriously in the running. The two were Ingham and the Bishop of Yukon, Ron Ferris — one progressive and one conservative — and the synod voted more on this polarity than for the "man." Ferris had shot out in front on the first ballot and increased his showing on the second, demonstrating that a campaign had taken place among the more conservative parishes of the diocese to solidify the traditional vote around one candidate. When synod realized what was happening, the votes started to increase for Ingham, who nearly doubled his showing on the second ballot, but Ferris remained in front after the votes were tallied. As candidates withdrew from the running before the third vote, five remained on the slate. Ingham started to worry. If Ferris carried the day, he would be his dean, and he foresaw difficulties arising from their differing theologies; if not, he would likely be the next bishop himself.

When the third-ballot results were announced, Ingham was within five votes of Ferris. In the "withdrawing" room, it dawned on Ingham that he was going to win the election, because the losing candidates, who were liberals, would move their votes to him on the fourth ballot. He noticed a sea change in mood before the crucial, final vote. Supporters amongst the unsuccessful candidates suddenly came and sat with him, and one even congratulated him prematurely, saying, "You're obviously going to be the one." [253] Ingham also discerned a shift of relationship taking place, because "power is real and bishops have power." He was filled with "an almighty sense of dread."[254]

On the fourth ballot, Ingham carried the day, earning 226 votes (66 per cent) to Ferris's 150.* The Diocese of New Westminster had opted for the progressive candidate to lead them into the new millennium. When the results were announced, observers noted that Ingham's face was hard to read, but he was speechless. Ingham remembers the moment as if it were yesterday, and recalls that he was coping with contradictory emotions. On one hand Ingham experienced "a feeling of unworthiness . . . to lead a diocese as large and diverse as [New Westminster]" and, on the other, he had a sense of acceptance: "If this is what God wants me to do, I know I can do this."[255] The bishop-elect declined addressing synod (he couldn't think of a thing to say), and chose to offer the closing blessing instead. "I was happy and full of dread all at the same time. It was a huge affirmation of me, but I had a real sense that I had been handed this very hot potato: 'You've won, congratulations; you've inherited the Gordian knot, commiserations!'"[256] Then the media scrum engulfed Ingham and he realized that nothing was ever going to be the same again.

Ingham was forty-four years old, young for a bishop, the same age as Hambidge was when elected in Caledonia. In fact Ingham was the youngest Anglican bishop in Canada in 1993. Since he was known to be progressively liberal in his theology, conservative Anglicans were disappointed and worried by the election result. In his first episcopal "sound bite," Ingham repeated to reporters at the close of the proceedings what he had said in his application to the nominating committee: "I will encourage the church to become more inclusive and welcoming."[257]

The primate, Michael Peers, phoned Ingham that night with his congratulations and gave him some welcome advice. They discussed how the day had gone and the polarization of the vote. Worried, Ingham commented, "I don't think the diocese is terribly together." Peers responded, "Well, that's always true on the day of an election; the next three months are a period of grace in which the diocese comes together around the new bishop. You will find that that will happen." Ingham soon discovered the primate was right — at least for while.

---

* Of 118 clergy votes, Ingham received 77; of 272 lay votes, 149.

Ingham's elation at being elected bishop of New Westminster was short-lived. Just after he arrived home and Gwen had flung her arms around him with delight, their phone rang. Four-year-old Cara, visiting friends, had sat on a wasps' nest and was in hospital with more than forty stings — a life-threatening situation for a youngster. The new bishop's elation evaporated instantly as they raced to see her, wondering if she would survive the ordeal. The scare put his elevation to the episcopate into perspective like nothing else could. Cara recovered and, at Ingham's consecration, managed to steal the limelight and have her picture splashed over the *Vancouver Sun*'s front page.

Ingham processing out of the Christ Church Cathedral after his installation. His daughter, Cara, could contain herself no longer and jumped into his arms. January 9, 1994. (Nick Didlick/*Vancouver Sun*)

The first thing Ingham did after the election was to contact his fellow candidates who had been unsuccessful. He knew that the process had hurt and bruised some of them, and he assured them that he valued them and would work with them all. Then, chuckling, he wrote two letters to and from himself. As rector of Christ Church Cathedral, he informed the commissary of the diocese that he was resigning; then, as commissary, he replied with a nice letter saying he had done a good job. Until his consecration, Ingham remained rector of the cathedral and continued with those duties, which he enjoyed. When Ingham processed into the cathedral on the first Sunday after the episcopal election, the congregation was unusually quiet. The bonds of affection between the new dean and his congregation had developed quickly, and now, as he was leaving them, both sides experienced a sense of loss. He immediately apologized for his short stay.

Ingham had a clear idea of what being a bishop was going to mean for him. His four years with the primate had shown him the implications, and so he was far from naïve about the office. Ingham knew that he had been elected, not for his managerial skills, but to give leadership in good times and in challenging times. He believed then, and still believes today, that one of the greatest temptations facing bishops in the midst of polarization and conflict is to abandon leadership and settle for the role of manager, because it is less stressful, easier on families, and better for the health. He vowed not to let it happen to him.

In the diocesan newspaper, the *Topic,* the bishop-elect wrote in his message to the clergy and laity, "I won't play games about what I really think on an issue, but I will allow other people the integrity of their own position. . . . I intend to be of good cheer and good courage as your bishop. I may not seek the safe places, and I may try to push the boundaries outwards in directions that will stretch us."[258]

The consecration on January 9, 1994, was a splendid affair, which Ingham's father was able to attend. Held at St. Andrew's–Wesley United Church in downtown Vancouver, because it held twice as many as Christ Church Cathedral, the service was filled with colour and incense, and magnificent music and singing from a huge choir. Michael Peers, the Canadian primate, preached a sermon that exhorted the new bishop to aim for the radical centre and to be strong when judged, caricatured, or criticized. Ingham found his consecration intensely personal in the midst of a huge public ceremony. He was uplifted, validated, and inspired by it and, at the same time, felt a great weight descending. "I wondered if I had any of the skills to manage the life of a diocese like this," he remembered.[259] Then the pipes of the Seaforth Highlanders led the new bishop in procession along Burrard Street to the cathedral for his installation.

Herbert, Ingham's father, was overwhelmed by the scale of the ceremonies and significance of the honour given to his only son. While he had always supported him in anything he wanted to do, he had not experienced anything like this before and was bursting with pride. Ingham, whose mom had died earlier, was thankful that his father could join the celebrations and be with him on such an important day in his life.

The reception that followed the official ceremonies took place at the Hyatt Regency Hotel. Ingham, surrounded by a gaggle of media, hardly had time to mingle with the guests and drink some orange juice. Gwen left the celebrations early to relieve their younger daughter's caregiver and to get a weary Cara to bed. When Ingham arrived home, Gwen asked him to change Robyn's diaper, so he trudged upstairs and, still dressed in his finery, did so. The baby promptly threw up all over him and the new bishop took it as a signal: "Don't take yourself too seriously!"[260] Life was returning to normal, at least at home.

Ingham managed to attend some of the excellent courses for new bishops run by the General Theological Seminary in New York City, but the pressure of work meant he could not take them all. He was busy putting his stamp on the diocese and working on a couple of initiatives that he hoped would improve its mission and ministry. One was the Spencer Commission that studied the rapidly changing demographics of the diocese and how the diocese could respond to the increasing immigrant population and exploding suburbs that were under-churched. This work resulted in the planting of new churches in areas of rapid growth in Abbotsford and Richmond, as well as an ecumenical ministry in Whistler, the international ski resort. The commission also identified churches that were struggling with small, declining congregations. The other initiative was the Rivers Commission, which looked at alternative models of ministry and new creative ways to take the Gospel to the world. Suggestions included the expansion of lay ministry in parishes, support for the restoration of the permanent diaconate, new methods of identifying and training young clergy, and models of church planting that would be more flexible than the customary church, steeple, and parking lot. However, before the work could be completed and the recommendations be implemented, the sexuality issue overwhelmed the diocese, and its financial consequences limited further growth and consolidation. The bishop had to spend much of his time interpreting the actions of the diocese to Canada and the rest of the world and steering the diocese through careful decision-making. Outreach programs and the revitalization of mission and ministry continued under the oversight and direction of diocesan staff and senior leaders, but he himself was not able to give them the attention in the second half of the decade that he had done in the first.

I'm not a binary thinker

After preaching his thirty-ninth sermon on confirmation in a parish church in his first year as bishop, Ingham conferred with his archdeacons and moved all confirmation services to the cathedral, where they now take place in five ceremonies during the Easter season. With eighty parishes, he felt it was not an effective model of episcopal ministry to go out to each individually and confirm as few as two or three. Ingham's decision was not well received by everyone, and turned into an early, though very minor, controversy in his episcopate. The resulting benefit was an important one though. When the bishop visits parishes now, which he does from September to December, he is able to meet the community and discuss the issues of the day.

By his third year in office, Ingham knew more of the matters touching the hearts of the people in the pews than before, and today he feels he has his finger on the pulse of the diocese. Also Ingham particularly enjoys the opportunity of preaching on the lections rather than solely about confirmation. He likes to offer his vision of the Gospel and what its imperatives are in the modern world. He preaches well, sometimes very well. His sermon at Easter 2005 achieved a standing ovation from a full cathedral, and a transcript of it raced round the world via e-mail afterwards.

Ingham posing a skill-testing question to the Education for Ministry graduates before he cut the celebratory cake, June 2005. (Julie H. Ferguson)

Ingham has developed his own way of thinking and preaching over the years since university. "I'm not a binary thinker and I'm deeply suspicious of either-or thinking. I recognize that is difficult for some people, so I've tried always to be clear, tried always to say where I stand and why, but always to say to people, 'You may have a different view and I'm really interested in hearing about that.'"[261] Regarding sermons, Ingham says, "I've never been impressed with preaching . . . that declines to take a position. To get up and say, 'On the one hand some people say . . . and on the other hand other people say . . . ,' and then to sit down again, is not leadership. It's deeply dissatisfying, spiritually and intellectually. I think it's okay to say: 'On the one hand these things can be said . . . on the other, those things can be said. Now let me tell you what I think.' . . . I [preach] in a way that allows others the space to come to their own point of view and I never ask people to agree with me. That way, in every parish I've been in, we've been able to live with a great deal of diversity [of opinion] . . . because [parishioners] knew that their positions were honoured."[262]

When he became bishop, Ingham resigned from many of the international and national boards and committees of which he was a member, so that he could devote more time to the diocese. But he remained the episcopal representative from Canada on the Anglican Consultative Council until the beginning of 2005. He is the Canadian representative on the governing body of the Episcopal Church of the United States, and he became a member of the Council of General Synod in 2004. Even so, Ingham still travels extensively — he attends the regular meetings of the Canadian and provincial Houses of Bishops, visits the companion Diocese of Taiwan occasionally, and is a sought-after speaker.

I cannot believe in a God who only saves Christians

Ingham's life-long passion for the interfaith movement and dialogue was sparked at the seminary in Edinburgh when Alistair Haggart encouraged him to read more widely on the subject. His passion is still in full flame, though not always visible. One of the evident signs of Ingham's continuing contribution was his book, *Mansions of the Spirit: The Gospel in a Multi-Faith World*, which caused a stir in 1997. Another was his active involvement in the visit of his friends, the Dalai Lama and Archbishop Desmond Tutu, to Vancouver in April 2004 for a series of public forums.

But first, a story about the deepening of his personal relationship with God in an unlikely setting. Michael Ingham's most recent profound religious experience occurred in 2000, not in a Christian church, but in a Hare Krishna temple in Bangalore, India. The bishop was on sabbatical in India as a visiting scholar studying interfaith issues in Indian religions and interfaith theology in Indian Christian churches. The temple, amongst many he visited, is devoted to the philosophy and religion of the Krishna consciousness. It is a large and impressive place, and Ingham was met at the entrance by an official who told him there were two ways of entering, "You can go through this door and say your prayers on your way in; it only takes ten min-

Ingham during his sabbatical in India, 2000.
(Ingham collection)

utes. If you don't have ten minutes, you can go straight in through this door."[263] The bishop of New Westminster naturally chose to go through the prayer door.

Inside Ingham discovered a kind of labyrinth marked out in tiles on the floor and, while standing on each tile, visitors repeated the Hare Krishna mantra, which loosely means "Please Lord, engage me in your service." He found out it was a breathing prayer, and everyone, as they finished, moved in unison to the next tile. Ingham quickly absorbed the inherent rhythm of the prayer. Initially he wondered what he was doing saying the Hindu prayer, but realized that he was not praying to Krishna but to God; the words were simply the external vehicle to an invisible and deep reality, which was, for him, Christ. By the time he had completed the labyrinth he was floating, detached from the immediate physical and material space and in deep communion with God. On his return to Vancouver, Ingham relayed this experience to some of his clergy. A few were horrified. They found his story difficult to hear because they believed any prayer offered in a pagan place should be ineffectual. Some even thought it was demonic, or evil.

During his Edinburgh seminary days, Ingham's principal had given him a paper to read by John Hick. It was Ingham's first exposure to "theocentric Christology," which explains the work of Christ in terms of the universality of God, rather than God in terms of Christ. Ingham became intrigued with Hick's theology and devoured his early books, which he found compelling and persuasive. Ingham's immersion in Judaism at the Hebrew University in Jerusalem in 1972 solidified his life-long investigation into other faith traditions. His first visit to India the following year, coupled with more reading, led Ingham to explore and assess other religions from a theological point of view.

Arriving in Harvard from Bombay, he discovered the Centre for the Study of World Religions and so, while studying American theology, he also signed up to take courses there. Ingham enjoyed learning about the philosophy of Hinduism and the various approaches in Christian theology to other world religions. The courses developed in him a broader base for exploring the validity of other traditions through a Christian lens, some of which he had already experienced. He was becoming hooked on the subject and, while he served his apprenticeship as an ordained priest in Ottawa and Burnaby, Ingham continued to read all he could find on the subject and to reflect on it. He also chose to become deeply involved in the social-justice issues of the day — global poverty, famine, homelessness, and refugees — and quickly grasped that interfaith connections were vital if any efforts to alleviate the starving and oppressed were to have an impact. Ingham attended conferences, led forums, and, in all the parishes he served as priest, worked on "Ten Days for World Development," an educational initiative of the national Church.

When Ingham got to the West Coast, Archbishop Somerville had asked him to start the diocesan unit for the Primate's World Relief and Development Fund, and Ingham set about it with a will. The unit's task was to educate parishes about the needs of the Third World and, as he focused on the task in the late 1970s to mid-1980s, Ingham was again made aware that inter-religious dialogue hovered in the background of all world-development issues. By 1993,

Ingham was doing more. He was a enthusiastic member of the Interchurch Interfaith Relations Committee of General Synod and attended, as a representative of the Anglican Church of Canada, the second Parliament of the World's Religions in Chicago. Double the expected participants turned up, overwhelming the organizers with over seven thousand attendees, representing more than one hundred faith traditions. Ingham was struck that the same problems, profound differences, and deep tensions between religions that were discussed at the first parliament in 1893 had not changed much. The experience galvanized him, and he vowed to take action somehow. In 1995 Ingham, mulling over his many experiences, said to an interviewer, "When you've encountered the same spiritual core in another religious tradition, it strikes you as more than simply coincidental. It strikes you that God's wisdom is poured out through the Earth, as the psalm says."[264]

When he wrote *Rites for a New Age* while rector of St. Francis in the Wood, Ingham had already felt a nudge to write a book about the interfaith issues that were emerging in an increasingly plural Western world. The subject had been tackled by others solely as a preparation for Christianity, but he wanted to approach it from a new and perhaps provocative direction. Once he was bishop, his wife, Gwen, urged him to get on with it, saying, "You should keep writing; it's one of your gifts." Attending the Parliament of World Religions in 1993 gave Ingham the final impetus, and he began to prepare. As the outline had been in his consciousness for years, and his reading and experience had converged, Ingham was ready to get it on paper. In 1996 he borrowed a boat from a priest friend and sailed alone to Silva Bay in the Gulf Islands, dropped anchor, and wrote on his laptop from morning till night for a week. Dishevelled and unshaven, he returned home with the bulk of *Mansions of the Spirit* written — and ready for a shower.

The main premise of *Mansions of the Spirit* is that Christians can, with integrity, affirm the differing paths of others to God. While staying with the Hindu family in Bombay in the 1970s, the young Ingham had set out, but failed, to convince his hosts that Jesus had removed the need for other forms of worship and belief. All along, his hosts had been interested in his words, but also encouraged him to see that the truth could not be confined to any single route.

"God's beauty and glory is demonstrated in many incarnations beyond the one called Jesus," [265] they explained politely.

Ingham's *Mansions of the Spirit* examines the different paths to God and the Christian response to them through the lens of multi-faith neighbourhoods. Prior to the twentieth century, cultures with different religious traditions rarely met each other. If they did meet, it was on the battlefield or in the mission field. Our Christian predecessors, like Bishop George Hills, fervently believing that the only path to salvation was through Jesus Christ, worked zealously to convert non-Christians and refused to accept the validity of any other faith. Today we live in a global village. We meet those different from ourselves over the garden fence and in our classrooms, which demonstrates that the relationship of Christianity with other world religions has become an integral part of our everyday lives. *Mansions* takes off from there.

Ingham maintains that not everyone believes in God in the same way. The book demonstrates that individuals can accept that other religions can lead to God, without embracing the doctrines of other faiths or rejecting their Christian beliefs. *Mansions* has chapters on Christian inclusivism and exclusivism, the history of the interfaith movement, religious pluralism, the mystical path, safe exploration of other faiths, and how to evangelize with tolerance.

As loving one's neighbours is a Christian imperative, to mutually understand and relate to them, Ingham writes, Christians have no choice but to educate themselves on the subject and engage in serious interfaith dialogue. Employing many sources from Scripture, modern scholarship, and recent theology, Ingham debates an easily understood argument for change in the Christian approach to other faith traditions through open dialogue and cooperation. He believes faith communities should be working in partnership, not competition: "We only have to look to places like Bosnia and the Middle East to see what happens when cultures and religions collide."[266] Ingham ends by saying that Jesus does not want "Imperialism in his name, but love and justice. Not conquest of other religions but mutual respect and tolerance. Not superiority but humility."[267] And he believes the task before us is urgent.

The Anglican Book Centre published *Mansions* in 1997 to considerable fanfare. The editor thought it would do well in the marketplace because it was breaking new ground. Indeed, if the pre-publication endorsements were anything to go by, the book was impressive. Praise and support came from many quarters, notably the Dalai Lama, the Most Reverend and Right Honourable Lord Runcie, who was a former Archbishop of Canterbury, and the eminent Rabbi Emeritus and author Gunther Plaut. Plaut wrote, "Michael Ingham has written a closely argued and highly readable book that is essentially a deconstruction of Christian exclusivism. . . . Christianity is not the only religion claiming that it alone represents the true way to God . . . therefore *Mansions of the Spirit* makes an important contribution to inter-religious rapprochement."[268]

The Anglican Book Centre hired a publicist to promote Ingham's second book. To the bishop's dismay the campaign used the headline "Bishop denies Jesus is the only way," which he was unable to veto. In fact, Ingham had not denied his own faith but had simply affirmed the different ways of others. The publicity roared across North America, leaving confusion in its wake. For example, a *Vancouver Sun* headline said Ingham had "ignited an Anglican controversy,"[269] and, in the *BC Report*, the sub-head of a critical article was "In an Anglican bishop's mansions, there is room for everything but truth."[270] Others called Ingham a heretic and an apostate. *Mansions* had certainly provoked debate.

Ingham was caught in the crosshairs once more, but this time was clearly targeted by more severe evangelical Christians who believed that it was scandalous to suggest that Jesus was not the only route to God. Many at the traditional end of the spectrum were deeply offended by both *Mansions* and its author, although two conservative bishops in England did tell Ingham they appreciated his viewpoint. Some clergy in the Diocese of New Westminster also reacted adversely and challenged their bishop's views. Ingham met with them and others to discuss his position and his belief that we have inherited a living tradition which requires engagement with the issues of the day. He told them, "I cannot believe in a God who only saves Christians."[271] A few were soothed by the dialogue, but a handful remained so distressed that they wrote Ingham a letter telling him he had broken his ordination vows because, as Jesus was the only path to salvation, the bishop was clearly not guarding the faith as he was required to do. The letter ended with a vague threat to sue him in ecclesiastical court for heresy. A trial has never materialized, but the experience demonstrated to Ingham once again that a percentage of clergy and laity were fearful of the increasing assaults on their faith tradition in the 1990s, and no longer felt safe and secure in the changing times. In retrospect, the bishop feels the distress produced by *Mansions* had a direct effect on the sexuality issue that soon followed.

Ingham was encouraged at the 1998 Lambeth Conference when the bishops embraced a form of pluralism by endorsing the "Thirty Theses on Inter-Faith Relations," a document that rejected conversion and proselytism, but allowed for witnessing to the faith. In his article published in the *Anglican Journal* in December 1999, he wrote, "Lambeth was clear that conversion is God's business, not the church's. . . . The exploitation of poverty or weakness by Christian (or any other) agencies to 'win souls' was declared unacceptable. So was the targeting of Jews, Muslims, or other groups."[272] This position was a far cry from that of the Victorian imperative in which the first bishop of British Columbia ministered.

A year later, to promote the Parliament of the World's Religions in Capetown, South Africa, in December 1999, more reviews and articles appeared about *Mansions.* A Jewish rabbi in Vancouver wrote, "Ingham goes beyond formal tolerance to develop an authentic (if radical) theology that embraces the existence of other faiths. . . . I found the author's frank writing to be stimulating, engaging, and challenging."[273] Ingham himself wrote an article for the *Globe and Mail,* published the same week, predicting major changes for the religions of the world: "The big emerging movement of the future — still young but now unstoppable — will be global interfaith consciousness."[274]

As Ingham has always believed that "theology is a clash of ideas, an engagement of opposites . . . an evolving discipline,"[275] he had been surprised and disappointed that more traditional-thinking Christians did not see the theological exploration in *Mansions* as part of the role of a bishop. As he wrote:

> *For me, a bishop is not disqualified by virtue of the office from undertaking theological exploration . . . to 'guard the faith' means to keep it alive, not preserve it*

in a museum. [The conservatives] tend to see revelation as finished and the job of the Church is merely repetition of what was handed down 2,000 years ago. . . . I sense from some of them that they cannot get out of their box . . . and that if there are no absolutes any more, they can't feel safe in the world.[276]

The controversial book meant Ingham was in demand, and he received more invitations than he could accept to speak around the world. He used the opportunities that *Mansions* provided to promote both interfaith dialogue and the plight of the world's disadvantaged and oppressed. Somerville came out firmly in favour of the book. "We are all believers. There is one God and many paths,"[277] he said recently. One Chinese reader wrote to say the book had relieved a long-held agony fostered by her Christian church: the fear that her parents had gone to hell at their deaths because they were Buddhists.

Ingham also started teaching a course on religious pluralism at the Vancouver School of Theology in 1999, bringing together both his academic and intellectual interests and his passion for interfaith dialogue. As part of the ongoing program, Ingham introduces the students to both the traditional arguments for Christian exclusivism and to the newly emerging theologians of the pluralist school. Instead of merely reading about other religions in textbooks and discussing them, Ingham's students get something quite different — they visit mosques, temples, and synagogues and meet other religious communities on their (holy) ground.

Just before the 1998 Lambeth Conference, Ingham received a letter from the Bishop of California, the Right Reverend William E. Swing, which was to step up his involvement in interfaith dialogue — in his diocese and internationally. Three years before, Swing had started the United Religions Initiative after he realized that the countries of the world customarily gathered at the United Nations, but that the world's faiths had no permanent organization or place to meet. Today the URI is the fastest-growing interfaith movement in the world. Swing read *Mansions* with increasing excitement, and after finishing it, wrote to Ingham saying, "You have the theology and I have the organization. We should get together."[278] They agreed to talk at Lambeth, discovered they both loved golf, and became firm friends. Ingham, galvanized once more, returned home and to establish a local chapter of URI. He has since attended several global assemblies of the URI, which continue to stimulate and feed him.

To get the chapter of URI operational in Vancouver, the bishop chose to make a personal approach to the religious leaders whom he already knew. He phoned them and suggested that they gather together for breakfast or lunch. Ingham's idea met with immediate support, and together Jewish, Sikh, Hindu, Muslim, and Christian leaders, among other traditions, formed the local URI chapter in early 2000. In an interview, Ingham said, "In a world where religions are often seen as part of the problem, we hope to show that interfaith cooperation is possible to ease tensions."[279] Although not the only interfaith organization in Vancouver, URI was the first in which the religious leaders participated; other groups were comprised of various faiths' members. The members of URI's Vancouver chapter became mutually supporting, and drew much satisfaction from their regular association with each other. It was just in time.

The best-known outcome of this interfaith group took place after terrorist planes destroyed the World Trade Center in New York and damaged the Pentagon in Washington, D.C., on 9/11. The new URI chapter enabled Ingham to quickly bring together all the religious leaders in Vancouver in response to the tragedy and provide an interfaith service at Christ Church Cathedral. Letters to the editor in the Vancouver newspapers demonstrated how much comfort citizens drew from the prayers of the Sikh, Jewish, Islamic, and Christian traditions. URI in Vancouver also organized a multifaith public forum to demonstrate that religions could be part of the solution to 9/11, not the problem. Another outcome was the 2004 round-table discussion, which Ingham moderated, of the Dalai Lama, Archbishop Desmond Tutu, Sto:lo Dr. Jo-Ann Archibald, Rabbi Schacter-Shalomi, and the Iranian feminist and 2003 Nobel Peace Prize winner, Shirin Ebadi. Tickets to the event sold out in hours, and it was an overwhelming success that received much front-page ink and air time.

The visit of the Dalai Lama and Archbishop Tutu served as inspiration for the proposed Interspiritual Centre of Vancouver (ISCV), in which Ingham is enthusiastically involved. This centre will put into practice what he has always preached: a partnership among faith communities, rather than competition. Approached by Vancouver Rabbi

Ingham moderated a couple of interfaith forums, April 2004, during the Dalai Lama's visit to Vancouver. L to R: Tutu, Ingham, Archibald, Schacter-Shalomi, unknown, Ebadi, Dalai Lama (his interpreter is behind him), Dr. Pitman Potter (UBC). (Carey Linde)

David Mivasir and others who realized that the proposed development of seven thousand housing units for the southeast corner of False Creek in Vancouver had no space set aside for devotional purposes, Ingham rallied his interfaith contacts. Their vision is for a permanent sacred space that could be shared by many faith traditions for worship, education, and fellowship. Ingham is one of the directors of the centre, in the company of like-minded Roman Catholics, aboriginals, Buddhists, Hindus, Muslims, and Jews, as well as community and business leaders. So far, the concept has been accepted by the City of Vancouver, and planning is under way, with considerable participation from the Diocese of New Westminster. The diocese's business administrator, Mike Wellwood, sits on the project committee and said, "It's truly exhilarating to be working so closely together, while honouring our differences."[280] All hope to see the interspiritual centre finished in time for the 2010 Winter Olympics, because part of this development will contain the athlete's village.

Ingham is also an active participant in a dialogue between the Pacific branch of the Canadian Jewish Congress and local Christian leaders. At a monthly breakfast they listen to a speaker (Ingham has presented) and participate in lively discussions. Initially the group built confidence and trust rather than tackling contentious issues, and spent time in mutual inquiry and study. Now they attempt to unravel questions around topics like Israeli–Palestinian relations, suicide bombers, settlements in the West Bank, and other thorny issues. "It is one group I most enjoy going to," says Ingham. "And one of the paradoxes is that the Vancouver Jewish community has been very supportive of minority rights for gays and lesbians . . . they have long had a passion for social justice."[281]

"I've found my contacts in other religious communities to be life-giving,"[282] and Ingham builds them into his heavy schedule, both at home and overseas. "There is a remarkable spirit of goodwill among us,"[283] notes Ingham, as he explains the fellowship he enjoys with other religious leaders in Vancouver. In 2004, Ingham was invited to speak at the fourth Parliament of the World's Religions in Barcelona, Spain. Ten thousand delegates from every imaginable faith tradition met amid tight security and provided another heartening experience in the interfaith movement for the bishop.

"If this sexual orientation were indeed a matter of personal choice, the homosexual persons must be the craziest coots around to choose a way of life that exposes them to so much hostility, discrimination, loss, and suffering."[284]

Desmond Tutu

Both Christian and world opinion caught Ingham in the crosshairs for the third time over the issue of human sexuality, and they have held him there. This issue has proved to be the longest and most difficult challenge of his episcopate. However, despite repeated shots being fired at him since 1998, Ingham has not ducked once. He has been unwavering in his stance of inclusion. He has also remained serene, at least on the outside, while deflecting the bullets flying at him.

Issues inherent in human sexuality have engaged humankind for millennia but only recently have they been so openly discussed. Frank debate regarding sexuality became increasingly acceptable in society after the Second World War, as scientific research escalated and modern communications disseminated the growing body of knowledge to a fascinated public. The complete array of sexual orientations and practices, which many had previously ignored or knew nothing about, hit the mainstream. The diversity in the expression of human sexuality caused reactions in society that encompassed everything from acceptance to disgust.

Christian churches knew they had to respond, but spent considerable time discerning the will of God before they took public positions on human sexuality. The majority did so carefully and with respect. In many denominations, the "study mode" has reigned supreme since the 1980s — and, in large measure, still does. Serious inquiry soon exposed sexual and gender double standards in religious institutions. The results of the deliberations often mirrored the societal responses, which ranged from tolerance through denial to horror. The one constant in the myriad discussions was, of course, emotion. The debate on sexuality provoked strong reactions, some passion, and always vehement disagreement.

Although homosexuality has felt a bit like the only issue on the table since the early 1980s for Anglicans of the western world, it was simply one of many sexual topics being grappled with globally, including polygamy, lobola,* and genital mutilation, for example. By the time the 1988 Lambeth Conference convened, individual gays and lesbians were gaining some acceptance in western church life, but same-sex unions were not. Lambeth discussed the issue of human sexuality and passed a resolution (see Appendix II for the full text) that acknowledged the wide disparity of opinions on homosexuality and encouraged further study. The world's Anglican bishops wondered if the issue might play out the way the ordination of women had: "we could be faced in the future by one province allowing what other provinces fundamentally disagree with."[285] But diversity seemed alive and well, although some predicted the possibility of a threat of division over homosexuality.

Gay-lesbian rights became an issue for the Anglican Church in North America long before Ingham became bishop of New Westminster, and has been under discussion in Canada for over quarter of a century. The first, unofficial liturgy for the blessing of same-sex unions appeared in New York in 1973, following the American Psychiatric Association's removal of homosexuality from

---

* The practice of paying a price for the right to marry a woman.

the list of mental diseases. The Anglican Church of Canada, through the House of Bishops, made its first interim pronouncement on sexuality five years later, after three years of intensive study, but ahead of the proclamation of the Canadian Charter of Human Rights and Freedoms. The House of Bishops' guidelines of 1979,[286] which were pastoral not doctrinal, stated that homosexuals, as children of God, had full rights to the love, acceptance, and pastoral care of the Church. However when it came to the admission of gays and lesbians to ordained ministry, because they did not condone active homosexual behaviour, the bishops decided that homosexual priests and deacons must remain celibate. The bishops also decided, "We do not accept the blessing of homosexual unions."[287]

Study and discernment continued throughout the 1980s at the national, diocesan, and parish levels in Canada. The Church authorized for study the "Report on Human Sexuality," published by the National Executive Council in 1986 to assist the congregations and parish discussion groups, and it was widely used. As Anglicans learned more of what it meant to be homosexual in the church and in society, many clergy and laity saw the bishops' 1979 guidelines as outdated and called for reform. General Synod held its first open forum on homosexuality in Toronto in 1992 (organized by Ingham while he was Principal Secretary), and passed a resolution to conduct an immediate study of homosexuality and homosexual relationships for delivery at the next General Synod. A second forum, with live-feeds to Montreal, Toronto and Vancouver, took place at the 1995 General Synod, where delegates also voted to ask the House of Bishops to amend their 1979 guidelines on human sexuality. Several resolutions were carried at the same synod on the issue of homosexuality, including one calling for consultations on how to liturgically recognize committed same-sex unions.

The Diocese of New Westminster itself had also been engaged in serious discussions about sexuality for several years. In fact, the diocese's synods had received motions on the subject as early as 1987. While Ingham was in Toronto working with the primate, the synod passed a resolution urging the House of Bishops to revise their guidelines on sexuality after the diocese previously had gone on record as disagreeing with the Canadian Church's official position of 1979 on homosexuality. In his last year, 1992, Hambidge appointed a task force on human sexuality after synod resolved to press the House of Bishops for changes that would standardize the requirements for ordination for both heterosexuals and homosexuals. The task force reported in 1993 and this resulted in a two-year program of study throughout the diocese, as well as a renewed task force. The pressure was rising.

When Archbishop Hambidge resigned and the Diocese of New Westminster went looking for his successor in 1993, the topic of human sexuality was included in the process. Some episcopal candidates, when interviewed on videotape, were required to give their opinion on the bishops' guidelines on homosexuality and their own. Ingham was one of those asked, and his response to the Church's position had been "Yes and no." He said that, as bishop, he would support the House of Bishops' guidelines until they were changed, but he would actively work towards reform. Ingham also clearly restated his insistence on full inclusion for everyone in the Anglican Church, including gays and lesbians. Archival records show he hid nothing. Another, unofficial process, instigated by some of the more traditional, conservative parishes in the diocese, circulated a questionnaire to the candidates that also focused on the human sexuality issues. Not all the candidates filled it in, but Ingham completed it as a courtesy.

Having clearly articulated his position on the sexuality issue, Ingham insists that he had no intention of leading the charge on gay liberation, inclusion, or the blessing of same-sex unions. In 1993 "it was not even on [my] horizon," he said.[288] However his involvement in it began to take shape even before he was consecrated. Ingham met with many groups who visited to introduce themselves to the bishop-elect; one such group who called on him was Integrity Vancouver, the local chapter of the international organization working towards the full inclusion of gay and lesbian people in the life of the Anglican Church. Ingham invited them to march in the procession at his consecration and carry their banner — just as he had invited every parish and group to do. But it was a first for Integrity.

In his remarks at his installation, Ingham told the diocese that "We must be a changing church for a changing world,"[289] and went on to emphasize his determination to exclude no one. Ingham incorporated his passion for interfaith dialogue and his admiration of Trudeau's vision of a just society when he said, "I will work with anyone — of any race, sex, or political opinion, anyone of good will whatever their religious faith or belief, whether Christian or non-Christian — who wants to build a society of justice and peace."[290] His words, "Whether you are brown or white, Asian or black, heterosexual or homosexual, abled or disabled, rich or poor, you are welcome here,"[291] caused one of the visiting bishops to frown suddenly. The next day the bishop of the companion diocese of Northern Argentina, Maurice Sinclair,* sought out Ingham in some distress. He expressed his strong opposition to the new bishop's willingness to work with gays and lesbians, but did not give Ingham the opportunity to explain his position.

Not long after that incident, Ingham realized that some of the conservatives in the diocese were more disturbed than he had anticipated with the direction he was taking. Ingham intentionally reached out to these members of his diocese. He began to study up on evangelical Christianity, and made a point of visiting all the conservative parishes in his diocese as soon as he could. He reread everything that had been written by evangelical proponents, such authors as Alistair McGrath and John Stott,‡ and reflected on their positions. Ingham admits to being discouraged at the end of a year of study: "It felt like a return to . . . pre-Enlightenment thought . . . [the authors] totally ignored or dismissed the last two hundred years of biblical scholarship. In those years we have learned a great deal. . . . In fact, modern liberalism was driven by [recent] biblical scholarship." [292] Ingham knew that the majority of Anglicans who favoured the evangelical expression of their faith were not opposed to inclusivity, and did not see it as a deal-breaker; however, the core of the opposition to it was certainly amongst their number, and, for this minority, the issue was definitely a communion-breaker. Ingham also understood that, in modern pluralistic societies, there are always some individuals who "define who they are by kicking other people out,"[293] and any hint of

---

* This visiting bishop, who later became the Primate of the Southern Cone, led (until his retirement) the group of primates who oppose gay-lesbian rights and are now working towards expelling North America from the Anglican Communion.

‡ See Web sites: http://resources.theology.ox.ac.uk/staff.phtml?lecturer_code=Amcgrath and http://www.johnstott.org//

inclusion of those who are different becomes a highly charged, emotional situation, in which rational thought and discussion often deserts healthy debate.

So concerned were some of the conservatives in Canada that they established Anglican Essentials in 1994, by combining the memberships of Anglican Renewal Ministries, the Barnabas Ministries, and the Prayer Book Society into a federation of "orthodox" Canadian Anglicans. Essentials's goal was to thwart the perceived threat from the progressives to the traditional side of the Anglican spectrum, and Ingham became one of their targets after his consecration. One way Essentials hoped to counter the liberal shift in the national churches of North America was to ensure the election of conservatives to the council and committees of General Synod, and another was to organize conferences to rally like-minded Anglicans from around the world.

The new bishop moved quickly to get the members of the diocese informed about recent thinking and research on sexuality. Before Ingham's episcopacy, several parishes in the Diocese of New Westminster had participated in a national study on homosexuality called *Hearing Diverse Voices, Seeking Common Ground* (Anglican Book Centre, 1994). Ingham established a second diocesan task force on human sexuality that spent two years developing resources to encourage open dialogue on the issue for use in parishes. In 1997, prior to the release of the House of Bishops' amended guidelines, the Diocese of New Westminster held two public forums to discuss scriptural, doctrinal, and ethical questions on the subject, and hosted a "Day of Dialogue on Homosexuality" for several hundred clergy and laity.

Ingham first spoke out publicly in support of the inclusion of gay and lesbian people as full and equal members of the Church in a speech he gave to Integrity in Toronto in October 1996. Integrity had approached several bishops prior to inviting Ingham, but none was prepared to speak out in public. The bishop of New Westminster considered carefully whether he should accept, but finally said to himself, "I should really. I'm supportive, so there's no point in being covert about it."[294] As he was driving to the engagement, Ingham knew his life was about to change: "It was a significant moment," he recalled.[295] It was significant for members of Integrity too.

Ingham was pleased to find the former primate, Ted Scott, amongst the audience, and then delivered his carefully crafted speech.[296] He talked about his own transformation in understanding homosexuality and said that "I have come to think that the basis for our continued denial of dignity and intimacy to gay and lesbian people is not theology but pathology." Having told the audience, "While acknowledging that celibacy is a viable, courageous choice for some [inside and outside ordained ministry]," Ingham went on, "I no longer believe sexual abstention can be required of an entire class of people, simply because of their sexual orientation." Then he spoke eloquently and in depth about how the church and society has mishandled human sexuality over the centuries and predicted a liberal use of biblical proof texts by opponents as the debate intensified. Towards the end of his speech, Ingham expressed his hope that the church would soon allow parishes and dioceses to choose whether they want to bless same-sex unions, but admitted that he feared it would be a while before any took place. After the speech, Ingham received a wildly enthusiastic standing ovation from the audience. This mood changed abruptly during the question-and-answer session when the bishop clarified that gays and lesbians need not rush to Vancouver immediately to get ordained or to have their unions blessed simply because he supported their cause. Ted Scott went up to the microphone and helped Ingham out, confirming that the bishop of New Westminster did not have the authority to change the Church's rules by himself. Disappointed at the time, Integrity only later recognized how pivotal Ingham's speech and public support were to be in their march to equality in the Anglican Church

Before he flew to Toronto, Ingham was fully aware that some Anglicans would be upset by his words: "And, yes, I knew what would follow. I know the church fairly well. Whenever someone proposes change, it's met with a fairly strong reaction from traditionalists."[297] The secular press picked up the event, and Ingham was a front-page story. Ingham's predicted reactions followed in short order.

In an interview[298] given a few days before the speech, Ingham had denied that dioceses would move unilaterally to bless same-sex unions without the approval of the House of Bishops, of which he was now a member. He explained that Canadian bishops were working colle-gially on the issue, and he hoped that their amended guidelines, due the next year, would reflect considerable reform. However Ingham admitted recently that he privately feared that change might end up being more cosmetic than substantive.

In 1997, the House of Bishops finally issued their amendments to the guidelines for both lay and ordained lesbians and gays. Their new position was their old position with a few updates in light of recent "pastoral awareness" of homosexuality. The new guidelines, which car-ried substantial moral authority within the Anglican Church of Canada, still did not permit the blessing of same-sex unions or the ordination of partnered gays and lesbians. Despite considerable effort, the bishops had been unable to achieve unanimity or, failing that, even a consen-sus. Two-thirds of the thirty-three members had opposed the move to more inclusivity, and their votes easily preserved the *status quo*. Their stumbling block was whether or not homosexual relationships and activity could possibly be expressions of God's will and purpose.

In other words, the Canadian House of Bishops was telling gay and lesbian clergy they could never have a sex life, because the Church could not figure out a way to recognize their unions. Not all Anglicans, lay or ordained, could tolerate such a double standard; Somerville, in retirement, was one. He had recently admitted to ordaining several gays, who may or may not have been celibate, dur-ing his 1969–1980 episcopate. Ingham was another for whom the double standard was anathema. He refused to support the new guidelines and, when the vote for approval of the amended guide-lines was called, he abstained. "The Church restricts sexual activity to marriage and then restricts marriage to heterosexual people, and it leaves gay and lesbian people with no options other than absti-nence or loneliness," said Ingham sadly. "I think such a double stan-dard is doomed to failure in the long run, but . . . we would need to follow proper processes."[299] Ingham used the latter phrase to set the stage for managing the issue, something that he knew was going to confront the Diocese of New Westminster the following year.

The 1998 General Synod further discouraged Ingham. The pro-gressives' social agenda at that synod was stalled by a groundswell of traditionalism from members of the newly established Anglican Essentials, which included several conservative clergy and laity from the Diocese of New Westminster. This tipped off Ingham to what the future might hold.

This then was the context* for the momentous synods of the Diocese of New Westminster that Ingham had to handle. The issue played out from 1998 to 2005 on the West Coast of Canada, moving after that to higher, international levels in the Anglican Communion. Ingham, conscious of the myriad implications if his synod chose a policy of inclusion, braced himself for controversy and nastiness. As bishop, he could have refused to entertain the motion calling for the blessing of same-sex unions and handed it over instead to the national Church to tackle. However, any denial of democracy such as this carries immense implications that few bishops would contemplate seriously. Ingham also knew that to refuse the motion could delay a decision for another generation. So, with his eyes wide open, Ingham allowed it to reach the synod floor when others would have shied away.

Should Anglicans resist the changing values of society?

What exactly is meant by the blessing of same-sex unions? First, it is not marriage; the Anglican Church does not perform marriages of same-sex couples. Canadians, and others around the world, often confuse the word "union" with marriage, and regrettably the media use the words interchangeably. The debate in the secular world, which was (and is) running concurrently, centres on same-sex *civil marriage* and has furthered the public's misunderstanding of the church's struggle. The New Westminster resolution in 1998 proposed a pastoral act, not a sacrament, which would bless same-sex unions, recognize the gift of love between two people, the dignity and sanctity of their relationship, and would allow the couple and the community of their family and friends to celebrate the relationship.

---

* The possible causes of homosexuality and theological arguments for and against the blessing of same-sex unions and ordination of practising homosexuals are not within the scope of this book. Many authors, on both sides of the debate, have tackled these questions with insight, balance, and respect. Some of their books and useful Web sites are in the bibliography and endnotes to point inquiring readers in the right direction, but by no means are all listed.

Ingham addressing a synod of the Diocese of New Westminster.
(Neale Adams/*Topic*)

In his charge to the 1998 New Westminster synod, Ingham called on the delegates to reflect deeply on the blessing of same-sex unions. He posed tough questions to them: "Should Anglicans resist the changing values of society? Were current values in conflict with Christian ethics? And how might God be speaking through changing values?" When the pertinent motion came to the floor, the bishop was in the chair and laid down the rules for the debate. Ingham expected delegates to discuss carefully, treating everyone with love and respect. He limited speakers to three minutes each at the microphone, banned applause, and determined that the vote would be by secret ballot.

The final Motion 9 stated after a preamble:

> *BE IT RESOLVED THAT the synod of the Diocese of New Westminster asks the bishop to authorize clergy in this diocese to bless covenanted same-sex unions, subject to such conditions as the bishop deems appropriate.*

The mover, Mr. John Brewin (a former NDP member of parliament) introduced the motion, saying that some consider homosexuality to be a moral issue, and others a justice issue. While acknowledging that the issue was divisive for the church, Brewin told synod that all Christians must discuss it and discuss it immediately. The Reverend

Robert Korth of Christ Church Cathedral seconded the motion and urged delegates to vote in favour, as the time had come to bless same-sex unions. Both the mover and seconder were careful not to equate same-sex unions with the Anglican understanding of marriage being a sacrament between a man and a woman, because a diocese does not have the authority to alter that understanding or practice.

The debate, at times heated, took two hours; speakers were passionate on both sides of the issue. Some spoke powerfully, others spoke simply, and sincerity was also evident on both sides. Ingham listened intently, showing no reaction; his demeanour was neutral throughout the tense time. Delegates were deeply attentive and respectful and most were aware of the significance of the debate and its potential outcome. Ingham thanked each speaker by name as they finished. Commenting about the way the debate played out, he said, "I was proud of the synod. It was the Church at its best. I was astonished to read some of the comments afterwards — that it had been 'intimidating' or 'bullying.'"[300]

When the time came to vote on the motion, Ingham rejected a request to vote by orders (clergy and laity voting separately), explaining that it was unnecessary because the matter was pastoral not doctrinal. The stress escalated as Ingham prepared to announce the result. Motion 9 carried, but only just — those in favour, 179, and those opposed, 170. It was a momentous result despite the narrow majority. New Westminster was the first diocese in Canada to pass a motion in favour of the blessing of same-sex unions.

The slim majority of 51 per cent surprised Ingham, as he had anticipated the motion's defeat, and he took the difficult decision to withhold his consent. He felt this decision was the "right thing to do because the Lambeth Conference was being held that year,"[301] but he promised the diocese to respond to the result after he had time to reflect on the way ahead. Then Ingham gave his word to act slowly and wisely, consulting as many as necessary, and to do what he could to preserve the unity of the church. He promised he would listen with an open mind to what the Canadian bishops had to say about the issue at their next meeting, and to the world's Anglican bishops at Lambeth later that year. Afterwards delegates expressed their profound respect for the way the bishop handled the debate and his decision to withhold his consent.

The reactions to New Westminster's synod vote ranged from delight that committed gay-lesbian relationships might one day be recognized to threats to sue the diocese. Some individuals came back to church, while others left, vowing never to return. The gay and lesbian community was especially encouraged by the first vote on the issue, and disappointed — but not surprised — that Ingham had withheld his consent. E-mails, letters, and faxes from the laity and clergy around the world, representing every point of view, poured into the synod office. A number threatened and abused the bishop; more were positive, praising and thanking him for his courage. The debate also triggered a torrent of questions from parishioners of the diocese, which Ingham promised to address in his response.

The media knew a good story when they saw one and were dogged in pursuit of the bishop and others. (Ingham had chosen earlier to allow the media's presence at synods to ensure openness and transparency.) The then-diocesan communications officer, Lorie Chortyk, provided the journalists with comprehensive backgrounders beforehand and afterwards stickhandled the inquiries from around the world that asked for more information and interviews with Ingham. The communications officer bore the brunt of the public-relations work that surrounded every contentious vote, and also arranged press conferences when required. However, the unprecedented reaction to the 1998 vote consumed everyone in the diocesan office, including the bishop. In the end Ingham told his staff, "Try to deal with sex only on Tuesdays,"[302] and insisted that the mission and ministry of New Westminster would continue normally despite these media preoccupations.

It was a General Synod year, and the 1998 national gathering took place immediately after the historic New Westminster synod. There, the Anglican Church of Canada elected to affirm the House of Bishops' guidelines, which many — including Ingham — thought inadequate.

Ingham took over six months to formulate a procedure that would move the Diocese of New Westminster forward. After the historic vote, Ingham attended the House of Bishops' meeting, where he put New Westminster's case. Many of his colleagues were unmoved, and the House restated their opposition to the blessing of same-sex unions and stressed that it would be inappropriate for a bishop and diocese to go it alone. Ingham was now firmly caught between his loyalty to the House of Bishops and his duty to the diocese that elected him. (Current thinking, in a confederal Church such as Canada's, is that decisions on issues like this are a diocesan matter.[303])

Then came the 1998 Lambeth Conference in August, Ingham's first, held at the University of Canterbury, south of London. Although these gatherings are sometimes intimidating for new bishops, the bishop of New Westminster was at home there from the beginning. He knew most of the primates from his time with Michael Peers, many of the other bishops, and the staff of the Anglican Consultative Council from London. And one thing was crystal clear — many had heard of Ingham. Ingham enjoyed most of the Lambeth experience, which achieved much, but he was upset by the "sordid debate"[304] on homosexuality.

The last week of the conference "turned sour and nasty to the point of being . . . horrendous!" recalled Ingham. Lambeth debated a resolution[305] (1.10) that confirmed that the Anglican Church was not prepared to bless same-sex unions or ordain active homosexuals, and which called for a moratorium on such practices. Resolution 1.10 also affirmed that gays and lesbians are full members of the Body of Christ and that the Anglican Church must listen to them. When some of the African bishops heard this latter demand for the third time since 1978, they balked, erupting in a most unepiscopal show of intolerance and derision. Repeatedly drowning out the supporters of gay-lesbian rights with catcalls and hissing, they compared homosexuals to child molesters and those who practise bestiality. The derision poured over the North American bishops was an ugly display of prejudice and bad manners that shocked many. "It was an appalling scene,"[306] remembered Ingham. Considering that Lambeth had previously made an accommodation to the cultural reality of polygamy in Africa, many hoped the Africans would extend similar consideration towards the western dioceses' reality. However, in the end, that courtesy never materialized, and the conservative forces easily amended the final resolution* to include the words "*while rejecting homosexual practice as incompatible with Scripture.*" This passed with a huge majority (526 voting in favour, 70 opposed, and 45 abstaining). In speaking to

---

* See Appendix 4 for the wording of Resolution 1.10.

reporters by phone after the vote, Ingham said, "The vote has caused a lot of pain. Very strong language was used. But anyone who thinks this is over because of the [result] has to think again."[307] Ingham and other progressive bishops concluded that Lambeth's Resolution 1.10 had closed the door on any hope for Anglican international dialogue on homosexuality. His realization had a profound effect on how he was to handle the issue at home in the coming years.

Additionally, throughout the conference, Ingham had been aware of a current swirling below the surface. A group of U.S. bishops from the conservative American Anglican Council, had been running a separate agenda in parallel to the official business of the gathering. This group of American prelates, discontented that they had not been able to influence their progressive leadership at home, rented a building on campus and invited African and other bishops from the developing world to join them every evening. Over barbecued chicken and convivial conversation, the Americans coached the Africans on how best to oppose the progressives. They are alleged to have encouraged support for their right-wing agenda with offers of money to dioceses that were strapped for cash. But the Third World bishops definitely benefited from the Americans' gifts like free cell phones and overseas calls, help with their speeches, and free flights to Texas in 2003, in return for their votes. This might have been fairly normal behaviour in American convention politics, but it was inappropriate at Lambeth and left a nasty taste in the mouths of many. Retrospectively Ingham observed, "It was all very murky and . . . obvious that the political drive had begun to manipulate the Anglican Communion."[308] The debate on homosexuality had split the Anglican bishops of the world like no other issue had done, not even the ordination of women. The road to division was being paved.

The decennial conference ended by reaffirming that scripture and tradition teach that God intends human sexuality to find its expression between a man and a woman; and also that marriage between a man and a woman was sacred, instituted by God, and blessed by Christ. But the world's bishops, just like the Canadian House of Bishops, could not reach an agreement on gay and lesbian relationships and how they could be expressed. They probably never will.

By evolution rather than by revolution

After returning to Vancouver, Ingham prepared to respond to the New Westminster synod vote on Motion 9 in light of what he had heard from the Canadian bishops and those at Lambeth. He gathered a "council of advice" around him that included representatives of both sides. Ingham worked on, with assistance to be sure, but ultimately he had to decide alone. In November, New Westminster's diocesan council urged the bishop not to delay his response to Motion 9, despite a request to do so from the House of Bishops, who had just had a meeting that Ingham was unable to attend. "I'm in an awkward position,"[309] replied Ingham. In the end, Lambeth's outcome convinced him that to delay his response would gain nothing, and he presented it to the diocese and the Canadian bishops in January 1999. Ingham admitted that he had struggled with several factors in formulating the way forward. His paper[310] provided context, an update on the worldwide situation, and explained his 1998 decision to withhold consent for the blessing of same-sex unions. The response also detailed Ingham's plans on how to handle the issue, given the strident opposition from other provinces within the Anglican Communion.

Ingham stated that the recent reactions of the House of Bishops and Lambeth had clearly indicated that the diocese should slow down before unilaterally authorizing the blessing of same-sex unions, although neither body had any power to govern New Westminster. He wrote, "The majority of bishops, in Canada and throughout the world, were opposed to partnerships between people of the same sex,"[311] despite 185 bishops, nine of whom were primates, signing a pledge to continue to work for full inclusion of gays and lesbians in the Church.* Although New Westminster was leading the way, Ingham cautioned the diocese to view his decision to wait as neither a victory for the synod vote nor a defeat. He simply wanted to proceed "by evolution rather than by revolution."[312] Ingham was well aware that whatever happened on the West Coast of Canada would have a significant impact on the whole Church, nationally and globally.

---

* The Canadian primate, Michael Peers, and three Canadian bishops, including Ingham, signed the pledge.

His plan, following New Westminster's vote of 1998, had six parts, each interwoven:

- The diocese would maintain the *status quo* for two more years out of consideration for the House of Bishops, Lambeth, and those locally who were struggling with the vote's implications. Synod would not vote on the issue again until 2001.
- Intentional dialogue on the blessing of same-sex unions would take place at "twinned" parishes, with support from the diocese, so that those in the pews could study and understand the issue before the next vote.
- A Bishop's Commission on Gay and Lesbian Voices would provide "twinned" parishes with the opportunity to hear the experiences of homosexual Anglicans. (Ingham expected every parish unit to invite and listen to them, as required by Lambeth's 1998 statement.)
- A Bishop's Commission on Faith and Doctrine would assist parishes in reflecting on the Scripture and tradition related to the issue, using insights of modern biblical and theological scholarship to guide them.
- A Bishop's Commission on Legal and Canonical Matters would offer guidance to the bishop on the legality of the diocese authorizing the blessing of same-sex unions upon resolution of a future synod.
- A Bishop's Commission on Liturgy would develop a sample rite for the blessing of same-sex unions, to be used only if the diocese voted to proceed.

The bishop emphasized most strongly that, during the months prior to the 2001 synod, there were to be no alternative programs running in the diocese, such as lobby groups, parallel symposia, or conferences, or literature that sought a particular outcome. It was to be just one process. Ingham asked the gays and lesbians in the diocese to continue to be patient: "I am asking you to help us understand more clearly your spiritual vocation within the Body of Christ. I am asking all members of the church to listen to our brothers and sisters in Christ with compassion."[313] The bishop was conscious of their deep disappointment.

At the bishop's news conference in January 1999, Ingham told the media that he had overridden the slim majority in the diocese *and his own conscience* when he decided to delay further action and another vote for two more years. He also again acknowledged the presence of a significant number in the diocese who were strongly opposed to the blessing of same-sex unions and who were worthy of respect. "But I think it's going to happen," predicted the bishop, ". . . the trend is clear."[314] The Dean of Christ Church Cathedral, the Very Reverend Peter Elliott, also spoke, expressing disappointment at the delay but reminding everyone that the bishop had not said no, but rather "Let's have another vote in 2001." Most of the clergy who disagreed with Motion 9 were supportive of Ingham's plan for parishes to study and discuss the issue in depth over the next two years, as well as of his four commissions.

A few clergy and lay members of New Westminster accused the bishop of weighting the commissions with liberal Anglicans and for working to a predetermined timetable of his own. Others complained of Ingham's "obvious political gamesmanship," and claimed that he had carefully planned out everything so his diocese would eventually proceed. In other words they believed the blessing of same-sex unions was a foregone conclusion driven by the bishop, and that Ingham was just going through the motions of consultation. In fact, the commissions reflected a diversity of opinions that were evenly balanced, with the exception of the Voices commission. But even that one had an ex-lesbian priest whom Ingham appointed over several objections. The diocese also hired an external consultant — a Mennonite from the conservative Fraser Valley — to oversee and direct the whole process, so it would be as impartial as possible.

During 1999 to 2001, work in the Diocese of New Westminster carried on: the synod office dealt with mountains of correspondence; the bishop was in high demand to speak around the world; the commissions worked on their reports for the congregations; and the parishes studied.

On the world scene, the conservative opponents to the ordination of gays and lesbians and the blessing of same-sex unions had begun gathering their forces, and they coalesced into groups, some more powerful than others. For example, in 2000 a gathering of senior international Anglican leaders, including bishops from Africa and Asia, met in Uganda to stop the "moral drift" in North America. Ingham believes that this event was financed and politically managed by the conservative American Anglican Council, which enticed the Third World bishops at Lambeth 1998. So do many others, including Stephen Bates, an Oxford historian, journalist, and the author of *A Church at War: Anglicans and Homosexuality* (I.B. Taurus, 2004). The battle lines were being drawn.

Late 2000 saw the press reporting that the Diocese of New Westminster, after nearly two years of work, had written a proposed liturgy for the blessing of same-sex unions. Indeed it had, but only for Anglicans to see what one might be like, prior to voting on Motion 9 again at the synod of 2001. The rite was not for use, but still generated a flurry of negative reactions. "The idea is unchristian, un-Anglican and illegal,"[315] said Dr. Don Lewis, professor of church history at Regent College in Vancouver. The Reverend Paul Borthistle, who chaired the team that produced the rite, responded, "beginning from the first century, there is precedent for bishops to break new ground. Otherwise we never would have freed slaves or ordained women."[316] Ingham referred the proposed rite to the Legal and Canonical Commission for comment, and, as they felt it was too close to the marriage service to be within the jurisdiction of a diocese or a bishop to authorize, he later vetoed it.

Meanwhile the dialogue on homosexuality between the twinned parishes of New Westminster continued, sometimes smoothly and sometimes downright roughly. The process had varying outcomes. For the majority, it was a positive, though lengthy, experience, but a few parishes faced significant pain and dislocation. Some withdrew entirely, either refusing to discuss positions that they had already adopted and/or declining to meet Anglican gays and lesbians; others had to cope with difficulties with their clergy, who either did not participate or, conversely, dominated the dialogue; a few contended with rudeness and hostility.

It would be as obvious as a beautiful sunset

The 2001 synod of New Westminster took place in June, following the concentrated parish dialogue on the issue and consideration of the reports* from the bishop's four commissions. Delegates knew that the Legal and Canonical Commission report (released on April 22) had found no impediments to proceeding with blessing of same-sex unions, should the vote be in favour. They had learned about the theology involved and they had seen the sample rite developed by the Liturgical Commission. They had also read the results of the diocese-wide "Dialogue on Same-Sex Unions."[317] Thus prepared, the synod again vigorously debated Motion 9, as it had in 1999, but for longer and with more passion. It took eighty delegates' speeches and five hours before Ingham called for the vote. One speaker claimed the debate had unleashed "Satan the deceiver" to sow division in the diocese; another wept as she spoke of a young gay man attempting suicide; and one priest described the threats she had received because of her opposition to the motion. At the end, although many delegates were exhausted, all were on tenterhooks.

This time, out of 400 votes, 226 were in favour, with 174 opposed — a majority that moved from 9 in 1998 to 52, demonstrating increasing support. But Ingham again withheld his consent, saying that, although the diocesan lawyers considered that permitting the blessing of same-sex unions was within the scope of a bishop, the diocese needed more time for consensus to emerge. The bishop had also wanted a clearer and more substantial majority. Despite the trend in favour, Ingham did not feel a 56.5 per cent majority was enough to change the practice of the church. He did not pinpoint the magic number, saying, "It would be as obvious as a beautiful sunset — hard to define, but you know it when you see it."[318] Many surmised Ingham wanted at least two-thirds of synod, if not more, to support the motion before he would give his consent.

The bishop spoke after the announcement of the vote, and again requested patience to allow some members of the diocese to have the

---

* www.vancouver.anglican.ca/default.asp?Menu=101&SubMenu=7&Item=0&
Content=SameSex/Archives.htm provides downloads of the reports of the
bishop's commissions on the blessings of same-sex unions. Click on "Archives"
and then select the report on the left-hand navigation column.

chance to come to terms with change. He further explained that his refusal to consent was "in part a pastoral one to those who now find themselves in a minority situation with the result."[319] Ingham ended his address by talking directly to the gay and lesbian Anglicans of New Westminster, "I ask that you accept the need of this family to ponder these matters a while longer, to wait upon the Holy Spirit a bit more."[320] The bishop did not plan to reintroduce the same Motion 9 at the 2002 synod. The conservatives left that day anxious and troubled by the increase in support. The gay and lesbian delegates were frustrated and bitterly disappointed that Ingham had again asked them to wait. Several left in tears.

Anglican Essentials (the conservative organization) intentionally held their first major event in seven years in "the most divided diocese in Canada," and deliberately timed it for two weeks after synod. The seven hundred delegates converged on Langley, B.C., and heard a pledge of support from the Archbishop of Canterbury, George Carey, read out at the opening. Ingham was there to welcome them all to the diocese as a matter of protocol. In his brief remarks he told the delegates that, as the diocese had always been interested in dialogue with those of differing views, he had invited the attending Primate of the Southern Cone, Maurice Sinclair, to meet and engage in dialogue with his clergy. (This was the same archbishop who had objected to Ingham's remarks about inclusivity at his consecration.) Ingham went on to tell Essentials that Sinclair had been candid at the meeting and that he was claiming the same privilege on their conference platform. "I think the Church needs fewer rallies and more dialogue . . . among members of the Body of Christ in its diversity," said Ingham.[321] The Primate of South East Asia, who also attended, responded, "The bishop . . . should know we're interested in truth, not dialogue."[322] At the conclusion of his welcome, Ingham garnered no applause, instead the delegates prayed for him. As he was leaving, about thirty individuals approached him and said that they were concerned that Essentials was becoming more of a political vehicle in the Canadian Church than a place for theological reflection, which was its original intent.

Essentials' organizers had denied Integrity Vancouver's request to set up a literature table at their conference. When Integrity wrote back asking for reconsideration of their decision, Essentials again refused Integrity's small ministry. Conference planners had decided that, if there was space left after all their groups had been accommodated, only those organizations that were willing to sign onto Essential's Montreal Declaration of 1994, would be welcome. This declaration confirms, among other things, that homosexual unions are intimacies contrary to God's design. Part of the long e-mail from Essentials explained, "Your request for a display table is not being turned down because of who your group is but for who you are not. You are not able to freely sign onto the Declaration."[323] Of course, Integrity could not possibly do so. They vowed to work towards having their table ministry at future Essentials' conventions to provide their voices for delegates to hear, as three Lambeth Conferences had resolved.

Ingham was now in a difficult position. In 1996 he had publicly stated that dioceses should not move unilaterally on the blessing of same-sex unions without the backing of the Canadian House of Bishops. Now he was likely to have to do so. It was simply a matter of time (perhaps as soon as the next year) before his diocesan synod voted in sufficient numbers to reach the majority he needed to give his consent. Both his heart and his mind confirmed what he must do: Ingham would implement what synod would surely decide. A couple of weeks after the 2001 synod, Ingham met with the traditionally conservative clergy in the diocese for discussions, hoping to ease their anxieties. He promised them he would ensure a conscience clause in the 2002 resolution on the matter, as well as the provision of an alternative bishop for their pastoral care.

In 2005, Ingham reflected back on that impending decision, "I think that, if Lambeth [1998] had set up a commission . . . that would have said to gay and lesbian people throughout the world that we are trying to find a way to listen to your concerns, I would have taken the position in New Westminster that we must wait. . . . But they didn't, and neither was there any movement in the [Canadian] House of Bishops, and it was then, I think, that we begin to explore the possibility of a local option. . . . To me there's no question that synods have more authority than the House of Bishops' guidelines."[324]

We have voted not to compel, but to permit[325]

The next synod, in 2002, was the defining moment in New Westminster, and both the primate, Michael Peers, and the metropolitan, Archbishop David Crawley, attended. It provoked even more media attention and public reaction than previous synods, in Vancouver, Canada, and around the world. In the run up, reporters from London (England), New York, and Toronto visited Vancouver to interview the bishop, as well as others on both sides of the issue, and wrote set-up stories. As synod neared, Ingham refused all media interviews to prevent influencing the votes. Afterwards, he did make himself available to answer questions, provide interviews, and have his photo taken, both at synod and later.

For months ahead, groups on both sides of the debate developed strategies for success. Aware of the probability of an increased majority if the issue went to another vote and the possibility of division if that happened, Ingham worked towards fairness. The resulting Motion 7 for 2002 (renumbered from 9) included several new and salient provisions. It contained a conscience clause to extricate those who were adamantly opposed to the blessings of same-sex unions. It included provisions for blessings to occur only in parishes where the priest was willing and parishioners had voted by an 80 per cent majority to be a place of blessings. It also stated that no clergy would be discriminated against in ordination, appointment, or advancement because of his or her position regarding the blessing. Additionally, the motion provided for a temporary "episcopal visitor," a bishop other than Ingham, to give pastoral care to those who disagreed with the diocesan decision if the motion passed. This "visiting" bishop would be accountable to the diocesan bishop and paid for by the diocese, but would be unable to perform confirmations and ordinations.

Nearly eighty delegates spoke to Motion 7. The Reverend Silas Ng of the Church of Emmanuel in Richmond, was the most dramatic, suggesting that passing the motion would be like shoot-ing bullets into the Church: "Bang! Bang!" he yelled. "Please say no to the Deceiver who wants you to pull the trigger."[326] A young delegate from St. Paul's in the West End of Vancouver, who was proud to be both gay and Christian, proclaimed: "This is my real-ity, and I make no apology for it. I believe that God affirms me as I am created. God's creation is far more diverse that we're giving credit for."[327]

The atmosphere was more heightened than at previous synods, and the delegates were completely engrossed by the speeches and mindful of history in the making. The media, hoping for some drama, trained their cameras on the speakers and the bishop. The metropolitan, commenting at the end, called the debate "a moment not just of high drama but of great dignity; a dignity of debate and decision that the bishops of the whole Anglican Communion did not even remotely approach at Lambeth [1998]."[328]

After the vote on Motion 7, with 215 in favour and 129 opposed (a majority of 62.5 per cent), Ingham finally gave his consent to the blessing of same-sex unions in the Diocese of New Westminster, knowing full well what to expect. Synod went wild

Members of dissenting parishes walk out of synod in 2002 after Ingham gave his consent to the blessing of same-sex unions in the Diocese of New Westminster. (Neale Adams/*Topic*)

— some with delight and others with anger and dismay. Under the glare of lights from four TV cameras and in front of a scrum of reporters, a group of clergy and lay delegates from eight of the eighty parishes walked out in protest, waving banners that they had brought with them in anticipation of losing the debate. The new provisions and the conscience clause had not been enough. The parishes that left included:

- The Church of the Good Shepherd (Rev. Stephen Leung), Vancouver
- The Church of Emmanuel (Rev. Silas Ng), Richmond
- St. Andrew's (Rev. Barclay Mayo), Pender Harbour
- St. John's Shaughnessy (Rev. David Short), Vancouver
- St. Martin's (Rev. Timothy Cooke), North Vancouver
- St. Matthew's (Rev. Trevor Walters), Abbotsford
- St. Matthias and St. Luke (Rev. Simon Chin), Vancouver
- St. Simon's (Rev. Ed Hird), North Vancouver

"It was a very emotional scene [like] the break-up of a family," recalled Neale Adams, the communications officer who had taken over in 2000.[329] The expectant mood earlier that day suddenly turned to despondency. As the parishes walked out, the rest of synod sat quietly, very distressed by the protest. Their faces were sombre and a few had tears streaming down their cheeks. Those who remained passed a resolution expressing their sadness over the departure of the eight parishes and inviting them to continue to pray and discuss together.

Although they comprised only 10 per cent of the New Westminster parishes, those that walked out of synod represented 15 per cent of the diocesan membership, and became known as the "dissenting parishes." They formed a group calling itself the Anglican Communion in New Westminster (ACiNW), declaring that they were in "impaired communion" with their diocese and bishop and asking for another bishop. In June they stopped sending their required financial allotment to the diocese, a loss of a quarter of a million dollars annually, which forced curtailment of some diocesan programs. These included hospital chaplains, Christian-education work, diocesan office staff positions, and support for the work of the national Church both overseas and in northern Canada.

"Here we stand on the fault line. The earthquake is coming."[330]

An explosion of mail* tore through the bishop's office after he gave his consent to the blessing of same-sex unions. The invective and animosity in some of it was so alarmingly unChristian that it cannot be recorded in this book. A distraught parishioner in Vancouver wrote, "To remain in [Ingham's] jurisdiction is totally unacceptable." The dissenting parishes called the vote a "schismatic act of synod," and some clergy described the decision as "a contravention of clear scriptural teaching and orthodox Christian tradition." One Canadian bishop, in a particularly upsetting letter, told Ingham he was a "self-declared schismatic." However, not all mail objected to the synod's vote or to the bishop. There were poignant letters of thanks from gay and lesbian Anglicans all over the world, both lay and ordained. Dozens from inside and outside Christianity offered prayers for Ingham. And still more correspondents expressed their support and encouragement. A few sent brilliantly argued positions in favour of the motion. Communications like these, from humble parishioners and primates, from gay priests and straight theologians, from politicians and ordinary citizens alike, helped Ingham stomach the attacks. But, there were no letters of support out of Africa.[331]

For a couple of days after the 2002 synod vote, both the bishop's and the communications officer's phones never stopped ringing. They both worked long hours. Most calls were rerouted to the communications officer, Neale Adams, who quickly got a sore ear, but plodded on, correcting misinformation and determining what journalists wanted of the bishop. When the initial flood of phone calls decreased, he began to answer all the e-mails directed to him, except those that were abusive, and forwarded them to Ingham to read. Then Adams turned his attention to the internal communications required for the benefit of the diocese. A new and important task also occupied him as other dioceses requested material on the blessings of same-sex unions and information about New Westminster's procedures. He developed packages and circulated them around the world.

---

* The bishop made every email and letter on the issue of same-sex unions available to the author

The bishop handled the onslaught well. Certainly, he got weary of it, but he kept his spirits up and, his staff reported, was rarely as stressed as they were. However, when a camera crew from a conservative national TV station invaded his doorstep to film as he was about to drive his daughters to school, Ingham was visibly angry. Fortunately, it only occurred once. Ingham usually handled the media with composure. He rarely prepared statements ahead of time for any of the anticipated media activity that resulted from New Westminster's decision, because he thinks well on his feet. Ingham's ability to make rapid analyses and quick decisions means he has an excellent instinct for speaking "on the record." The rest of the diocesan staff quickly learned to refer journalists back to the communications officer and, overall, New Westminster delivered a consistently professional approach to the media, which dealt with issues and not personalities.

Ingham in a media scrum after consenting to blessing same-sex unions at synod 2002.
(Adams/*Topic*)

As Ingham anticipated, over the next eighteen months there was a gathering storm of protest from conservatives in the diocese that he had to weather. He coped with bitter criticism at home and abroad, as well as internal strife in the diocese. Thirteen Canadian bishops even signed a public statement opposing Ingham's and the diocese's decision and saying that the bishop had acted improperly, because "matters of morality" are beyond the jurisdiction of a diocese. "There has been a great diverting of energy," said Ingham at the time. "And we are in danger of losing our sense of mission."[332] The bishop also worried about the weakening of the church's credibility, especially to youth who were saying, "Why should I join your church if it's so bigoted, so homophobic, and so intolerant?"[333] The potential loss of the church's credibility was the concern that disturbed Ingham's sleep, not the personal attacks and hate mail as they rose to a crescendo.

Two months after the Diocese of New Westminster's 2002 synod, the retiring Archbishop of Canterbury, George Carey, and his successor, Rowan Williams, issued a joint public statement, saying that unilateral blessings of same-sex unions were a threat to the unity of the worldwide Anglican Church. Intended or not, this was definitely a slap in the face to the Canadian diocese and the Anglican Church of Canada. This and a previous public statement from Carey asking for prayers for the opponents only, as well as a letter calling Ingham to account, earned Canterbury a severe rebuke from the primate and the metropolitan on behalf of the bishop of New Westminster.

As promised at synod, Ingham appointed the newly retired Bishop of Fredericton, William Hockin, as the episcopal visitor to minister to the dissenting parishes. But, even though he was a conservative, all the dissidents rejected Hockin's pastoral care. St. Clement's, a conservative parish that had chosen to stay within the diocese, accepted the offer. At the outset, the others had demanded alternate episcopal oversight (sometimes known as a "flying bishop") that had real episcopal power — a bishop with authority to perform confirmations, ordinations, and make clergy appointments, etc., without reference to the diocesan bishop. These parishes stated at the time that, if Ingham would agree to this type of bishop, reconciliation might become possible. When Ingham did not acquiesce to their demand, the dissenting parishes refused to recognize his authority and appealed to the world Church for help.

Archbishop Emmanuel Kolini, Primate of Rwanda, and three others responded. Kolini offered episcopal oversight to the dissenting parishes and invited them to join the breakaway Anglican Mission in America of conservative churches that he led. The New Westminster dissenting parishes considered the offer. It was not the first time this and other primates had interfered in another bishop's jurisdiction, but it made resolution in the Diocese of New Westminster that much more elusive. Three days later, Canterbury pleaded for calm and urged other bishops to keep their noses out of New Westminster. The African and Asian primates paid no heed.

At the beginning of September 2002, the opposing forces held a "Celebration of Global Anglican Fellowship" to rally support at a Baptist church situated in the Diocese of New Westminster. The primates of Central Africa and South East Asia, along with representatives of the American Anglican Council and other groups, joined the dissenting priests and parishes in attendance. Right in his backyard and highly irregular though it was, Ingham did not react. But three weeks later, at another event, he did.

Ingham faced scathing public condemnation from the retiring Archbishop of Canterbury, George Carey, at the Hong Kong meeting of the Anglican Consultative Council. The bishop of New Westminster attended ACC as the elected representative of the Anglican Church of Canada, not of his diocese. At the opening session, while listening to Carey's presidential address, Ingham heard himself singled out for censure. Canterbury blamed him and two Americans for driving the Anglican Communion towards fragmentation through their actions over homosexual issues. Ingham quickly rebutted Canterbury's accusations publicly, saying, "His remarks about the Diocese of New Westminster fail to honour the careful way the synod and I have made decisions about the blessings of same-sex unions. . . . It is not correct to say that New Westminster has 'acted without regard.' I have twice withheld my consent . . . in part because of the potential impact on other areas of the Communion. . . .[334] I think [Canterbury] sincerely believes his remarks today will further our unity. My expectation is that they will do the opposite."[335] It was a hard-hitting response, delivered with his usual courtesy.

Anticipating the possibility of a public rebuke in Hong Kong, Ingham had earlier asked the general secretary of the Anglican Consultative Council for an opportunity to tell the New Westminster story if necessary. The diocesan chancellor and the metropolitan of British Columbia and Yukon had blocked off time just in case, and, after Carey's address effectively put the issue on the agenda, Ingham phoned them and asked them to pack their bags and fly to Hong Kong to take part in a hastily gathered panel. In addition to those three, the Canadian primate and the three Canadian delegates* to the Anglican Consultative Council joined the team, and the Archbishop of Armagh (Ireland), Robin Eames, moderated the panel.‡ As the agenda was too full, and the panel had been squeezed in over a lunch break, the Canadians expected a slim turnout. They were gratified when almost everyone attended and missed lunch — but the primate of Nigeria, though a member of the ACC, was conspicuously absent.

The panellists gave a detailed account of how and why the Diocese of New Westminster had arrived at their controversial decision and how it was possible for a diocese to take such action in Canada. The response of those that attended the panel was one of immense interest, which provoked much subsequent conversation. Some said that they supported New Westminster privately but felt unable to do so publicly. The panellists were questioned throughout the ten days of meetings, and many continued to field questions afterwards via e-mails and letters. After the session ended, the Anglican Consultative Council reported that it still could not establish a common Anglican view of homosexuality.

The Canadian House of Bishops convened in October during the resulting uproar. Sitting around the table, Ingham included, they endeavoured to reach a consensus on the blessings of same-sex unions in light of New Westminster's vote. But they were still unable to do so and referred the hot potato to General Synod to handle in 2004. Ingham supported the motion, which, among other things, called for a professional mediation process to be set up in New Westminster and asked the dissenting parishes to respect the authority of the diocesan bishop and synod. The House also requested that

---

* The Canadian lay delegate just happened to be the former dean of law at McGill University, who sat on the General Synod task force on jurisdiction, which had investigated whether dioceses could act unilaterally and bless same-sex unions.

‡ An illicit recording of the event was posted on a conservative Web site soon afterwards. The transcript is still available, but does not contain the question-and-answer session. See http://listserv.episcopalian.org/scripts/wa.exe?A2=ind0209c&L=virtuosity&D=1& H=1&O=D&P=2403

bishops outside New Westminster respect the integrity of the diocese's reconciliation process and not intervene. The bishops encouraged other Canadian dioceses to avoid making individual decisions on the blessing of same-sex unions, and to uphold the 1997 guidelines on human sexuality. Ingham's comment on all of this was "The Anglican way is not [one of universal] consensus. We [can and do] act to change things one diocese at a time, and I hope more Canadian dioceses will join us in acting. The idea of a local option, where no one is forced to do something they cannot in conscience participate in, protects the conservative minority. . . . The unity of the church cannot be preserved on the basis of injustice and exclusion."[336] Ingham was, by now, totally committed to seeing the issue through to its conclusion in New Westminster, even if the Canadian House of Bishops could not or would not support him and his diocese. He saw no benefit in further delay.

Back on the West Coast again after much of a month away, Ingham set about supporting the local reconciliation process in New Westminster and delayed issuing his rite for the blessings of same-sex unions at the request of the metropolitan, Archbishop David Crawley. The diocese and the eight dissenting parishes of the ACiNW agreed on a facilitator and started work. After three meetings, the process collapsed in March 2003 when yet another bishop interfered. This time the Bishop of Yukon, the Right Reverend Terrence Buckle, contrary to canon law and the House of Bishops' October appeal, disrupted the course of action by writing to Ingham, offering to provide alternate episcopal oversight (as a flying bishop) for the ACiNW parishes. Ingham declined Buckle's offer, having already asked the Bishop of Fredericton to assist him under the terms of the 2002 Synod's resolution, and a week later issued an inhibition order against Buckle. This warned him not to exercise any ministry within the Diocese of New Westminster by invoking a section of Canon 18, the church law pertaining to the discipline of the clergy. But three weeks later, in violation of the inhibition, Buckle contacted the eight dissenting parishes directly, and seven voted to accept his offer. (The parish vote at St. Martin's, North Vancouver, failed by a small margin.) After all this, the reconciliation process never recovered.

After Buckle's intervention, the Diocese of New Westminster delayed no longer, and Ingham issued the liturgy for the blessings of same-sex unions. (The final order of service differed from the sample rite circulated at synod 2001, which Ingham had ruled out, and had been written by the Reverend Dr. Richard Leggett, Professor of Liturgical Studies at the Vancouver School of Theology.) Ingham reiterated that the rite was a blessing of permanent and faithful commitments between persons of the same sex and was not a marriage ceremony, or even similar to one. Couples seeking the blessing had to receive preparation and instruction and had to be supported and sustained by their parish throughout their lives together. Initially, six parishes in the diocese voted to be places of blessing — St. Margaret's Cedar Cottage, St. Mark's Kitsilano, St. Paul's, and Christ Church Cathedral, all in Vancouver, and St. Agnes, North Vancouver, and St. Laurence, Coquitlam, both in the suburbs. Over the next two years, two more parishes (St. Hilda's in Sechelt and St. Barnabas in New Westminster) voted to join the roster. But, in contrast to the flood of gays and lesbians pouring into secular provincial jurisdictions that had legalized civil same-sex marriages during this period, only seven blessing ceremonies were conducted in the diocese from mid-2003 to mid-2004.

On May 28, 2003, after the world's primates had gathered for their regular meeting in Brazil, and three days after Ingham approved the rite, the first blessing took place in the Diocese of New Westminster. The Reverend Margaret Marquardt blessed the twenty-one-year relationship of two gay parishioners of St. Margaret's, Cedar Cottage, Vancouver, in front of their friends and families. As it was a public ceremony, several conservative Anglicans went and witnessed the occasion, but their reasons for doing so were unclear. Although the media attended, they interviewed and photographed the couple afterwards outside the church and did not intrude on the blessing itself. However, their reports and images raced around the world via the Internet and were featured on television newscasts and in newspapers in Europe, the United States, and elsewhere.

Several primates from Africa, Asia, and Latin America once again accused Ingham of being willing to split the Anglican Communion. They called the first blessing of a same-sex union "a defining moment in which the clear choice has to be made between remaining a communion or disintegrating into a federation of churches."[337] Ingham responded, "All of this fuss is a bit puzzling because [hundreds of] same-sex blessings have been happening in the United States [and the United Kingdom] for years with the tacit and/or explicit consent of the bishops. What's different here is that we are doing it publicly, openly, and in the light of day."[338]

When interpreting New Westminster's decisions, Ingham has repeatedly referred to the cultural reality in North America that surrounds the gay-lesbian question, especially in relation to his urban diocese in British Columbia. Culture is one of the factors that Anglicans can apply when discerning how change should or should not evolve in the Church. The three guiding principles that theologians, scholars, clergy, and laity look at when establishing a position include: what the Bible has to say about an issue; what church tradition brings to the subject; and what sensible reasoning offers to the question under scrutiny. Culture — the society and customs in which we live — is not a constant in the equation; it varies from Anglican province to province. While fairly well-accepted in the major urban centres in Canada, gays and lesbians still face considerable discrimination and risk in the smaller, rural communities in Canada. Many have moved to cities like Vancouver to find welcome and a safer place to live, work, and worship, though they still face risks there. The culture in African countries is often radically different from that of western nations. There homosexuals can be demonized, cast out of society, and actively imprisoned, maimed, and persecuted by both governments and religious leaders. These cultures, which believe homosexuality is an abomination and which are competing for converts with Islam, provide part of the motive for the ferocity of some African primates when reacting to New Westminster's position.

Further reasons for the strident Third World voice opposing homosexuality revolves around the Christian background of the countries that were converted by the mostly evangelical-conservative mission movements of the past. Their understanding of scripture and the theological teaching they have received has not incorporated much of modern scholarship, and still does not. African churches, and other developing countries, are supplied with materials from and supported financially by conservative Christians in the United States who believe in the faith as it was first revealed. Archbishop Hambidge, who has lived and worked in Africa, explains the continent's frustration with progressive Christianity. African clergy say, "When you first came to

Africa you told us to believe the Bible; now we do, you say we are wrong."[339] Akinola of Nigeria is more confrontational and says that, now Africa has come of age, it does not need the west to tell it what to believe or how to interpret scripture. These primates outnumber those of a more liberal stripe.

At the same time as the first blessing took place in New Westminster, the Church of England declared gay Canon Jeffrey John as their bishop-designate of the Diocese of Reading, outside Oxford, and, ten days later, the diocese of New Hampshire in the United States elected a bishop who was living openly in a same-sex relationship. Canon John withdrew as opposition mounted, but the ECUSA (Episcopal Church of the United States of America) General Convention* in August confirmed New Hampshire's election of Gene Robinson, which opened the way to his consecration. The primates in the developing world, notably Archbishop Peter Akinola of Nigeria, screamed, "Ungodly! A satanic attack on the Church of God." Akinola's outraged reaction worked. The new Archbishop of Canterbury, Rowan Williams, hastily called an emergency meeting of the primates to deal with North America's actions, which, he believed, would tear the Church asunder on his watch.

That same summer, in June, confusing the turmoil in the Anglican Church but applying the Canadian Charter of Rights and Freedoms, the civil courts of Ontario extended the right of civil *marriage* to homosexual couples (without a residency requirement), the first province to do so. Gays and lesbians from around the world travelled to Toronto to marry. Two Anglican deacons were among those who had made the legal challenge in Ontario, and, when it finally succeeded, they also married in a civil ceremony. Afterwards, their twenty-year relationship was blessed in the Church of the Holy Trinity in downtown Toronto in front of two hundred friends, even though their diocese had not yet voted to permit the blessings of same-sex unions. The Province of British Columbia followed Ontario on July 8, 2003, with a decision in the B.C. Court of Appeal, becoming the second province in Canada to allow same-sex couples to marry. All but a few of the other Canadian provinces followed suit.

---

* Equivalent to a General Synod.

As the Diocese of New Westminster tried to get on with its mission in the world after the first rite of blessing, Ingham had his hands full. The bishop had to take over St. Martin's in North Vancouver, which was incapacitated by a parish split over the issue. Two churchwardens from the same parish later sued the diocese in an unsuccessful attempt at reinstatement after the bishop had dismissed them by invoking Canon 15.* Ingham also closed a new mission church in the Fraser Valley in southern British Columbia, which was financially supported by the Diocese of New Westminster, after the congregation had voted to be the eighth to accept Bishop Buckle's offer of episcopal oversight.

Throughout the dispute, Ingham considered that the ACiNW parishes were still part of the Diocese of New Westminster, even though they did not — they no longer attended diocesan events, including synods, or submitted their financial assessments (and still do not). However, the bishop did not view the priests and the parishioners of St. Andrew's, St. Simon's, and the Church of Emmanuel to be part of the diocesan family any longer after they chose to accept the episcopal ministry offered by Rwanda.

On September 7, 2003, just before Ingham left for Hong Kong, sixteen hundred conservative Christians attended a second "celebration" service. Within Ingham's diocese and again right under his nose, two primates from Africa and India "commissioned" the Bishop of Yukon, Terrence Buckle, to provide oversight to the ACiNW parishes, six months after he had disrupted the reconciliation process. This was in direct contravention of the canons of the church, and of Ingham's inhibition order.

The primatial communiqué, which came out of the October 2003 emergency meeting at Lambeth, had strongly advised the American Church against consecrating Gene Robinson, but their dire warning failed to prevent it. Canterbury also struck the Lambeth Commission on Communion to study theologically and legal-

---

* Canon 15 enables a bishop to reorganize a parish "experiencing difficulties or a crisis which, in the opinion of the bishop, affects the orderly management and operation of the parish."

ly how to preserve unity in the cracking Communion and to discover a way forward. This commission resulted in the famous Windsor Report a year later. The ACiNW were heartened by the primates' call for adequate provision of episcopal oversight for dissenting minorities, which they believed supported their position. Ingham for his part welcomed the primates' refusal to expel New Westminster from the communion and their condemnation of those bishops who sought to divide the church by meddling in others' jurisdictions. Ingham also publicly urged more traditional dioceses to provide for their progressive minorities, just as he had for New Westminster's dissenting conservatives.

In October 2003, the diocesan communications officer dealt with another flurry of media coverage. New Westminster had announced that Ingham, no longer able to allow the dissident priests to continue their uncanonical actions within the diocese, would establish a commission of inquiry in accordance with the diocesan canons. This body would investigate the charges of disobedient and disrespectful conduct brought by the diocesan chancellor against the seven priests who had founded the ACiNW. They were accused of breaking their ordination oath of obedience to their bishop by creating a scandal, causing a schism, and other offences against the lawful authority of the bishop. The commission had three months to determine if the allegations were sufficient to take to an ecclesiastical trial (reminiscent of Bishop Hills and his unruly dean). A spokesperson for the ACiNW explained that the parishes did want to remain Anglican but, because they no longer recognized Ingham as an Anglican bishop and he had bullied them, their priests had sought an alternate. The diocese responded, "When priests are made priests, one of the things they do is pledge loyalty to the bishop. The charges, simply put, are that [these seven priests] haven't been loyal."[340] Ingham explained the action: "It's a matter of last resort . . . after we've exhausted every avenue of reconciliation."[341] Just before this, the metropolitan of British Columbia and Yukon, Archbishop David Crawley, began disciplinary proceedings against Bishop Buckle for his assertion of episcopal authority over the dissident parishes in New Westminster. If found in contravention of church law, Buckle faced suspension or dismissal for his uncanonical actions.

Also, in October 2003, the Canadian House of Bishops met. With Ingham on the hot seat, they devoted much of their highly charged meeting to the escalating situation caused by New Westminster. The bishops requested that the Diocese of New Westminster and its metropolitan implement a ceasefire by staying their legal proceedings against the dissenting priests and the Bishop of Yukon. Ingham and Crawley complied, but only on condition that Buckle withdraw his oversight of the dissenting parishes. He did so a week later, providing another chance at reconciliation for the diocese and its dissenting parishes. The House also set up a task force to investigate how to provide spiritual care to Anglicans who oppose the policies of their dioceses. They chose the Bishop of Edmonton, Victoria Matthews, as chair. The brinkmanship eased in the Canadian West, but the dissenting parishes in New Westminster were disappointed, because the institution of a task force meant they would not have episcopal oversight as soon as they wanted. They said that their need was too urgent to wait for a task force to study the issue.

A couple of weeks later, Ingham and the Bishop of Quebec flew to Durham, New Hampshire, to lend support to Gene Robinson at his consecration on November 2. Fifty other bishops also participated to show their solidarity. The moving three-hour ceremony was accompanied by the cheers and tears of four thousand who attended. Ingham said, "It was magnificent and also clear that the diocese had elected him because of his profound spiritual gifts, not because of his sexual orientation."[342] Afterwards, from Lambeth, Rowan Williams, the new Archbishop of Canterbury, expressed his "deep regret" over the divisions in the Anglican Communion that would result from the consecration. "Realignment has begun," commented the American Anglican Council. Akinola, also speaking for the primates of Global South, denounced American Anglicans for choosing "the path of deviation from the historic faith,"[343] and Uganda and Kenya severed relations with the entire United States Episcopal Church. Over one-third of the ecclesiastical provinces followed suit, and declared themselves out of communion with the Diocese of New Westminster as well. Denunciations ricocheted around the world. Division was looking increasingly likely, and had not been helped by Canterbury's earlier pronouncements. Observers noted that incomprehension and cowardice at the leadership levels in the Anglican Communion prevented action that might have supported both points of view and encouraged both sides to agree to disagree, thus defusing rather than inflaming the situation.

Responding to the growing conservative movement around the world, the gays and lesbians within the church stepped up the fundraising and networking to further their cause. In October 2003 they sponsored "Halfway to Lambeth," a conference in Manchester, England, designed to provide bishops and others in the church with a look at the experiences of homosexual people. The election of Gene Robinson injected a note of joy in the proceedings; many participants believed that it signalled their world was, at last, changing for the better. Ingham's keynote address[344] was one of many highlights of the three-day-long meeting. In a well-argued speech, he reclaimed Christian orthodoxy from those conservatives who had labelled the actions of the dioceses of New Westminster and New Hampshire as "unorthodox." Members of Integrity Vancouver presented two workshops, telling the New Westminster story and emphasizing what it meant to gays and lesbians in their North American context. The Canadian delegates knew how different their struggles were from those in other countries, but they discovered that others saw them as islands of hope for the future in a sea of bleak pessimism. Integrity Canada members found themselves encouraging the rest, a new experience for them.

Retired Archbishop Somerville, who had kept his own counsel for several years, waded into the turmoil in November 2003. He wrote a short, but important, letter to the editor of *Topic*, New Westminster's diocesan newspaper, firmly supporting the diocese and its bishop. "The whole brouhaha about sexuality is disastrous. It is hard enough to interest young people in the church today. Most of them think the Christian way is irrelevant and narrow-minded. They cannot understand why gay women and men should be shunned and denied the blessing of their faithful, committed unions." Somerville reminded everyone that the decision to bless same-sex unions was taken at three synods, and Ingham had acted with courage and compassion. He ended by saying, "in the Gospels Jesus does not mention homosexuality, pro or con. What he does both teach and demonstrate is inclusiveness and love."[345]

So 2002 and 2003 had proven most difficult for Ingham personally, as well as for his family. The bishop had received threatening telephone calls at his office and his daughters were taunted in the schoolyard. Ingham defused the latter by teaching Cara and Robyn to debate, providing them with simple rejoinders for those who assailed them. But Ingham stresses he was never afraid for his personal safety. He often said, "I think it is far more dangerous to be a gay or lesbian person in our society than to be someone advocating for human rights."[346] However he did try to mitigate the risk to his wife and daughters by refusing to allow his family to be photographed or interviewed. The continual barrage of nastiness was lessened by more than twice as many supportive e-mails and letters from cabinet ministers, business leaders, and judges, as well as from clergy and laity inside and outside the Anglican Communion. Ingham told *BC Business* magazine in August 2003, "I've learned how important it is to take the high road and not get down in the ditch with people who want to throw mud. I've also learned to be patient. . . . If you asked me even ten years ago if I'd become well known for supporting gay and lesbian equality, I would have laughed. This wasn't the major issue on my plate, but it's become that."[347]

Although some bishops struggle with the overwhelming workloads and high stress levels inherent in any episcopate, Ingham handles them well. "I have a strong instinct for self-preservation. . . . I've never had any difficulty drawing boundaries around myself, either defending myself or protecting my inner life."[348] He builds time off into his schedule for both himself and his family — he used to play squash twice a week until injuries ended that pastime, and he now plays golf and plays it well. Ingham says, "[Golf] is a spiritual discipline that can teach you much about God and your own soul — about how to deal with failure, anger, and frustration."[349] Ingham also relaxes with books; he is a voracious reader of both theology and spy novels. The bishop enjoys cooking and has taken courses in Asian cuisine. He and Gwen like to go to the theatre and, before they had Cara and Robyn, used to have season tickets to the Vancouver Symphony Orchestra. Now they listen to classical CDs at home and their radio is tuned to CBC Radio. Ingham nurtures his spiritual life carefully and works hard at avoiding the traps of arrogance and despair by ensuring it remains joyful and thankful.

Ingham relaxing on the golf course.
(Julie H. Ferguson)

What troubles Ingham most is the infighting that besets the Church locally, nationally, and internationally: "The public bitterness [towards organized religion], coupled with our internecine nastiness are costing us credibility. How can we proclaim a message of good news, peace on earth, goodwill to all . . . when we can't even demonstrate it to ourselves? . . . the manner in which the Church is dealing with [disagreement] is a fundamental obstacle to evangelism and mission. That worries me more than the issues themselves."[350]

If Ingham gets angry — and he does admit to it — it is in private. Mostly, it is because of his impatience. Time-wasting, slow decision-making, and cowardice are all sources of irritation. Intense anger is a rare emotion for him but, when it happens, it has been a result of feeling personally wounded by unjust attacks during the last few years. He also believes that righteous anger has a place and can move individuals towards promoting change. He feels this most when he considers the unfair treatment of gay and lesbian clergy around the world and the dreadful persecution of homosexuals that continues in many countries. When frustration reaches a point of anger, Ingham goes to the driving range and hits golf balls as a healthy way to get it out of his system.

Lending credence to the stresses borne by Ingham for five years and especially in 2003, the Religion Newswriters' Association of North America voted the chaos caused by both New Westminster's decision to bless same-sex unions and New Hampshire's consecration of a gay bishop as the top religious story of 2003.

"A trial separation with a hope of reconciliation"

The new year of 2004 dawned on a splintered and fractious Anglican Communion that, according to some, had been worsened by feeble leadership at the international level. The storm that had savaged Ingham was blowing into the international arena and moderating in Vancouver. The bishop was still standing, but bloodied, his career stalled.

In the calmer waters, Ingham again offered the five rectors, who still opposed him but had chosen to remain in the Canadian Church, the opportunity to come to the table again and find out if reconciliation was possible. The priests declined, writing that they would be happy to talk when the diocese renounced its position and repented. Three priests from the original eight dissidents, and one other who was on leave, were not included in the invitation, as Ingham had received notification from them that they were leaving the Anglican Church of Canada for good. They were the rectors of St. Andrew's of Pender Harbour, St. Simon's in North Vancouver, and the Church of Emmanuel, which the dissenters renamed Christ the Redeemer, in Richmond. These priests, frustrated at the long delay in receiving temporary alternative episcopal oversight from the Anglican Church of Canada, accepted it from four Third World primates who had formed an alliance to enable it. They formed the new so-called Anglican Communion in Canada (ACiC), leaving the ACiNW to the five parishes who had not accepted the offer. The Reverends Ed Hird, Barclay Mayo, and Silas Ng now considered themselves "missionaries" to North America under the jurisdiction of Archbishop Kolini of Rwanda. The first two, however, continued to use the church buildings in Pender Harbour and Deep Cove for worship and other activities, which was an affront to the diocese that owned them. As Ng's former parish in Richmond worshipped in rented facilities, no dispute threatened over church property.

Too late for Hird, Mayo, and Ng, the Primate's Task Force on Adequate/Alternative Episcopal Oversight for Dissenting Minorities released its report in March 2004. Bishop Matthews, who chaired the task force, likened the scheme to a "trial separation with a hope of reconciliation."[351] The task force recommended temporary episcopal oversight for dissenting parishes for a maximum of six years, with biennial reviews, which, it was hoped, would prevent a separate jurisdiction developing. The program would provide a bishop with full authority to parishes who voted for it by a margin of 80 per cent, the cost being borne by the diocese. Unlike the scheme Ingham had offered the dissenting parishes, the diocesan bishop would have no input into the appointment or the jurisdiction of the alternate. The application of this alternate oversight was reserved for dissenting parishes in dioceses that had approved the blessing of same-sex unions, but not for any other controversial synodic decisions or minorities.

Needless to say the recommendations met with a cool reception in New Westminster. Ingham said, "[The report] seems to raise a great many questions which are not worked out. We have to ask how the temporary partition of dioceses along theological lines is going to contribute to unity."[352] The rector of St. James' in Vancouver, Archdeacon David Retter responded, "It seems as if they are recommending an alternate church."[353] The Reverend Paula Porter-Leggett of St. Faith's, Vancouver, observed, "It appears that if you are a liberal diocese you have to protect the conservatives, but if you are a conservative diocese you don't have to protect the liberals."[354] The Diocese of New Westminster felt unfairly singled out because, unless other dioceses voted to perform blessing of same-sex unions, it was the only one to be affected by the recommendations.

The Canadian House of Bishops received the report too, but failed to reach agreement on it at their April 2004 meeting. Favouring the model of an episcopal visitor (which had been accepted by the Diocese of New Westminster at its 2002 Synod), rather than an alternate bishop, they eventually agreed to defer further discussion until their fall meeting. This deferral ensured the task force's recommendations did not reach the floor of General Synod in June 2004. The bishops' deliberations on the proposed temporary episcopal oversight revealed unease with the proposed concept, which provoked outsider comments about division in the bishops' ranks. Ingham said, "If the jurisdiction of bishops can be divided up along theological lines, we are no longer shepherds of the flock, but leaders of theological parties." The chair, Bishop Victoria Matthews, was disappointed at the delay and complained, "We have chosen to not to have a safety net [for the conservatives] in place as we go into the debate and voting at General Synod"[355] on the issue of blessing of same-sex unions.

Ingham had received a letter in the spring from Bishop Hockin, whom he had appointed as the episcopal visitor to the dissenting parishes in New Westminster. Hockin resigned, effective in June, having completed his commitment. "I had hoped I could be an agent for conciliation, but the conditions of alienation and fear did not allow that," he said in an interview. "I told Bishop Ingham that I would do it for a year and I did, but the distance [from New Brunswick] was just too far and I was disappointed that only [St. Clement's, North Vancouver] took advantage of the offer."[356] Ingham confirmed that he would find another episcopal visitor to minister to St. Clement's and another parish, St. Thomas' in Chilliwack, which had requested assistance. But before he took further action, he wanted to hear the House of Bishops' decision on alternative episcopal oversight in October 2004.*

Also in the spring of 2004, eighteen Global South primates, representing fifty-five million Anglicans, and the conservative American bishops met in Nairobi. Chaired by Archbishop Akinola of Nigeria, they affirmed their unequivocal opposition to ECUSA's decision to consecrate Robinson as bishop and called for the still-deliberating Lambeth Commission on Communion to demand that ECUSA repent for its support of homosexuality. In case ECUSA did not repent, they asked Canterbury to suspend, and if necessary expel, them from the Anglican Communion. The council wanted the same treatment meted out to the Diocese of New Westminster if it failed to measure up to similar demands.

---

* A couple of months after the House of Bishops announced a revised scheme called Shared Episcopal Ministry, St. Clement's held a parish vote and decided they did not need an alternate bishop any more.

After that, for Ingham, came the New Westminster synod of 2004. Unlike the previous three, this one was not controversial and got on with other business, despite the non-attendance of the remaining dissenting parishes. St. Martin's of North Vancouver had since reorganized under the faithful ministry of an eighty-year-old priest, Canon Don Willis, and was back in the fold. Focusing mainly on the mission of the diocese, this synod did not attract any media, and delegates welcomed their absence. Members did hear three presentations that derived from the same-sex issue. One was a moving update from the same-sex couple whose union was blessed first, a year before. Another came from St. Clement's, the only dissenting parish that accepted the episcopal visitor offered by Ingham, which described how valuable Bishop Hockin's ministry had been. The last presentation was delivered as a prelude to General Synod the following month. Reverend Canon Eric Beresford, a consultant for both the Anglican Church of Canada and the Anglican Consultative Council, provided a summary of the consequences of the same-sex decision of 2002 and explained the complex motion on same-sex unions going before General Synod. He surprised many when he told the delegates that sixteen dioceses in the Church of England bless same-sex couples routinely behind closed doors and have provided the rite to nearly five hundred pairs of gays and lesbians. New Westminster also decided to persevere with the reconciliation process with the residual dissenting parishes and established a task force to study the best ways of restoring the relationship. The bishop asked them to report their findings and suggestions at synod 2005.

General Synod, the "one to be watched" that year, was held in St. Catharines, Ontario. This is the triennial meeting of the Anglican Church of Canada, attended by over three hundred clergy and laity from every diocese in Canada. Ingham, of course, was there as the head of the delegation from New Westminster. The main item on the agenda was the election of a new Canadian primate to replace Michael Peers, who had retired.

Ingham was not one of the four nominees — too controversial, perhaps, noted the editor of the newspaper of the Diocese of New Westminster,[357] and too similar to Peers, said his executive archdeacon[358] — but many delegates wondered why. With the primatial candidates on both sides of the sexuality issue, observers expected the selection of the new primate to signal the direction the Anglican Church of Canada would follow on the matter. General Synod stepped down the middle path and chose Andrew Hutchison, the centrist, but gay-positive, Archbishop of Montreal.

While the national gathering was engaged with many resolutions, two motions came to the floor on the issue of same-sex unions that had resulted from the House of Bishops' referral in 2002. Delegates' packages contained background information to assist them in decision-making, and most had done their homework. The special-interest groups on both sides of the issue had reserved booths, and some delegates had prepared strategies to further their positions on the floor and garner votes. Interest was avid inside and outside the Anglican Church, Canada, and the wider world. The media again were lined up, with eyes pushed to their viewfinders and microphones at the ready, just as they had been in New Westminster in 2002. Would the Canadian Church follow the American Episcopalians, who had voted for the local option in August 2003?

The five-part procedural motion (see Appendix 3 for the final wording) on the blessings of same-sex unions was not an attempt to establish the national Church's position on same-sex blessings, but asked the key question: Can a diocese permit blessing ceremonies for gay couples? It included acknowledgement of the diverse views on the issue, the level of disagreement, the need for more study, and the intention to provide pastoral care for all Anglicans, as well as episcopal oversight for dissenting parishes. However, the relevant section (Part 2) read, "this synod affirms the authority and jurisdiction of a diocesan synod, with the concurrence of its bishop, to authorize the blessing of committed same sex-unions," a statement that, if passed, would confirm the "local option" in a confederal church. Passing Part 2 would also imply that the issue was pastoral, not doctrinal. This implication, that the matter was pastoral, became the crux of the ensuing debate.

In their first action, General Synod voted to detach Part 2 from the other sections, for debate as a separate motion. An amendment added a sixth section to the main motion to reinforce that the church welcomes gays and lesbians and affirms their relationships. The first motion passed with the amendment that read that General Synod affirmed "the integrity and sanctity of committed adult same-sex relationships." The amendment caused an outcry from the world's conservative Anglicans over the use of the word "sanctity" (or holiness), which had also caused considerable difficulty for some synod delegates. Ingham was not a major player in the debates: "In the main, I wanted to see how the national Church would deal with the matter. I felt we had made our own position clear as a diocese, and that we now needed to listen to the rest of our Church in Canada."[359]

Then General Synod voted to defer consideration of Part 2 of the original motion until 2007, leaving the jurisdictional question unresolved. After a polite and vigorous debate, only 54 per cent of the clergy and laity, but 68 per cent of bishops, voted in favour of deferral, hardly a landslide decision. Delegates also approved the addition of a request that the primate ask his Theological Commission to investigate and give an opinion on whether blessings of same-sex unions constitute a matter of doctrine and report back in 2006.

The compromise decision sent mixed messages. On one hand, by inferring that no more dioceses would be able to employ the "local option" until 2007, the Canadian Church seemed to be defusing the threat of a division at home and saying it was unsure if the issue was doctrinal or pastoral. On the other, by affirming the "integrity and sanctity" of committed same-sex relationships, the Anglican Church of Canada was perhaps indicating its growing awareness that homosexuality was part of God's creation and not a sin. Only one message continued to ring out clearly: the Canadian Church was still struggling with the issue. One other vote sent a strong message. The dean of Christ Church Cathedral in Vancouver, Peter Elliott, was elected Prolocutor (chair) and second-in-command of General Synod. Elliott had recently "come out" as a gay man living in a long-term relationship.

Ingham said after the vote, "It's appropriate that we take the time that people need and, while we take that time, it's important to hold people in mutual respect."[360] This was not just a statement given for public consumption, but an honest response; Ingham "thought the debate was fair, and the outcome reasonable. After all, it took us many years in New Westminster to get to the place we did, and I could see the same process unfolding, albeit more slowly, at the national level."[361]

Home again, the bishop issued a statement that demonstrated his tenacity. He announced that the Diocese of New Westminster would "continue to allow priests, in parishes that wish to do so, to bless permanent, faithful, same-sex relationships, and we will continue to respect the conscience of those clergy and parishes who feel they cannot." He also said he was encouraged by the approval of the amendment, noting that the word "sanctity" was used in a pastoral and not a doctrinal way. Overall, Ingham was relieved that General Synod had not defeated the second motion outright, but had simply deferred it. Hope for eventual reform had not been entirely extinguished, nor had New Westminster been left out on a limb.

Archbishop Rowan Williams of Canterbury acknowledged the Canadian decision to defer with some relief, perhaps hoping it might ease tensions in the Anglican Communion. Canadian gays and lesbians, of course, were disheartened with the deferral of Part 2 of the motion. Integrity Vancouver's well-informed president said, "It was the third General Synod since [1998] and they [the national church] still had not made any indication of whether or not this was their issue."[362] A group of bishops stood up after the vote and spoke out against Synod's affirmation of the "integrity and sanctity of committed adult same-sex relationships." Conservative Anglican leaders reacted harshly to the same words. So did twenty-two Global South primates who, bristling with outrage, again demanded that Canterbury eject Canada from the Anglican Communion. However, this remained unlikely to happen because, as the newly-elected Primate Andrew Hutchison pointed out, Canada had in fact made no final decision, but remained in a conversation both nationally and internationally on the question. The issue was moving further into the ambit of the national and international churches, a development that Hutchison's actions at the primates' next meeting in February 2005 would confirm.

Given the eruptions around the world caused by the decision to proceed with blessing of same-sex unions in the Diocese of New Westminster and then the non-decision at General Synod, many wondered aloud why Ingham had chosen to go it alone. Judge John Spencer, a former chancellor (legal advisor) of the diocese, now retired from the bench, provided an explanation. Ingham had had two choices in 1998. He could have backed away from the inherent risks and sent the gay-lesbian issue directly to General Synod, where it would have taken decades to reach a decision, if ever. Or, he could have taken it on within the diocese and secured a decision at the beginning of the new millennium. The first option was the easy way out, although it would have diminished the democratic process of a synod; the second was much riskier for the diocese and for the bishop's career. The risk in taking on the issue jeopardized the diocese, which, if it split, could result in a smaller and less economically viable organization with fewer funds to support the range of outreach ministries that New Westminster does so well. However, Spencer also believed that once Ingham chose to follow the local option, it allowed synod to decide to provide justice for a group that was much discriminated against within society and the Anglican Church in a reasonable time frame.

As to Ingham's chances of advancement, many insiders acknowledge that, but for this issue, he could have been elected Canada's primate in 2004. As it was, he was not even nominated. In November 2005 the provincial synod of British Columbia and Yukon sought a new metropolitan to replace the retired Archbishop David Crawley. Opinion was divided on whether or not the senior bishop in the province, Michael Ingham, stood a chance. As it turned out, Bishop Terry Buckle, aged sixty-four, won the three-way election and became archbishop. Although Ingham was only one vote behind Buckle in the first ballot, when Bishop Cowan withdrew after the second ballot, all his votes went to Buckle.

On his return to Vancouver from St. Catharines, the bishop still had a few issues from the earlier diocesan synod votes to clear up. He settled down to write some important letters that he had intentionally delayed until after General Synod. On June 25, 2004, he informed Hird and Mayo, two of the dissenting priests who had joined the Diocese of Rwanda the previous spring, that over the summer they must seek alternate worship space. This request aimed to recover the church property, so that any parishioners who wished to remain in the diocese could worship in the Anglican parish churches. (While parishioners and priests can choose to leave the diocese, "parishes" cannot.) In the same letter, Ingham again offered reconciliation. The two priests did not respond but defied Ingham in the press. For example: "We own the premises and we're carrying on as usual," said the Reverend Ed Hird of St. Simon's in Deep Cove, North Vancouver. Ingham was not unduly concerned with their attitude. The canons of the church are clear that dioceses hold in trust parishes and their buildings.

Another letter went to the Church of Emmanuel (now known as the Church of the Redeemer) in Richmond, extending the olive branch again. Ingham invited members of this parish, which did not have a church building and whose priest had also left, to a meeting to give them an opportunity to return to the Anglican Church of Canada. The bishop hoped they would at least be willing to discuss their situation further. They did not reply either. Diocesan council then considered whether to close down the parish, in the legal sense, meaning that, while parishioners might continue to worship together, it would not be under the name of the Anglican Church of Canada.

Anglican Essentials held another conference in September 2004, and the organization was handled differently than previously. This time all delegates had to "embrace" a revised version of the Montreal Declaration of 1994, as well as repudiate the decision at General Synod two months earlier that affirmed the "integrity and sanctity" of same-sex unions. This action kept more moderate conservatives away and prevented the primate from attending. Once again Essentials refused Integrity their table ministry, because its members could not meet their conditions. Conference organizers also barred the media from attending and, when pressed hard by two reporters from the *Anglican Journal* and *Crosstalk*,* asked them also to sign the Declaration. They refused, needless to say, as any professional journalist would.

Deftly vague

Anglican clergy and laity around the world eagerly anticipated the release of Lambeth's Commission on Communion, known as the

---

* Newspaper (monthly) of the Diocese of Ottawa.

Windsor Report, in mid-October 2004. Important to all the stake-holders, both conservative and progressive, it was especially so to New Westminster. With provocative timing, two weeks before the due date, the Nigerian primate, Akinola, announced plans to estab-lish a non-geographic Nigerian diocese on American soil, separate from the Episcopal Church of the United States. Speculation swirled through both camps as the deadline neared. Far-right conservatives hoped that ECUSA and the Diocese of New Westminster would be forced to repent and to overturn Robinson's consecration and to cease to bless same-sex unions. They also hoped that the North American churches would be disciplined; some even speculated that Ingham would be barred from attending the next Lambeth Conference in 2008 and other important Anglican Communion meetings around the world. Those more liberally inclined hoped for a moderate response, which might keep the Communion whole, but would not offend the Africans. Most agreed that both sides had to be willing to make concessions. Ingham wanted a more accurate his-torical analysis of the situation.

A year before, the Archbishop of Canterbury had directed the Commission on Communion to provide recommendations for how member churches of the Anglican Communion could maximize unity. Chaired by the Irish Archbishop Robin Eames, who is known as the "divine optimist," the commission had a challenging task in the face of alienation over issues like homosexuality and the provinces' widely varying cultures and values. A Canadian served on the thirteen-person commission, but no gays or lesbians. Eames, in the final report's fore-word, emphasized that the committee's opinion was not a judgement but "part of a process" towards reconciliation and healing.

As it turned out, the ninety-three-page Windsor Report* took a less punitive path than some had demanded, and which church schol-ars described as "deftly vague." In brief, the commission invited both ECUSA and the Diocese of New Westminster to "express [their] regret that the proper constraints of the bonds of affection were breached" [363] by the results of their decisions. Dioceses that already per-formed blessings of same-sex unions were asked to impose a moratori-

---

* Available for download at www.anglicancommunion.org/windsor2004/down-loads/ index.cfm

um on future blessings, and those that were about to start doing so, were asked to wait. The bishops who had interfered in others' jurisdictions were also called upon to express regret and to cease intervening in dioceses that were not their own. The Canadian member of the commission clarified this further: the report does *not* call for apologies for actions but, rather, regret for the consequences. Lastly, the Lambeth Commission acknowledged there was a real danger that, if reconciliation was unsuccessful, provinces with differing positions in the Anglican Communion might go their separate ways.

Many on both sides of the conflict judged the requests to express regret a serious rebuke of the dioceses that had removed barriers to homosexuality in advance of agreement from the whole Church, which canonically they did not need. The report said that the Diocese of New Westminster, among others, had acted unilaterally by authorizing the blessing of same-sex unions. However, it did not challenge the diocese's right to have made the decision, only the *wisdom* of doing so. The day after the report's release, Ingham delivered his preliminary reaction, "I welcome the report and greatly appreciate that [it] focuses on reconciliation."[364] Without hesitation he publicly offered his regrets for the consequences of the diocese's decision to bless same-sex unions, which, he acknowledged, had dismayed some Anglicans. However he stopped short of apologizing for the blessings themselves and told the world that the diocese would continue providing the rite for same-sex couples. Ingham expressed his concurrence with the Windsor Report's criticism of the bishops who had intervened in the Diocese of New Westminster and ECUSA.

Conservative Anglicans and the dissenters called the report "toothless" and ambiguous. Gays and lesbians felt that "expressions of regret" would not help their plight at all and that their "bonds of affection" with the Church were already strained to breaking point. "We will not wait quietly, nor will we apologize for the work of God in our lives," said the president of Integrity Vancouver. He also noted that the primates, as one of the major "instruments of unity" of the Anglican Communion, had never once met with any gays and lesbians. "We will continue to press toward our full inclusion in the Anglican Church of Canada."[365] Not one expression of regret was heard from the bishops who interfered in the Diocese of New Westminster and other jurisdictions — indeed, they felt the very idea of offering apologies was offensive and indicated they would continue to act on calls for episcopal oversight by parishes outside their dioceses.

After its release, the Windsor Report enjoyed a long life, as it was studied minutely. Various international Anglican bodies needed time to thoughtfully consider it, the Canadian primate asked parishes and others to submit their reactions to it, and the Diocese of New Westminster planned to prayerfully work out their reply to it over six months. Ingham asked two priests in the diocese, one progressive and one conservative, to develop a response, which would be debated and voted on at the next synod in May 2005. But the crucial response that everyone anticipated was that of the world's primates' meeting in February 2005; many expected Global South to stage a protest. In advance of it, the provinces of Uganda, Nigeria, Central Africa, and South East Asia boycotted meetings that the Anglican Church of Canada and ECUSA attended.

But before the primates deliberated, the Canadian House of Bishops had also to respond to the Windsor Report. They met in November 2004 in Saskatoon for the first time under the leadership of the new primate, Archbishop Andrew Hutchison. Most bishops, including Ingham, agreed that the House met in a heightened spirit of cooperation, allowing for more collegiality and decision-making. The bishops considered the Windsor Report in small groups. Parts of it received marked criticism, including the recommendation to reduce national churches' independence by increasing the authority of the Archbishop of Canterbury. However, in the end the House passed a unanimous resolution, commending the report for study, as well as recognizing its importance.

The thirty-eight bishops also formally approved a revised scheme to provide alternate bishops for dissenting parishes, which they had struggled with in the spring, and renamed it "Shared Episcopal Ministry." The House agreed that bishops should work with each other across theological lines to ensure the pastoral care of everyone in the Church. This included all dissenting minorities — both conservative and progressive. The "Shared Episcopal Ministry" document was substantially different from the scheme proposed earlier by the Bishop of Edmonton's group, and it gained almost unanimous support from Canadian bishops, including Ingham. He reacted immediately by pointing out that the model was closely parallel to the one already put in place in New Westminster, and that it avoided the one-sidedness of the earlier proposal. At the same meeting in Saskatoon, Ingham obtained a personal promise from Bishop Buckle that he would respect the traditional role and authority of bishops in their own dioceses and would not interfere again in the Diocese of New Westminster. At once Ingham publicly lifted the inhibition he had placed on Buckle in 2003. This move was warmly welcomed both in New Westminster and across the national Church. Afterwards Ingham noted, "The Church is looking for important signs of reconciliation. At this meeting, it feels like the corner has been turned. This period has called us back to our roots and people are seeing that relationships are more important than issues."[366]

In mid-November 2004, the lay and clergy delegates of the Diocese of Niagara approved blessings of same-sex unions, becoming the second diocese in Canada to do so. However, the bishop withheld his consent, as Ingham had done the first time the Diocese of New Westminster voted on the issue, and for much the same reasons. In December, Canada's largest diocese, Toronto, voted to defer a decision on the blessings of same-sex unions, but only by a very narrow margin (51.4 per cent), until after the primate's Theological Commission had delivered its opinion on the doctrine involved in the issue. Also around the same time, three other Canadian dioceses had either voted against similar motions or made it clear that they were not going to move towards blessing same-sex unions for a while. Still others were planning to bring the issue to their synods for debate.

Ingham then sorted out two remaining issues before the diocese. After receiving no replies from the three priests who had become missionaries in North America under Rwanda's jurisdiction, the diocese concluded that they had abandoned their ministry within the Canadian Church. Ingham sent formal notices to this effect on November 30, 2004, to the Reverends Ed Hird, Barclay Mayo, and Silas Ng, and expressed his hope that they would reconsider. Ingham also restated the diocese's legal position: the parishes which they had served, including any associated properties, remained part of the Diocese of New Westminster. Eventually the diocese had to serve legal notice to the two congregations to recover the property, with a demand to vacate by April 1, 2005.

The bishop again sent letters of invitation to the rectors of St. John's Shaughnessy (Rev. David Short), Good Shepherd (Rev. Stephen Leung), St. Matthias and St. Luke (Rev. Simon Chin), and Holy Cross (Rev. Dawn McDonald), all in Vancouver, and St. Matthew's (Rev. Trevor Walters) in Abbotsford, who had not abandoned their ministries over the blessing of same-sex unions, but had been withholding their diocesan assessments. He invited them to return to the table to see if reconciliation might be worth another try. The basis of this third invitation was the shared episcopal ministry plan, which the Canadian House of Bishops had adopted, 35 to 3, the previous month, and his own promise to work with the acting metropolitan, Bishop Buckle. "Let us make our best efforts," wrote Ingham, so the diocese could once again focus on its work of community outreach and care for parishioners. Their reply disappointed the bishop. They told him that, without a moratorium on the blessings of same-sex unions, they could not see any basis for reconciliation. Ingham remained hopeful for the long-term, however. "The differences may take years to resolve. We must always be open,"[367] he said, demonstrating a capacity for patience that some in the diocese find hard to accommodate.

Ingham welcomed the Canadian primate on his first visit to the Diocese of New Westminster in December 2004. Hutchison made his support for Ingham, the diocese, and the local option abundantly clear. "[It] was a decision made in conscience," the primate said publicly. "We must act locally with courage and integrity. You may be doing something prophetic. That should be reassuring. This was not a wildcat move by a maverick diocese."[368] Ingham was pleased with, and not a little surprised at, Hutchison's candour.

The new year of 2005 saw further recovery in the Diocese of New Westminster and lessening of anxiety, as the consequences surrounding the blessings of same-sex unions wound down. In Holy Week, the congregations of St. Simon's and St. Andrew's voted to vacate their parish churches rather than undertake a costly legal battle with the diocese. They finally moved out on May 31, 2005, after they had found alternative worship space. This result enabled the diocese to restore the two parishes to the Anglican Church of Canada. The bishop assigned the rector of nearby St. Clement's, North Vancouver (a conservative-leaning parish), to take charge of St.

Simon's, and the rector of St. Hilda's in Sechelt (a progressive parish) to the additional duty as priest-in-charge of St. Andrew's. Ingham also announced that he was formally dissolving Richmond's Emmanuel parish, an action that the Diocesan Council had earlier encouraged, but which did not involve property.

At the end of February 2005, the deeply divided Anglican primates convened to respond to the Windsor Report in Northern Ireland. Ingham was out of town at the time, visiting the companion diocese of Taiwan, but he followed events closely on the Internet and by telephone. Seen as a turning point for the Anglican Communion, the session was expected by informed observers to be fraught with deliberate intransigence from Global South, sufficient perhaps to break the Communion, given the aggressive statements some provinces had recently issued. All but three African primates were furious that the Windsor Report had neither called for disciplinary action against the ECUSA and the Anglican Church of Canada nor demanded their repentance for consecrating a gay bishop and blessing same-sex unions. However, it should be said here that not all the bishops and laity in Africa support their primates' strident views, but they dare not publicly oppose them. The western, liberal churches went armed to do battle over the recommendation to increase Canterbury's authority, which would limit the traditional independence of the provinces and dioceses.

Archbishop Andrew Hutchison, Canada's primate, was in the thick of it, hoping that other primates had consulted their Churches before the meeting and would speak for them. Before leaving for Northern Ireland, Hutchison explained, "The primacy operates quite differently in some countries. There are some primates who have enormous personal authority, jurisdiction, and power in a way that we don't. We're very consultative [in Canada]. When I speak it [is] the voice of the church."[369] On arrival in Dromantine, the primate insisted that the blessings of same-sex unions be treated as a Canadian Church issue, not a diocesan issue — and that he, not an individual diocese or bishop, was responsible for the actions of the Canadian province. This was a significant pronouncement, for it signalled that all future dealings on the

Archbishop Andrew Hutchison, primate of the Anglican Church of Canada, 2005.
(Julie H. Ferguson)

matter would be with the Anglican Church of Canada and not with the Diocese of New Westminster, effectively removing much of the burden from Ingham. Hutchison also expressed his desire that the meeting should provide a moderating influence on a Communion in crisis.

Some media sensationalized their reporting on the primatial meeting and caused many Christians to fear schism was imminent. Certainly the sessions were difficult and sometimes even touch-and-go, but the participants did manage to express a desire to remain united. To gain some breathing space for the Communion, the primates' final communiqué included, but was not limited to:

- Acknowledgement that both ECUSA and the Diocese of New Westminster had followed proper constitutional procedures with respect to their decisions to remove barriers to homosexuality;
- A repeated call for consultations on human sexuality that, up till then, had not taken place everywhere in the communion;
- Caution regarding the possible increase in authority of the Archbishop of Canterbury; most primates opposed the idea fearing it might create an international jurisdiction that would override current provincial autonomy. Global South worried that it might result in a loss of the leniency towards polygamy that they had achieved at Lambeth 1988;
- Voluntary withdrawal of the U.S. and Canadian churches from participation in the meetings and standing committees of the Anglican Consultative Council prior to the next Lambeth Conference in 2008;
- Protection for dissenting groups in the form of a "Panel of Reference," which would supervise episcopal ministry for them (Canada's primate offered to provide Canada's model that the House of Bishops had recently adopted); and
- A moratorium on future blessings of same-sex unions and consecrations of any practising gay bishops.

Hutchison was saddened by the behaviour of a dozen or more primates during this important gathering. Not only did the Global South primates abandon a working session to have dinner with conservative U.S. Episcopalian supporters, they also boycotted the final Eucharist because the Canadian and American primates attended it. Afterwards the Canadian primate spoke forthrightly about the Archbishop of Canterbury's lack of leadership in handling this show of disrespect. After he returned home, Hutchison also commented about the way the Church of England had failed to confess to blessing same-sex unions clandestinely in much greater numbers than Canada had ever blessed openly.

When the communiqué was released, it was as Ingham expected, and he responded from the Far East. The bishop of New Westminster reassured Anglicans that there was no schism yet in the Anglican Communion, despite inflammatory and erroneous media reports that Canterbury was planning to "uninvite" certain bishops to the next Lambeth Conference. However, Ingham did counter the request for the voluntary withdrawal of North American churches from the next Anglican Consultative Council meeting: "It should be firmly resisted," he said.[370]

Most reaction from other Anglican leaders in Canada was directed at Hutchison, who had signed on to the primates' final plan despite some reluctance and his impassioned pleas to keep North America at the table of the Anglican Consultative Council. Liberals were dismayed that he had agreed to all the points, but he maintained it was part of the pain to be endured to avert an almost-certain split, at least for now. Conservatives said that the final decisions were a validation of their position and sent a clear message that the Canadian Church had erred and should repent. Some clergy accused Hutchison of betraying gays and lesbians by endorsing the call for a moratorium on blessings, but many Anglican lesbians and gays themselves hoped that the decisions might, at last, result in their voices being heard around the world. Not a few observers surmised that the primates were setting themselves up to lay claim to future decision-making by changing the composition and agenda of the Anglican Consultative Council, the only instrument of unity with laity included in its membership. All this was unnerving for the parishioner following events from the pew, and reinforced for the unchurched that they wanted nothing to do with organized religion. Even after all this, the primates' meeting had by no means laid the homosexuality issue to rest. It was still front and centre, particularly internationally, and being used to gain power. Neither had they accomplished much on the unity front.

In March 2005 the Executive Council of the Episcopal Church of the United States officially expressed their regrets over the consequences of the consecration of a gay bishop and agreed to withdraw from full participation in the Anglican Consultative Council's triennial meeting in June. However, it had been a struggle in discernment for them, which illustrated a willingness to retreat from their more adamant position prior to the primates' meeting. ECUSA also pledged that their House of Bishops would not authorize any new dioceses to bless same-sex unions until 2006. Those bishops, who had jurisdiction, agreed to suspend consecrating *any* bishop before their next General Convention of 2006 and to delay any more episcopal elections until after it. Additionally, the American bishops of five dioceses agreed to reschedule pending consecrations till 2006. This was a clear indication of the Episcopal Church's willingness to provide time and space to strengthen the bonds of affection in the Anglican Communion.

Meanwhile the work on New Westminster's response[371] to the Windsor Report proceeded apace, and it was released in April 2005 for discussion. Ingham organized a "Windsor Report Study Day" for its presentation to the delegates who would be attending Synod 2005. In an interesting pairing, the two priests who had prepared the response were on opposite sides of the debate on blessing of same-sex unions. Richard Leggett, Professor of Liturgical Studies at the Vancouver School of Theology, was a progressive and John Oakes, rector of Holy Trinity, Vancouver, and Web master of "New Vision," was a staunch conservative. Both men "shelved their personal preferences,"[372] demonstrating that it was possible to do so, even given the issue, and produced a document of considerable value to the diocese. Ingham was pleased with the result.

The study day for synod delegates (about 250 attended), which Ingham chaired, opened with an introduction to the Windsor Report by Archdeacon Jim Boyles, the retiring general secretary of the Anglican Church of Canada. He told the participants that it was generally well accepted within the Communion as a way to remain united, but concern had arisen over suggestions that Canterbury's role be strengthened. Although this solution might lead to easier resolution of international disputes, it could also mean that the Anglican Communion might become too centralized, bureaucratic, and legalistic, usurping diocesan independence. Boyles also told synod delegates that the conflict caused by the removal of barriers to homosexuality was, at its most fundamental, a "breakdown of trust."

Then Leggett and Oakes took over. They helped the delegates to understand their thirty-five-page response to the Windsor

Report and its recommendations, which synod would be voting on in three weeks. It contained affirmations of twelve recommendations of the historic report, three areas of disagreement, and one proposed resolution for synod. Both men cautioned that, if no response to the Windsor Report was forthcoming from the diocese, it would further alienate the traditional members locally and was a risk not worth taking.

The challenge concerned the Windsor Report's call for a total moratorium on the blessing of same-sex unions and, while admitting they disagreed with each other, Leggett and Oakes recommended that the diocese tread a middle path. They suggested that the blessing of same-sex unions remain limited in New Westminster to the parishes that were already authorized to perform them, at least until General Synod 2007. Leggett and Oakes explained that completely ignoring Windsor's call for a moratorium could play into the hands of those who would like to see the Diocese of New Westminster and its bishop expelled from the Anglican Communion altogether.

Vigorous group discussions resulted in a favourable overall response to the joint paper, especially the section on resisting an increase in Canterbury's authority, but distinct differences emerged over whether or not to limit blessings of same-sex unions. As the day drew to a close, Leggett and Oakes promised to revise their paper to reflect the comments of the day before presenting it to synod in May for discussion and vote. When Ingham generously suggested that they could revise the section on limiting blessing of same-sex unions, both men smiled, and Leggett shook his head.

Ingham joined the Canadian bishops at their spring meeting armed with New Westminster's revised response to the Windsor Report. The bishops' main agenda was to develop a response to the February primatial communiqué and to formulate a written statement for wide distribution. They voiced cautious support for a moratorium on blessing of same-sex unions, publicly saying, "we commit ourselves neither to encourage nor to initiate the use of such rites until General Synod has made a decision on the matter." On the question of the primates' request to voluntarily withdraw from full participation in the Anglican Consultative Council session in June, the House of

Bishops referred the decision to the Council of General Synod, meeting the following week.

The Council of General Synod (CoGS), consisting of thirty-seven elected clergy and laity, makes policy decisions for the Anglican Church of Canada in the years when General Synod does not convene. Ingham has been a member since 2004. As usual, many items were on the agenda, but one concerned the bishop of New Westminster the most. CoGS was to decide the action the Anglican Church of Canada would take over the primates' request that it withdraw from full participation in the Anglican Consultative Council until 2008. (The Council meantime had invited Canada, along with ECUSA, to give ninety-minute presentations at the June meeting to explain how they arrived at their current positions on human sexuality. Both had accepted.)

Ingham wanted the Anglican Church of Canada to refuse to withdraw from the Anglican Consultative Council meetings and helped to write a resolution to that effect. Integrity Canada delivered a presentation[373] to CoGS on the subject, requesting that a practising gay or lesbian person be a part of the Canadian presentation team to Nottingham. The ensuing debate, like so many surrounding the issue of sexuality, was long and passionate, sometimes even anguished according to the *Anglican Journal.* Hutchison, the primate, having signed on to the idea in February, urged CoGS to take the strategic high road, because he believed it would prevent those opposed to blessing of same-sex unions leaving the table. Ingham energetically challenged his position, explaining that, in doing so, he was not implying lack of respect: "it's really important for us to say that we respect our primate, but, if we take a different position, it's not thumbing our nose at him."[374] Ingham spoke spiritedly and from the heart, saying, "God has given the Canadian Church a prophetic voice to speak in this matter and the ultimate cowardice is not to speak the words you've been given to speak."[375] He also expressed concern that agreeing to withdraw from the Anglican Consultative Council could open the floodgates to further demands. "It won't be the last request that will be made of us. There will be further requests to repent, to turn our backs on gays and lesbians," he said.[376] Ingham urged CoGS to assume the "prophetic role" that God has set out for the Canadian Church to play within the Anglican Communion. "I think we are living at a moment in history which probably none of us wants to choose but here we are," he concluded.

The CoGS debate did not increase agreement in the Canadian Church — afterwards it was still divided along the usual progressive-traditional lines. Despite Ingham's heartfelt presentation urging the contrary, CoGS voted (20 to 12) that the Anglican Church of Canada would "attend but not participate fully" in the Anglican Consultative Council session in England in June.

Just before New Westminster's 2005 synod convened, and a year ahead of schedule, The Primate's Theological Commission on the Blessing of Same-Sex Unions released its findings in the St. Michael Report.* A year before, Canada's new primate had instructed this group to provide an opinion on the doctrinal implications of blessing same-sex unions, and fourteen members (gays and lesbians were represented) of the commission struggled with the question. They decided, after much study, that the blessing of committed, adult, same-sex unions is a matter of doctrine, but neither core nor creedal doctrine.‡ This viewpoint means that blessing same-sex unions touches on the traditional teaching of the Church regarding sexual ethics, but not on the Church's primary beliefs about God or salvation. The commission wrote in their conclusion that it is a type of doctrine "that does not hinder or impair our common affirmation of the three historic creeds,"[377] which means it could be open to change by General Synod. The report's summary, in part, said, "It is now for the church to decide whether or not the blessing of same-sex unions is a faithful, Spirit-led development of Christian doctrine."[378]

The St. Michael Report was distributed to the Canadian House of Bishops and dioceses, and Ingham described it as "a confusing document. It says that the blessing of same-sex unions is a matter of doctrine, but it cannot say what doctrine it is a matter of. . . . They imply a hierarchy of doctrine which requires much more explanation."[379] He said a great deal more too, including, "It strikes me as

---

* The St. Michael Report can be downloaded at www.anglican.ca/primate/ptc/
StMichaelReport.pdf.

‡ These doctrines include the Incarnation and the Trinity, for example.

discriminatory." Gays and lesbians responded through Integrity Canada. They saw this doctrinal opinion as marginalizing them once again because, if it is affirmed by General Synod, all blessings of same-sex unions would have to cease until the national Church acts upon it. According to Ingham, because the report carries the considerable moral authority of an eminent body, any motion on the blessing of same-sex unions at General Synod will likely fail and delay the full acceptance of homosexuals into the church by another twenty-five years.

Peter Elliott, the dean of Christ Church Cathedral, who is developing a response to the St. Michael Report, said that neither side of the doctrinal debate found it a satisfactory document. However, he is more optimistic than Ingham over timing, especially as no one anticipated the speed with which same-sex marriage has become a social reality in Canadian society. He also points to the success of the Diocese of Niagara's resolution that factored in civil marriage prior to a rite of blessing as evidence that the church is moving in the same direction. Elliott believes that the St. Michael Report is also "gesturing, in a highly nuanced way, toward marriage for same-sex couples"[380] given that the writers said that blessings are "analogous to marriage." Others will disagree. Elliott hopes that the Anglican Church of Canada will eventually do the same as the U.S. Episcopal Church and let priests be free to decide whether or not to perform the rite of blessing for couples, gay or straight. Whatever happens, the opinion provided by the commission is only one analysis of the issue among many, and the range of opinions is diverse. One thing the report does achieve is that it starts the debate again.

If General Synod decides that the matter is doctrinal *and* votes (most unlikely) to permit the blessing of same-sex unions throughout the Anglican Church of Canada, the canons of the church will need to be changed. This process would take a minimum of six years, as changes to canons require two consecutive votes at General Synod earning a two-thirds majority in all three orders (bishops, clergy, and laity) to pass. The earliest the national decision could be made on the issue would be 2010. However, the degree of opposition to the blessing of same-sex unions within the Canadian Church indicates that this level of support will be impossible to reach that quickly. Achievement of acceptance of the blessing of same-sex unions nationwide as a doctrinal matter might take half a century or more — but for the youth factor. They will be in the driver's seat by then and the opponents, who are now mostly in their fifties and sixties, will have left the field.

I stand with your bishop

Ingham returned from the string of meetings in the east to chair his own synod in mid-May, to which he had invited the primate, Archbishop Andrew Hutchison, as synod partner. Although not as ground-breaking as the synods of 1998, 2001, and 2002, the 103rd session did have one controversial resolution to debate: the one about the proposed moratorium on the blessing of same-sex unions requested by the world's primates. Hutchison preached at the opening Eucharist and encouraged the entire synod with his words of praise for the diocese and its actions. "You are one of the strongest dioceses in the country." He honoured Ingham, praising his leadership and commitment, and ended with the words, "I stand with your bishop."[381]

The bishop of New Westminster focused synod delegates before getting down to business by reminding them that "it's time to pay attention to relationships and the strain our actions have caused."[382] To that end the Task Force on Reconciliation presented its report about the distress in the diocese over the implementation of the blessing of same-sex unions and how best to manage it. Their findings showed that the distress was, and is, experienced mostly by those who opposed the blessing of same-sex unions. The task force also found some anxiety among the supporters of the issue, and surmised that these feelings had been caused by the outside events over which they had no control taking place around the issue. (A previous national report had identified this anxiety as stemming from concern over what would happen to the whole Anglican Church.) Recommendations called for more opportunities for the two sides of the debate to worship and plan together, through diocesan events and joint parish activities, for increased use of the resources for pastoral care for dissenting clergy and parishioners, and for the definition of the word "reconciliation" to be understood as "re-establishing cordial relations," rather than agreeing with each other. All four resolutions derived from this report dealt with mechanisms to intentionally reach out to strengthen these relationships in the diocese. Two speakers rose to address the motions. "Reconciliation is an intentional decision people make. It doesn't mean compromise," reminded Reverend Al Carson of St. Cuthbert's, Delta. Vancouver's archdeacon, Andrew Pike, commented, "one party doesn't want to have reconciliation, they want to have capitulation."[383] The motions to implement the recommendations carried easily.

The debate on the diocesan response to the Windsor Report's proposed moratorium on the blessing of same-sex unions was polite and respectful. Although there were speakers with strong positions on both sides, it never reached the level of passion that the debates of previous years had seen. Perhaps New Westminster had become more practised over the years in discussing emotionally charged matters, or perhaps delegates simply did not feel the moratorium debate was as significant as the one over the blessings themselves. As it was, Ingham never had to exert control over the speakers or delegates, and the debate was not protracted. The primate hung on every word.

Three resolutions came to the floor on the question of a moratorium. The vote in favour of no moratorium at all required a count to determine that the motion was defeated 192 (65 per cent) to 104. An overwhelming majority, requiring no count, voted against a total moratorium, which sent a strong message of support for the diocese's previous decisions. In the end, synod opted for the partial moratorium, as recommended by the Leggett–Oakes report, which would limit the blessing of same-sex unions to the parishes already authorized to do so. Less than one-third of the delegates opposed this motion. The final result meant that no more parishes would be added to the roster until after General Synod reconsidered the blessing of same-sex unions in 2007, after which New Westminster would again decide together what to do next.

Understandably, most gay and lesbian Anglicans, as well as the youth delegates, spoke in favour of no moratorium. They believed that a partial version would send a negative message to all gays and lesbians and their supporters, whether churched or not. Concern was expressed that the press would perceive the Diocese of New Westminster as backing down if any other course was taken. Steve

Schuh, president of Integrity Vancouver, supported those sentiments, but was more willing to accept a limited moratorium, although he did not believe it would influence the international scene. Schuh acknowledged that a limited moratorium might encourage more local communication with the loyal conservatives (those who still belonged to the diocese). He hoped it might allow more understanding of the conservative position within the diocese and where they were hurting, as well as permit development of relationships with them. "I would be willing to listen. . . . I have a lot of time for those folks," he said.[384] Overall, Schuh was willing to create some space for these opportunities to take place, but cautioned synod that the space must be filled with constructive work by *both* sides to cultivate the relationship. "Gays are willing to [support a limited moratorium], but not for free — make the coming years productive!"[385] he urged.

After the vote, Ingham wrapped it up: "We must now put the same effort into re-building broken relationships that we put into ending the discrimination against some people in our church."[386] The primate, in his final remarks to synod, told New Westminster that it was no longer isolated by its decision to bless of same-sex unions. "There is a movement across the whole church that cannot be reversed. . . . Hats off to you!" he said.[387] Hutchison reminded delegates that sixteen dioceses in England have blessed over four hundred same-sex unions unofficially, calling them "episcopal exceptions." With his usual frankness, he said, "No one is ever disciplined. But when we do it, openly and publicly, [they] feel it is reprehensible. I feel it is a case of duplicity."[388] Then the primate again praised Ingham, noting the gentle, effective way he had conducted a holy synod and acknowledging one of the best displays of chairmanship he had ever seen. The primate also said, to much applause, "The same-sex issue has clearly not hijacked the Diocese of New Westminster's ministry, and it will not hijack my primacy either."[389] Hutchison was referring to the ministries in the diocese that provide shelter for a thousand people every night, cook eighty-five thousand meals a year, and distribute tons of food through its food banks, for example.

At the end of May 2005, the Anglican Church of Canada announced the team that would make the presentation at the Anglican Consultative Council in Nottingham, England, in June. Heading it up was the Very Reverend Peter Elliott, Dean of Christ Church Cathedral in Vancouver, an openly gay priest and prolocutor of General Synod. Integrity Canada had got their wish. Both the primate and Ingham expressed hope for the meeting, because the Anglican Consultative Council tends to be more open and curious than the primates and "has been less quick"[390] to make judgements on human sexuality.

That having been said, the signs remain clear that the differences in the Anglican Communion might be irreconcilable, unless cooler heads prevail at the international level. Ingham believes that the local divisions in New Westminster might have been healed but for the international campaign and other bishops meddling in his jurisdiction. But God may have some surprises in store.

"There seems to be no skill level among the primates"

What is really going on with the worldwide Anglican Church? How can this conflict be happening in a Church that prides itself on living united in diversity; a Church that shuns dogma, that breathes reason, and that has the *via media*? How can human sexuality be the cause of such chaos?

As Hugh McCullum observed in *Radical Compassion*: "On the surface, the problem is what to do with gay and lesbian members — bishops, priests, deacons, and laity." Deeper down, the crisis is pure politics, the desire of some ecclesiastical provinces and primates to establish a conservative, more protestant, world body that decrees what its members believe and enforces a uniformity of practice, rather like the Roman Catholic Church does.

So what we have going on is a power struggle — the traditional protestants in the Anglican Communion want to oust the progressive liberals and deliver the Church back into their own hands. They tried to achieve it over the ordination of women to the priesthood and failed; now they are trying again, using the issue of human sexuality, more particularly homosexuality. The present climate and timing are more suited to the success of their cause than before, and they anticipate winning.

The complexity of factors that impinge on this collision of historical forces in the Anglican Church is confusing and neither well reported nor explained in the popular media. The brouhaha, as Somerville calls it, over the blessing of same-sex unions is just the visible tip of the iceberg. Ingham observes that "there have been deep undercurrents of unease in the Anglican Communion for some time, and they are rising to the surface now."[391]

The historic polarity between the liberal-progressive and traditional-conservative wings of Anglicanism, which have held together in a state of tension since the Elizabethan Settlement, is breaking down. This collapse derives, in part, from a significant decline in the more catholic voice in the Anglican Communion since the Second World War. This decline has accelerated recently with the negative reaction to the ultra-conservative papacy of John Paul II and a marked growth in the protestant wing around the world. The causes of the increasing popularity of more protestant principles in Anglicanism include the resurgence of the fundamentalist Christian-right in the United States; Islam's growth, especially in Africa, in which the competition for souls demands a more protestant theology with respect to sexual ethics to succeed; and the decrease in the credibility of the Christian churches in North America and Europe following their growing irrelevance in a secular society.

The Anglican churches of the western world lean to the progressive, liberal side of the spectrum, and are far more focused on social justice than the churches in the Third World, which still operate in the missionary mode. The protestant traditionalists of the West, who want to reassert control, see a way to swing the balance over to their position by harnessing the emerging energies of the more protestant Anglicans in Africa and Asia. It is these traditional groups who are using the gay-lesbian issue to ramp up support in the developing countries. It is these groups who are using the decisions of New Hampshire and New Westminster to demonstrate how profane the West is becoming. It is these groups and the church in developing countries who maintain that homosexuality is an abomination and forbidden by Scripture. And it is these groups of the Christian right in the United States who are funding the Third World ecclesiastical provinces to assert their doctrines in the Anglican Communion.

These then are the strategies, not only to bolster the African and Asian protestants in the Anglican Communion, but also to squash the "broad church" moderates in the centre, who are now the only group left to stop the takeover. The militant protestant activities are likely to succeed, because the more conservative African and Asian bishops and primates vastly outnumber those from the West. Additionally, other international liberal members of the Anglican Communion seem unable or unwilling to assert any leadership. Ingham says, "There has to be an alternative to capitulation or defiance. There seems to be no skill level among the primates, for example, for finding a way through this."[392] If it cannot get North America expelled, the traditional movement is likely to separate from a Communion that has maintained its diversity and bonds of affection for over four centuries, leaving the liberal West in one church and the protestant and Third World Anglicans in another.

Traditionalists believe they can finally rid the Anglican world of progressive liberalism using the issue of homosexuality after they failed to do so with their opposition to the ordination of women. Why? The gay-lesbian community is a small and often despised minority that is more easily dismissed, whereas women comprised the majority of the congregations during the previous debate. Homosexuality is still a crime in some African nations, and many of their churches refuse to even discuss it, except for the Province of Southern Africa, Tutu's former archdiocese, and a couple of others. Archbishop Akinola of Nigeria leads both the desire and the movement to separate over the gay-lesbian issue, while demanding that he be allowed to deal with polygamy in his own way in his own cultural milieu (Lambeth 1988). He is on record as saying the "issue is not a temporary cessation of [blessings and ordinations of gays and lesbians] but a decision to renounce them and demonstrate a willing embrace of the same teaching on matters of sexual morality as is generally accepted throughout the Communion."[393] Akinola wants a "unity" in the Anglican Communion that is actually "uniformity" and a uniformity that excludes an entire group in society, to boot. He also wants to be a leader.

A quick look into Rwanda's ecclesiastical province alarms many Anglican observers as well. Rwanda took three of New Westminster's dissenting priests and their congregations into its fold, and recently ordained two more priests in North Vancouver. The previous Rwandan primate publicly supported the mass slaughter of Tutsis in 1994 and had to flee for his own safety after the massacre. Kolini, the current archbishop there, is an aggressive, conservative evangelical, who has consecrated several American bishops uncanonically to further the protestant cause. His activities are funded by American conservative Anglican and other right-wing organizations.

It is not good enough to be treated as a "pastoral exception"

Despite his earlier reluctance, the Canadian primate, Andrew Hutchison, did attend the crucial meeting of the Anglican Consultative Council in Nottingham, England, in June 2005, as an observer. Ingham, no longer the Canadian episcopal representative after his term expired in Hong Kong, stayed at home. Two Canadian teams went to England. One was the official delegation, comprising a bishop, a priest, and a layperson. These representatives of the Anglican Church of Canada no longer had a presence, a voice, or a vote in the proceedings, since the primates had asked both the American and Canadian Churches to withdraw to allow some breathing space in the Communion. The other group, headed by Dean Peter Elliott from Christ Church Cathedral in Vancouver, went solely to deliver the presentation that explained New Westminster's decision-making process for blessing same-sex unions. Another consequence of the withdrawal, of course, was a change in the balance of power by the removal of the six American and Canadian votes from the floor. At the opening of the Anglican Consultative Council, the world's representatives of seventy-seven million Anglicans heard the archbishop of Canterbury describe the state of the Church as catastrophic — hardly an inspiring remark for an already-tense gathering.

The religious affairs correspondent of the British newspaper the *Guardian*, described how the North Americans, in a merciless atmosphere, were "paraded like naughty school [students] before the . . . meeting."[394] Less-gloomy media wrote that the United States and Canada had managed to overcome the conservative call to expel them from the council altogether. The Canadian impression of the event was more positive.

Elliott, concluding the presentation for the Anglican Church of Canada, openly told the delegates that he was a gay priest living in a committed relationship. The story of his Christian journey was potent and he felt able to tell it "because of the courageous ministry of our church." He also said, "I believe that all of God's children are called into holiness of life. . . . [It is not] good enough to be treated as a 'pastoral exception' as if the presence of gay Christians is an embarrassment to the church."[395] Elliott informed the meeting that New Westminster had actually blessed only fourteen same-sex unions since 2003, when Ingham gave permission for the rite, six of which he himself had conducted in the cathedral, but that no new parishes will offer blessings until after General Synod of 2007. ECUSA affirmed its support for gay clergy and the blessing of same-sex unions, taking a similar, though less placatory, line to the Canadians.

"People were grateful for the candour and appreciated that we try to accept different viewpoints in the [Canadian church]," Elliott told the *Vancouver Sun* by telephone immediately afterwards.[396] He also wrote a letter to the cathedral parish when he returned from England, giving more detail. Elliott spoke of the respect with which the council listened to the presentation and how many delegates thanked him for his remarks and the delegation for its honesty. "It was a most refreshing and supportive time," he wrote.[397] Noting that the struggle is less about sexuality and more about power in the Anglican Communion, Elliott said, "Those of us who value an inclusive church will have to continue to articulate our theology."[398]

The loss of the six North American votes made the passage of resolutions less predictable. The next day, the primate of Nigeria, the loudest opponent of the ordination of homosexuals and the blessing of same-sex unions, put forward his expected resolution to ban the North American churches from participation in any international Anglican bodies until Lambeth 2008. As the council debated for several hours in a closed session, the most punitive demands in the motion were removed and the resolution morphed into one with few teeth, which carried with a tiny majority (in favour — 30, against —

28, and 4 abstentions).The Canadians and Americans have been
asked only to withdraw from meetings of the council until 2008
(there are none) and not to sit on the two standing committees (we
have no members).

Ingham, talking about the result the next day, said that he had
predicted the inherent risks if Canada and the United States agreed
to withdraw. The loss of the Canadian and American votes enabled
the African and Asian delegates to push more of their agenda at the
council. They did succeed with another vote that changed the face of
the Anglican Consultative Council forever — from now on the
world's thirty-eight primates (70 per cent of whom are conservative)
will join the council as voting members, thereby diluting the block of
lay delegates from half to one-third and easily overpowering the progressive vote from the western world. Next day, New Westminster's
executive archdeacon, the Venerable Ronald Harrison, commented,
"This is a retrograde step and it's mean-spirited."[399]

Ingham, in Vancouver, reflected on what was going on five thousand miles away. He talked about the Anglican Communion being like
the British Commonwealth — it is an "idea," and when members do
not want to meet, he thinks, they are saying that they want another
kind of communion. If a parallel communion is formed, Ingham is
convinced that the church-to-church long-term relationships will continue (for example, New Westminster's link to the Diocese of Taiwan
and grants being paid to and from churches around the world). He
feels the vote to ban the Anglican Church of Canada from the standing committees of the Anglican Consultative Council was symbolical-
ly significant, but carried no disadvantages for Canada for the next
three years.

The protestant conservatives at the international level have a Plan A
and a Plan B to deal with the progressive North American churches.
Plan A is underway, and is their attempt to get them expelled from the
Anglican Communion and take control. If that fails, and it likely will,
Plan B will involve the formation of a conservative version of the
Anglican Church, probably led by an African primate. Bates recently
revealed[400] that militant conservative Anglicans in Africa, Asia, and
North America have already developed a constitution for the "Anglican

Global Initiative," which is essentially a new and parallel Communion under the chairmanship of Akinola of Nigeria and/or Gomez of the West Indies. Although these organizers claim to respect Canterbury, no one knows how long this will last. Ingham said, "The existence of this constitution is scandalous. It suggests there is no willingness to engage in the conversations or the listening process called for by the primates at their Northern Ireland meeting" in February 2005.[401]

To further support Plan B's existence, following a meeting in mid-September 2005, the Anglican Church of Nigeria has removed all references to communion with Canterbury on its Web site and reaffirmed its ties only with ecclesiastical provinces that maintain that homosexuality is a sin. Primate Akinola of Nigeria told the primates in a letter that the Nigerian Church has "changed its constitution so that those who are bent to walk a different path may do so without us."[402] The split now looks almost certain. . .

Meanwhile, the Canadian Anglican Essentials 2005 conference in Toronto had been laying down plans to deal with Plan A or B, in the event of a division. One of the speakers at the event was the conservative bishop of Algoma, Ron Ferris, who had lost the election for the Diocese of New Westminster to Ingham in 1993. In a significant decision, Essentials established two new organizations — the Essentials Federation and the Anglican Network in Canada (ANC) — which individuals and parishes can choose to join. The federation is for members who, in conscience, are able to participate in their dioceses and the Anglican Church of Canada but hold a conservative theology. The ANC, in contrast, is for those who believe they are in impaired or broken communion with the Anglican Church of Canada and/or their diocesan bishop. This group intends to build an ecclesial body that can join either a changed Anglican Communion if the Canadian Church is expelled from it or the proposed Anglican Global Network if the conservatives form a parallel communion. Two priests from the Diocese of New Westminster were made "Convocation Deans" in the ANC — Reverend David Short, the rector of St. John's Shaughnessy, and the Reverend Trevor Walters, rector of St. Matthew's Abbotsford, both of whom Ingham still technically considers "in the fold."

On June 28, 2005, Canada became the third country in the world to legalize same-sex civil marriage, after the Netherlands and Belgium. Although the majority of provinces had already done so, the House of Commons voted on the issue and Bill C-38 carried, with 158 (52.6 per cent) in favour and 133 against. Several MPs voted against their party lines after polling their constituents and agonizing over their decisions. The majority saw the decision as one of equality rights, but those who opposed the measure did so mainly on religious grounds. The new bill continues to protect the rights of religious institutions that, as a matter of conscience, choose not to solemnize marriages for whatever reason, whether heterosexual or homosexual.

"This straitlaced intellectual has a spine of granite"

Ingham definitely reached celebrity status between 2000 and 2003. The media loved him. Ingham "on the cover" meant sales. In April 2000, the *Vancouver Sun* named Ingham the sixth most important religious leader in British Columbia's history, one whose world view had transformed spiritual communities and the wider society. In 2003, *Maclean's* magazine named him one of the top three Canadians to watch, and called his work on inclusivity the "Canadian social experiment number 2."[403] In August that same year, *BC Business* magazine featured him in their article "20 things to do before you die." His personal "thing" was to *Challenge the Status Quo*,[404] which, it could be said, he had already done. Douglas Todd, a widely respected and award-winning reporter of religious affairs, wrote a spread for the *Vancouver Sun* in February 2004 under the inch-high headline, "Tyrant. Dictator. Heretic. Totalitarian. Revisionist. Maverick. Renegade."[405] Some of his descriptions of Ingham bear repeating: "This straitlaced intellectual has a spine of granite. . . . Ingham is Anglicanism's most disliked heterosexual bishop." Todd quoted the bishop's response to all the upheavals and nastiness: "I look at them with a peaceful equanimity. This is how the Holy Spirit moves along. I knew we'd be in for a hard time, but I'm less concerned with short-term public opinion than the larger judgement of history."

I work for #2⟨X⟩3!

Ingham, the celebrity — a collage made up for fun for
an office T-shirt by the diocesan communications officer.
(Neale Adams)

Undeniably, Ingham has received a lot of exposure in the popular media over the last seven years, and not all of it has been about the blessing of same-sex unions. His moderately controversial books and speeches have also contributed to a pile of newspaper clippings in his office that is over twenty centimetres high.

Somerville, the gentle rebel, who guided the reform of ordained ministry and opened the priesthood to women, has been watching Ingham's episcopate with interest from his armchair. Since he started to comment publicly on the debate in 2003, he has contributed some interesting observations. In an interview in 2004, Somerville said,

"Michael is fighting not only [local] dissent but dissent that is being supported from a distance."[406] Somerville also supports the view that the militant conservatives, largely from outside the Diocese of New Westminster, are making local reconciliation impossible and are funded by the rich Christian-right parishes of the United States. He predicts that, in twenty years, people will say, "I wonder what *that* was all about."[407] Somerville greatly admires the current bishop and thinks he is handling the pressure and the issue superbly. "Michael is [allowing room for difference] extraordinarily well over the gay issue. He put it to synod three times before . . . he finally consented to it. Afterwards he sent round a letter saying 'I now authorize, in answer to the request from synod, the blessing of gay unions and anyone who doesn't want to do it is perfectly free. But those who do want to do it, please contact me and I will give you a letter of permission.' I thought that was a very good way to handle it."[408]

Archbishop Hambidge, ten years closer to the New Westminster episcopate than Somerville, declines to comment on the blessing of same-sex unions, but has said that he sees a division in the Anglican Communion as the inevitable consequence. Hambidge believes, "You can't act first and then say, 'Let's talk about it' afterwards to the international community."[409] A former chancellor (legal advisor) of the Diocese of New Westminster, Judge Spencer, said this: "Michael is a man of his age . . . and he let it come [to synod]. He gave it a rigorous test."[410]

Believing that the Diocese of New Westminster and its bishop are pariahs in North American Anglican circles is to be influenced by the notoriety that some media have created. The diocese's decision to champion the rights of gays and lesbians has resulted in positive outcomes and considerable encouraging attention from the secular world. Many abroad, in less progressive climates, see the diocese as a pioneer and a beacon of hope for their own churches. Many Christians believe, or have come to believe, that the diocese has acted properly on what is a Gospel issue. Many in New Westminster and elsewhere have seen gays and lesbians through a new lens and are beginning to act upon the discrimination against a whole section of society. Integrity has recently established three new chapters in Canada — Niagara, Montreal, and Halifax. Many parishes have rethought their positions and now provide a welcome and safe place for gays and lesbians to worship and minister alongside their straight brothers and sisters. Many highly qualified priests from around the world want to join the team in New Westminster. And, just in case readers conclude that the bishop hires only liberal progressives, Ingham has made forty conservative appointments to the diocese since 1998.

The negative consequences of the whole affair fell mostly on Ingham but, smiling broadly, he disagrees, "What better job is there than to be the bishop of New Westminster?"[411] His chances of becoming a metropolitan or even primate in the future have decreased since he championed equality rights for gays and lesbians but, publicly at least, he does not even ponder the potential loss. Ingham was the one at the receiving end of threats and hate mail, which climaxed after he gave his consent in 2002 and the first blessing took place in 2003, but many inside and outside the church still praise his courage and resolution. Ingham finds he is now also in great demand from industry and business to speak on leadership and managing change, an outcome he enjoys.

While the vigour of opposition to the blessing of same-sex unions has been similar to that which followed the ordination of women, the advent of e-mail increased the volume tenfold and made personal attacks easier. Ingham likens hate e-mail to electronic drive-by shootings, "I've felt targeted by people who have had no other desire than to hurt me."[412] But at least he never had to wear a bulletproof vest, unlike Bishop Robinson at his consecration. The Internet has also had a distorting effect on the discussions. It has drawn people into the debate from far away who do not understand North American culture or context, and it is so instantaneous that e-correspondents do not bother to reflect, they just react and click the send button.

For better or worse, I've been given a part to play

Ingham's tenure as bishop of New Westminster has been longer than he hoped and less focused on the priorities he established on assuming the mitre. He recently identified three phases of his episcopate, each about five years long. The first focused on restructuring and reorienting the diocese to the changing face of immigrant demographics and to alternative models of ministry. The second five years have been consumed with the sexuality issue. Ingham spent most of this time steering the diocese through a careful and responsible decision-making process and then interpreting it outside of Canada. The bishop hopes the third set of five years will be more peaceful and a time of consolidation of the initial plan.

Although Ingham predicted in 1993 he would be the bishop of the Diocese of New Westminster for only about ten years, he has served for nearly thirteen years. Now he considers it is inappropriate to move on: "it is not a good time to leave . . . the stakes are too high. For better or worse, I've been given a part to play in the Anglican Communion. I want to see it through a bit further."[413] Ingham wants to finish what he has been called to do on the sexuality issue. He judges that the controversial diocesan work on equality rights for gays and lesbians is largely completed, and the issue now resides in national and international Anglican bodies. Ingham looks forward to rebuilding the Anglican Church in the bottom left-hand corner of British Columbia — adding to and completing the changes that began in the first five years of his episcopate — and playing his part in interfaith work. But he does plan to do something else before retiring. Perhaps he will return to academe? Perhaps he will do more in the interfaith movement? Perhaps he will write more books? Many hope he will do all three.

Reflecting in 2005 over the second five years of his episcopate, Ingham said, "Episcopal life is very demanding, but these years have been extraordinarily demanding."[414] He believes that "Probably [my] greatest error was underestimating the power of pre-enlightenment religion to re-establish itself as an appealing alternative in today's world. I didn't think anybody would take it that seriously. . . . But I [did know] that, for people within that mindset, it held great magnetic power."[415]

Agents for change and those who disturb complacency are often pilloried. In the religious world today, movers and shakers are those who explore theology and take up new and unsettling positions. They are all individuals who push the envelope. Some like Richard Holloway and Jack Spong are feisty and perhaps seek to be contrary. The bishop of New Westminster is more like Somerville in leading change — he consistently projects a non-anxious, non-reactive presence as he moves forward. However, in his pursuit of social justice, Ingham is also as unyielding as a rock, as steadfast as a mountain, and has the patience of Job. Although he did not seek controversy, he accepted the equality-rights issue that landed on his lap and unhesitatingly took it on as his own. For Ingham, the path he treads is similar to that of all reformers — he faces the challenge of polarized ecclesiastical and world opinion and the resulting opposition. Most of all, he is just as "called" as his predecessors. The secular world would label it "driven."

Opponents brand Ingham a heretic, an apostate, and the bishop who risked the unity of the Anglican Communion. He has attracted wounding personal attacks because, once the conflict reached a certain level, discrediting him was the only way his opponents had left to try to stop him. Some gays and lesbians, though grateful, think Ingham must surely be crazy, because he has probably sacrificed his career for a "bunch of queers." Ingham is loved or hated, admired or despised, praised or vilified. Even those who dislike what he has done admit that he has stirred and shaken — not only the Anglican Church, but also the world.

Full face in public, Ingham is cordial in a conflict, respecting of differing opinions, patient, and careful not to overuse his episcopal power but willing to exert it when he has to. He is genuinely inclusive, intensely spiritual, and much respected by those who know him. He has shown his multi-faceted character in many ways while bishop — servant, yet leader; progressive, yet traditional; ordinary, yet extraordinary. But in private, Ingham confesses to bleak moments and mixed emotions. He has experienced much exasperation over the faint-hearted decisions of other Anglican bodies inside and outside of Canada, and has borne the pain of being perceived as the "heavy" in the diocese. In handling the "sex" issue, he has lived with steady persecution from some clergy and media, as well as the disappointment of having to shelve other consuming interests in his life. But, however much Ingham is frustrated, nothing is likely to stop him leading the way to equality rights for all.

There is also no doubt that Ingham holds the deep conviction that the Holy Spirit is behind the moves that the Diocese of New

Westminster has made to eliminate discrimination against homosexuals in the Anglican Church. Some call him a prophet — in the sense that he is discerning what God wants society to do. But, undeniably, Ingham will leave a public legacy in the Anglican Church. History will be the judge as to whether his legacy changed the Church and the world for the better, but everyone knows that Ingham willingly pushed the envelope.

Ingham after a confirmation service at Christ Church Cathedral, June 2004.
(Julie H. Ferguson)

APPENDIX 1

Excerpts from the letter of censure from Hills to Cridge, dated December 14, 1872, cited in the trial documents

PSA, reel 3, 28

Bishop's Close, Victoria, Dec. 14th, 1872

Reverend Sir:

Having offered you, with no good result, several opportunities of expressing regret at your conduct on the 5th of Dec., a regret which should be expressed to your Bishop, who was unhappily present, an eye and ear witness of the sad scene, to your brother minister, whom you openly insulted in the House of God, and to the congregation whom you disturbed and distressed, it now remains for me to discharge a most painful duty, the more painful considering your position as Dean of the Cathedral, and as senior clergyman of the Diocese, from whom might be expected at least an example of self control, propriety and order. . . .

   You have committed the grave offence which is described both in the Ecclesiastical Law and in the Statute Law of the Empire by the term of *brawling,* an act of disturbance of divine worship, punishable in a layman by fine or imprisonment, in a clergyman by suspension.

Moreover you violated the 53rd canon of the Church of England, which *forbids public opposition* between clergymen. . . .

No provocation is allowed to justify a violation of these laws. . . .

If, as was the case, you disapproved of the view [Reece] took of a particular subject you have abundant opportunities of teaching your congregation what you consider to be right, your attack upon him in the House of God was the more unjustifiable, since he had occupied the pulpit by your own suggestion, . . . is a member of the Cathedral body.

Considering all these circumstances, considering the public scandal you have caused, the outrages upon order and propriety in divine worship, and violations of the laws expressly framed to prevent such unhappy exhibitions, I should probably be justified in taking a course much more severe; considering however, also, your long and faithful service in the Church, that you were probably unaware of the laws which prohibit such actions, and that this is the first grave offence of any kind in the Diocese which I have been called upon to notice, I take the most lenient course I can adopt, and inflict upon you only a grave censure.

As your Bishop, then, I censure you for your conduct on Thursday, the 5th day of December, 1872, and I admonish you to be more careful in the future.

Witness my hand this 14th day of December, 1872,

        G. COLUMBIA

APPENDIX 2

Lambeth Conference 1988 Resolution
Sexual Orientation

153   Despite its basic assertions about marriage and family, there is much confusion in the area of the Church's doctrine and teaching about sexuality. *Transforming Families and Communities* witnesses to this on the basis of extensive Communion-wide consultations. Thus, on the vexed question of sexuality, it reports:

> The question of sexual orientation is a complex one which the Church is still grappling with: many Provinces have traditionally maintained that homosexuality is a sin whilst others are responding differently to the issue. As sexuality is an aspect of life which goes to the very heart of human identity and society it is a pastorally sensitive issue which requires further study and reflection by Church leadership.

154   We recognize that this issue remains unresolved, and we welcome the fact that study is continuing. We believe that the Church should therefore give active encouragement to biological, genetic, and psychological research, and consider these scientific studies as they contribute to our understanding of the subject in the light of Scripture.

155   Further study is also needed of the socio-cultural factors which contribute to the differing attitudes towards homosexuality, mentioned above, in the various Provinces of our Church. We continue to **encourage dialogue with, and pastoral concern for, persons of homosexual orientation** within the Family of Christ. (Resolution 64.)

Appendix 3

Final Resolution A134 — Blessing of Same-Sex Unions

**General Synod of the Anglican Church of Canada
June 2004**

Be it resolved that this General Synod:

Affirm that, even in the face of deeply held convictions about whether the blessing of committed same sex unions is contrary to the doctrine and teaching of the Anglican Church of Canada, we recognize that through our baptism we are members one of another in Christ Jesus, and we commit ourselves to strive for that communion into which Christ continually calls us;

Affirm the crucial value of continued respectful dialogue and study of biblical, theological, liturgical, pastoral, scientific, psychological and social aspects of human sexuality; and call upon all bishops, clergy and lay leaders to be instrumental in seeing that dialogue and study continue, intentionally involving gay and lesbian persons;

Affirm the principle of respect for the way in which the dialogue and study may be taking place, or might take place, in indigenous and various other communities within our church in a manner consistent with their cultures and traditions;

Affirm that the Anglican Church is a church for all the baptized and is committed to taking such actions as are necessary to maintain and serve our fellowship and unity in Christ, <u>and</u> request the House of Bishops to continue its work on the provision of adequate episcopal oversight and pastoral care for all, regardless of the perspective from which they view the blessing of committed same sex relationships; and

Affirm the integrity and sanctity of committed adult same sex relationships.

CARRIED

MOTION TO DEFER

That Resolution A134 be amended by:

1) Deferring consideration of section 2, *which reads "That this General Synod affirm the authority and jurisdiction of any diocesan synod, with the concurrence of its bishop, to authorize the blessing of committed same sex unions"* until the meeting of General Synod in 2007; and during the period of deferral:

2) Request that the Primate ask the Primate's Theological Commission to review, consider and report to the Council of General Synod, by its spring 2006 meeting, whether the blessing of committed same sex unions is a matter of doctrine;

3) That on receipt of such a report, the Council of General Synod distribute it to each province, diocese and the House of Bishops for consideration.

CARRIED

APPENDIX 4

The 1998 Lambeth Conference
Resolution 1.10 On Human Sexuality

This Conference:

(a) commends to the Church the subsection report on human sexuality;

(b) in view of the teaching of Scripture, upholds faithfulness in marriage between a man and a woman in lifelong union, and believes that abstinence is right for those who are not called to marriage;

(c) recognises that there are among us persons who experience themselves as having a homosexual orientation. Many of these are members of the Church and are seeking the pastoral care, moral direction of the Church, and God's transforming power for the living of their lives and the ordering of relationships. We commit ourselves to listen to the experience of homosexual persons and we wish to assure them that they are loved by God and that all baptised, believing and faithful persons, regardless of sexual orientation, are full members of the Body of Christ;

(d) while *rejecting homosexual practice as incompatible with Scripture* [my italics], calls on all our people to minister pastorally and sensitively to all irrespective of sexual orientation and to condemn irrational fear of homosexuals, violence within marriage and any trivialisation and commercialisation of sex;

(e) cannot advise the legitimising or blessing of same sex unions nor ordaining those involved in same gender unions;

(f) requests the Primates and the ACC to establish a means of monitoring the work done on the subject of human sexuality in the Communion and to share statements and resources among us;

(g) notes the significance of the Kuala Lumpur Statement on Human Sexuality and the concerns expressed in resolutions IV.26, V.1, V.10, V.23 and V.35 on the authority of Scripture in matters of marriage and sexuality and asks the Primates and the ACC to include them in their monitoring process.

INTERVIEWS BY AUTHOR

Mr. Neale Adams: June 23, 2005
Communications Officer,
Diocese of New Westminster

The Very Reverend Peter Elliott: July 10, 2005
Rector of Christ Church Cathedral and   (telephone)
Dean of the Diocese of New Westminster

The Most Reverend Douglas Hambidge: May 11, 2004
Retired   February 22, 2005
     March 3, 2005
     March 31, 2005
     August 29, 2005

The Venerable Ronald Harrison: June 23, 2005
Executive Archdeacon
Diocese of New Westminster

The Most Reverend Andrew Hutchison: May 13, 2005
Primate of Anglican Church of Canada

The Right Reverend Michael Ingham: December 9, 2003
Bishop of New Westminster   January 13, 2004
     November 18, 2004
     December 9, 2004

	January 12, 2005
	January 27, 2005
	March 9, 2005
	March 23, 2005
	April 7, 2005
	April 23, 2005
	June 23, 2005

Mr. Howarth Penny:
Cambridge, England
October 23, 2004

The Most Reverend T. David Somerville:
Retired
May 17, 2004
September 2, 2004
October 29, 2004
February 3, 2005
  (telephone)
May 20, 2005
  (telephone)
June 13, 2005
  (telephone)
September 1, 2005

Mr. Stephen Schuh:
President of Integrity, Vancouver
May 15, 2004
May 13, 2005
June 9, 2005
  (telephone)

Mr. Justice John Spencer:
Former Chancellor
Diocese of New Westminster
August 10, 2004

Mr. Garth Walker:
Archivist Emeritus
Provincial Synod Archives
July 27, 2004

Mr. Michael Wellwood:
Business Administrator
Diocese of New Westminster
July 5, 2005
  (telephone)

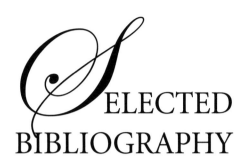

SELECTED BIBLIOGRAPHY

PSA   Archives of the Anglican Provincial Synod of British Columbia and Yukon

VST   Vancouver School of Theology

BOOKS

Bagshaw, Roberta L. *No Better Land: The 1860 Diaries of the Anglican Colonial Bishop, George Hills.* Victoria: Sono Nis Press, 1996.

Bates, Stephen. *A Church at War: Anglicans and Homosexuality.* London: I.B.Tauris & Co. Ltd., 2004.

Bawer, Bruce. *Stealing Jesus: How Fundamentalism Betrays Christianity.* New York: Crown Publishers Inc., 1997.

Berton, Pierre. *The Comfortable Pew: A Critical Look at the Church in the New Age.* Toronto: McClelland & Stewart Ltd., 1965.

Carrington, Philip. *The Anglican Church in Canada.* Toronto: Collins, 1963.

Collison, William H. edited by Charles Lilliard. *In the Wake of the War Canoe,* Victoria: Sono Nis Press, 1981. (Originally published by Musson Book Company Ltd. of Toronto as a memoir c.1915.)

Countryman, L. William. *Dirt, Greed, and Sex: Sexual Ethics in the New Testament and Their Implications for Today*. Philadelphia: Fortress Press, 1988.

Craven, Margaret. *I Heard the Owl Call My Name*. New York: Buccaneer Books, Inc., 1973.

Donnelly, Dody H. *Radical Love: An Approach to Sexual Spirituality*. Minneapolis: Winston Press Inc., 1984.

Dunn, Greig, and Chris Ambidge, eds. *Living Together in the Church: Including Our Differences*. Toronto: ABC Publishing, 2004.

Duthie, Rev. D. Wallace, ed. *A Bishop in the Rough*. London: Smith, Elder and Co., 1909.

Ferguson, Barry, ed. *The Anglican Church and the World of Western Canada, 1820-1970*. Regina: University of Regina, 1991.

Gibson, Paul. *Discerning the Word: The Bible and Homosexuality in Anglican Debate*. Toronto: The Anglican Book Centre, 2000.

Grove, Lyndon. *Pacific Pilgrims*. Vancouver: Fforbez Publications Ltd., 1979.

Hadley, Michael L. *God's Little Ships*. Madeira Park, B.C.: Harbour Publishing, 1995.

Hamilton, Catherine Sider, ed. *The Homosexuality Debate: Faith Seeking Understanding*. Toronto: The Anglican Book Centre, 2003.

Ingham, Michael. *Rites for a New Age: Understanding the Book of Alternative Services*. Toronto: Anglican Book Centre, 1986; 2nd ed., 1990.

_____. *Mansions of the Spirit: The Gospel in a Multi-Faith World*. Toronto: Anglican Book Centre, 1997.

SELECTED BIBLIOGRAPHY

Kimball, Charles. *When Religion Becomes Evil*. San Francisco: HarperSanFrancisco, 2002.

Knowles, Norman. *Stepping Stones: A Short History of Christianity in Canada*. Kelowna: Education for Ministry — Canada, 2001.

McCullum, Hugh. *Radical Compassion: The Life and Times of Archbishop Ted Scott, Tenth Primate of the Anglican Church of Canada (1971-1986)*. Toronto: Anglican Book Centre, 2004.

McCullum, Hugh, and Karmel T. McCullum. *Caledonia 100 Years Ahead*. Toronto: The Anglican Book Centre, 1979.

Murray, Peter. *The Devil and Mr. Duncan*. Victoria: Sono Nis Press, 1985.

Nelson, James B. *Embodiment: An Approach to Sexuality and Christian Theology*. Minneapolis: Augsburg Publishing House, 1978.

Parvey, Constance F. *Ordination of Women in Ecumenical Perspective*. Switzerland: World Council of Churches, 1980.

Patterson, Rosemary I. *Return of the Canoe Societies*. New York: Xlibris Corporation, 1999.

Peake, Frank A. *The Anglican Church in British Columbia*. Vancouver: Mitchell Press, 1959.

Pritchard, Allan, ed. *Vancouver Island Letters of Edmund Hope Verney, 1862-65*. Vancouver: UBC Press, 1996.

Somerville, Frances. *David: Bishop and Friend*. Vancouver: Best Business Solutions, 1991.

Vernon, C.W. *The Old Church in the New Dominion*. Toronto: Anglican Church in Canada, 1929.

Weir, Joan. *Catalysts and Watchdogs: B.C.'s Men of God, 1836-1887*. Victoria: Sono Nis Press, 1995.

Williams, David R. *Matthew Baillie Begbie,* Toronto: Fitzhenry and Whiteside, 2004.

SELECTED REPORTS, PAPERS, SERMONS, etc.
(Arranged chronologically)

The Life and Times of the Late Bishop Hills, by H. J. K. Skipton, unpublished manuscript, 1911, PSA 34.

"Edward Cridge and George Hills: Doctrinal Conflict, 1872-1874," by Susan Dickinson, unpublished thesis of 1964, VST Library.

Jack, 1955-81, scrapbook belonging to Mrs. Eleanor Bishop.

The Ordination of Women to the Priesthood: A Second Report by the House of Bishops for the General Synod of the Church of England. London: General Synod of the Church of England, 1988.

"Saturday Morning Address," Bishop Michael Ingham, Synod 2004, Diocese of New Westminster, May 14-15, 2004.

"Easter Sermon," Bishop Michael Ingham, March 27, 2005.

VIDEO

Anglican Diocese of New Westminster, *Somerville: Leader in a Time of Change.* 2001.

NOTES

ABBREVIATIONS

BCA   British Columbia Archives
DNW   Archives of the Anglican Diocese of New Westminster
PSA   Archives of the Anglican Provincial Synod of British Columbia and Yukon
VST   Vancouver School of Theology

PART ONE: GEORGE HILLS

1   Weir, Joan, *Catalysts and Watchdogs: B.C.'s Men of God, 1836-1887,* Victoria: Sono Nis Press, 1995.

2   Collison, William H., ed. Charles Lillard, *In the Wake of the War Canoe,* Victoria: Sono Nis Press, 1981, 8.

3   Cockburn, G.H., *Bishop Hills: Founder of the Church in British Columbia*, unpublished, PSA 59/11.

4   Meilleur, Helen, *A Pour of Rain: Stories from a West Coast Fort*, Victoria: Sono Nis Press, 1980.

5   Bagshaw, Roberta L., *No Better Land: The 1860 Diaries of the Anglican Bishop George Hills,* Victoria: Sono Nis Press, 1996, 50-51.

6   Peake, Frank, *The Anglican Church in British Columbia,* Vancouver: Mitchell Press, 1959, 29.

7   PSA Reel 4, SPG FP 1858-1867, letter to SPG, May 8, 1860.

8   Ibid., 191.

9   Ibid., 192.

10   Bagshaw, *No Better Land*, 51.

11   Ibid., 53.

12   Ibid., 72.

13   Duthie, Rev. D. Wallace, ed., *A Bishop in the Rough,* London: Smith, Elder and Co., 1909, 46.

14   Bagshaw, *No Better Land*, 110.

15   Ibid., 61.

16   Ibid., 83.

17   Ibid., 84.

18   Ibid., 90.

19   Ibid.

20   Ibid., 97.

21   Ibid., 97.

22   Ibid., 98.

23   PSA Reel 4, SPG FP 1858-1867, letter to SPG dated May 8, 1860, 197.

24   *The Sixteenth Annual Report on the Missions of the Church of England in British Columbia*, PSA, Reel 15, 108.

25   Bagshaw, *No Better Land*, 247.

26   Weir, *Catalysts and Watchdogs*, 101.

27   Ibid, 100.

28   Ibid, 101.

29   *Columbia Mission Report, 1860*, PSA Reel 17, 86.

30   PSA 59/11.

31   Ibid.

32   *Hills Journals*, PSA, B8, P215, code 352. 1862.

33   Ibid.

34   http://www.tseshaht.com/culture/timeline.htm.

35   Sillitoe, Violet E., *Pioneer Days in British Columbia: Reminiscences,* undated, PSA 59.

36   Ibid.

37   *Columbia Mission Report, 1872,* cited in Susan Dickinson's unpublished thesis of 1964, "Edward Cridge and George Hills: Doctrinal Conflict, 1872-1874," 1, VST Library.

38   BCA, MS-0320.

39   *Hills Journals*, PSA, B8, P215, code 352, 1873, 20.

40   Extract from letter from H. P. P. Crease to Cridge, December 18, 1872, cited in Susan Dickinson's unpublished thesis of 1964, "Edward Cridge and George Hills," 1.

41   *Hills Journals*, PSA, B8, P215, code 352, 1873, 20.

42   PSA, reel 3, Synodal Notes and Memo Book.

43   *Hills Journals*, PSA, B8, P215, code 352, 1873, 35.

44   Skipton, H. P. K. *The Life and Times of the Late Bishop Hills,* unpublished manuscript, PSA 34, chapter IX, 7.

45   PSA, reel 4, letter from Cridge to Hills, August 18, 1873, 30.

46   Fawcett, Edgar, "Reminiscences of Bishop Cridge," BCA, ADD MSS, 1055, 8.

47   *Hills Journals*, PSA, B8, P215, code 352, 1874, 1.

48   Dickinson, "Edward Cridge and George Hills," 84.

49   *Hills' Journals,* PSA, B8, P215, code 352, 1874, 20.

50   Paradice, Russ (History 350 student, Malaspina College, Nanaimo, B.C.), "Edward Cridge, 1817-1913," written in 1997, now published online at www.mala.bc.ca/homeroom/content/topics/people/cridge1.htm.

51   *Columbia Mission Report*, 1861, PSA 17, 29.

52   *Trial of the Very Reverend Edward Cridge,* cited in Dickinson, "Edward Cridge and George Hills," 99.

53   *British Colonist,* September 11, 1874, cited in Dickinson, "Edward Cridge and George Hills," 99.

54   Ibid., 108.

55   *Daily Standard,* September 18, 1874.

56   Skipton, *The Life and Times of the Late Bishop Hills.*

57   Ibid.

58   *Hills' Journals,* PSA , B8, P215, code 352, 1874, 31.

59   *British Colonist,* September 11, 1874, cited in Dickinson, "Edward Cridge and George Hills," 110.

60   *Hills' Journals,* PSA , B8, P215, code 352, 1874, 31.

61   BCA, ADD MSS 520, vol. 1/5.

62   *Daily Standard,* September 28, 1874, cited in Dickinson, "Edward Cridge and George Hills," 115.

63   Dickinson, "Edward Cridge and George Hills," 122.

64   Ibid., 123.

65   Letter from Begbie to Cridge, November 30, 1874, BCA, ADD MSS 320, Vol; 1, file 5 and 18.

66   Columbia Mission Society, *11th-20th Annual Reports*, 1869-1878, 22.

67   Williams, David R., *The Man for a New Country: Sir Matthew Baillie Begbie*, Victoria, B.C.: Gray's Publishing Ltd., 1977, 247.

68   *Hills' Journals*, PSA , B8, P215, code 352, 1874, 34.

69   Ibid., 35.

70   Ibid., 36.

71   Ibid., 36.

72   Columbia Mission Society, *11th-20th Annual Reports*, 1869-1878, 20, PSA.

73   Skipton, *The Life and Times of the Late Bishop Hills*, PSA 34.

74   Victoria *Daily Times*, March 19, 1888.

75   Cockburn, G. H. *Bishop Hills: Founder of the Church in British Columbia,* unpublished MS, PSA59/11.

76   Ibid.

77   Skipton, *The Life and Times of the Late Bishop Hills,* PSA 34.

78   Ibid.

79   Ibid.

PART TWO: T. DAVID SOMERVILLE

80   *Vancouver Sun*, June 8, 1966.

81   "Meet the New Bishop — A Sort of Quiet Radical," *Vancouver Sun*, August 21, 1971.

82   Audio tape of Lyndon Grove's interview with Archbishop T.D. Somerville, May 26, 1990, PSA 992-29P.

83   Author's interview with Somerville, September 2, 2004.

84   Author's interview with Ingham, January 27, 2005.

85   Author's interview with Somerville, May 17, 2004.

86   Ibid.

87   Grove, L. *Pacific Pilgrims*, Vancouver: Fforbez Publications Ltd., 1979, 151.

88   Anglican Diocese of New Westminster, "Somerville: Leader in a Time of Change." 2001 [Video.]

89   Ibid.

90   Audio tape of Lyndon Grove's interview with Archbishop T.D. Somerville, May 26, 1990 1991. PSA 992- 29P.

91   Ibid.

92   Grove, L. *Pacific Pilgrims*, 151.

93   Author's interview with Somerville, May 17, 2004.

94   Ibid.

95   Author's interview with Somerville, October 29, 2004.

96   Ibid.

97   Author's interview with Somerville, September 2, 2004.

98   Ibid.

99   Berton, Pierre, *The Comfortable Pew*, Toronto: McClelland and Stewart Ltd., 1965, 29.

100   Ibid.

101   McCullum, Hugh, *Radical Compassion: The Life and Times of Archbishop Ted Scott,* Toronto: ABC Publishing, 2004, 162.

102   Ibid.

103   Author's interview with Somerville, September 2, 2004.

104   Ibid.

105   "Meet the New Bishop — A Sort of Quiet Radical," *Vancouver Sun*, August 21, 1971.

106   Anglican Diocese of New Westminster, "Somerville: Leader in a Time of Change," 2001 [Video.]

107 Ibid.
108 Author's interview with Somerville, May 17, 2004.
109 Author's interview with Somerville, September 2, 2004.
110 Author's interview with Somerville, May 17, 2004.
111 Ibid.
112 Anglican Diocese of New Westminster, "Somerville — Leader in a Time of Change," 2001 [Video.]
113 Author's interview with Somerville, May 17, 2004.
114 Ibid.
115 Ibid.
116 Ingham, Michael, *Rites for a New Age: Understanding the Book of Alternative Services,* Toronto: Anglican Book Centre, 1986.
117 Author's interview with Somerville, May 17, 2004.
118 Audio tape of Lyndon Grove's interview with Archbishop T.D. Somerville, May 26, 1990 1991. PSA 992- 29P.
119 Ibid.
120 Pastoral letter from Bishop Somerville, December 10, 1972, PSA 317.
121 Audio tape of Lyndon Grove's interview with Archbishop T.D. Somerville, May 26, 1990 1991. PSA 992-29P.
122 Ibid.
123 Fletcher-Marsh, Wendy, *Beyond the Walled Garden: Anglican Women and the Priesthood*, Dundas, Ont.: Artemis Enterprises, 1995.
124 McCullum, *Radical Compassion*, 162.
125 "Commission on Women," *General Synod Journal, 1969*, 262-265, PSA.
126 Bays, Patricia, ed., *Partners in the Dance: Stories of Canadian Women in Ministry*, Toronto: Anglican Book Centre, 1993, 40.
127 Fletcher-Marsh, *Beyond the Walled Garden*.
128 *General Synod Journal, 1971-73*, PSA.
129 McCullum, *Radical Compassion*, 271.
130 *General Synod Journal, 1975*, M 66.
131 Fletcher-Marsh, *Beyond the Walled Garden*.
132 *General Synod Journal, 1975*, 73-75.
133 Fletcher-Marsh, *Beyond the Walled Garden*, 241.
134 Audio tape of Lyndon Grove's interview with Archbishop T.D. Somerville, May 26, 1990 1991. PSA 992-29P.
135 Fletcher-Marsh, *Beyond the Walled Garden*, 106.
136 Author's interview with Somerville, May 17, 2004.
137 Ibid.
138 "More Women Stepping into Protestant Pulpits" *Ottawa Citizen*, August 7, 2004.
139 Anglican Diocese of New Westminster, "Somerville: Leader in A Time of Change." 2001 [Video.]
140 Ibid.
141 Audio tape of Lyndon Grove's interview with Archbishop T.D. Somerville, May 26, 1990 1991. PSA 992- 29P.
142 Ibid.
143 Somerville, Frances. *David: Bishop and Friend*, Vancouver: Best Business Solutions, 1991.
144 Author's interview with Ingham, January 27, 2005.
145 Author's interview with Somerville, May 17, 2004.
146 Anglican Diocese of New Westminster, "Somerville — Leader in A Time of Change." 2001 [Video.]
147 Author's interview with Ingham, January 27, 2005.
148 Ibid.
149 Ibid.
150 Ibid.

PART THREE: DOUGLAS W. HAMBIDGE

151   Author's interview with Hambidge, February 23, 2005.
152   Ibid.
153   Ibid.
154   Ibid.
155   Ibid.
156   Ibid.
157   Ibid.
158   Ibid.
159   Ibid.
160   Ibid.
161   Ibid.
162   Ibid.
163   Author's interview with Hambidge, May 11, 2004.
164   Ibid.
165   Author's interview with Hambidge, February 23, 2005.
166   Ibid.
167   Ibid.
168   Ibid.
169   Ibid.
170   Ibid.
171   Author's interview with Hambidge, March 3, 2005.
172   Author's interview with Hambidge, March 31, 2005.
173   Author's interview with Hambidge, March 3, 2005.
174   Ibid.
175   Ibid.
176   Ibid.
177   McCullum, Hugh, *Radical Compassion: The Life and Times of Archbishop Ted Scott*, Toronto: ABC Publishing, 2004, 243.
178   Quoted by Roberta Bagshaw in an email to the author, July 14, 2005.
179   Chief J. Gosnell's speech to the B.C. Legislature, February 12, 1998.
180   Hambidge, Archbishop Douglas. "Justice for Canadian Aboriginal Peoples," for St. Lawrence's Anglican Church, Coquitlam, B.C., November 17, 1990, [audio tape], in Hambidge's possession.
181   Author's interview with Hambidge, March 31, 2005.
182   Ibid.
183   Ibid.
184   *Citizens Plus: The Nisga'a People of the Naas River in North Western B.C.*, Nisga'a Tribal Council, undated, 13.
185   Ibid.
186   Author's interview with Hambidge, March 31, 2005.
187   Ibid.
188   Ibid.
189   Author's interview with Hambidge, May 11, 2004.
190   Author's interview with Hambidge, March 31, 2005.
191   McCullum, Hugh, and Karmel T. McCullum, *Caledonia 100 Years Ahead*, Toronto: ABC Publishing, 1979.
192   Author's interview with Hambidge, March 3, 2005.
193   Ibid.
194   Ibid.
195   "Hambidge Calls on Church to 'Change Face of Society,'" *Topic*, January 1981, 1.
196   Author's interview with Hambidge, March 3, 2005.
197   Ibid.
198   Ibid.
199   Ibid.

200	Archbishop's Charge to the Synod of Diocese of New Westminster, 1985, PSA 789, 8/4.
201	Bagshaw, Roberta L., "One Sows, Another Reaps: The Diocese of New Westminster and Native Peoples, 1879-1997," the Diocese of New Westminster, 1998.
202	Gosnell, Joseph, Speech to the Canadian Club, Toronto, May 15, 2000, http://www.kermode.net/nisgaa/speeches/speeches.gosnell2.html.
203	Author's interview with Hambidge, March 31, 2005.
204	Hambidge, Archbishop Douglas, Charge to the Synod of New Westminster, 1991, Hambidge's audio tape.
205	Author's interview with Hambidge, May 11, 2004.
206	E-mail, Hambidge to author, June 28, 2005.
207	Ibid.
208	Author's interview with Hambidge, March 31, 2005.
209	Quoted in McCullum and McCullum. *Caledonia 100 Years Ahead*.

PART FOUR: MICHAEL C. INGHAM

210	Interview with Ingham, January 1994, DNWA, box "Videos Ingham."
211	Author's interview with Ingham, November 18, 2004.
212	Ibid.
213	Ibid.
214	Ibid.
215	Ibid.
216	Ibid.
217	Ibid.
218	Author's interview with Ingham, March 9, 2005.
219	Author's interview with Ingham, December 9, 2004.
220	Ibid.
221	Ibid.
222	Ibid.
223	Ibid.
224	Ibid.
225	Ibid.
226	Author's interview with Ingham, January 13, 2005.
227	Ibid.
228	Ibid.
229	Ibid.
230	Ibid.
231	Ibid.
232	Ibid.
233	Ibid.
234	Ibid.
235	Ibid.
236	Ibid.
237	Ibid.
238	Author's interview with Ingham, December 9, 2004.
239	Author's interview with Ingham, January 13, 2005.
240	Ibid.
241	Ibid.
242	Author's interview with Ingham, March 9, 2005.
243	The Diocesan Profile, Diocese of New Westminster, 1993, PSA, Biography Collection 12-I.
244	Ibid.
245	Ingham's response to the Diocesan Profile of 1993, 3.
246	Ibid.

247   Ibid, 5.

248   Ibid, 5.

249   Ibid, 7.

250   Author's interview with Ingham, April 7, 2005.

251   Ingham's response to the Diocesan Profile of 1993, 8.

252   Author's interview with Ingham, April 7, 2005.

253   Ibid.

254   Ibid.

255   Ibid.

256   Ibid.

257   "The Very Rev. Michael Ingham Elected Bishop," *Topic*, October, 1993.

258   Quoted in "New Anglican Bishop Told Job Won't Be Easy," *Vancouver Sun*, January 10, 1994.

259   Author's interview with Ingham, June 23, 2005.

260   Author's interview with Ingham, January 27, 2005.

261   Author's interview with Ingham, March 9, 2005.

262   Ibid.

263   Author's interview with Ingham, January 27, 2005.

264   Todd, Douglas, "The Bishop at Home," *Western Living*, May 1995, 22.

265   Ingham, Michael, *Mansions of the Spirit: The Gospel in a Multi-Faith World*, Toronto: Anglican Book Centre, 1997, 12.

266   "New Book on Multi-faith Dialogue Sparks Debate," *Topic*, November 1997, 1-2.

267   Ingham, *Mansions of the Spirit*, 140.

268   Ibid, back cover.

269   "Vancouver Bishop's Book Ignites an Anglican Controversy," *Vancouver Sun*, October 7, 1997.

270   "Open-plan Theology," *British Columbia Report*, October 20, 1997, 34.

271   Author's interview with Ingham, January 27, 2005.

272   *Anglican Journal*, December 1999.

273   Cohen, Martin S., "Bishop Speaks of Living with Disparate Faiths," *Vancouver Sun*, August 29, 1998, D5.

274   Ingham, Michael. "And the Walls Come Tumbling Down," *Globe and Mail*, December 1, 1999.

275   Author's interview with Ingham, April 20, 2005.

276   Ibid.

277   Author's interview with Somerville, October 29, 2004.

278   Author's interview with Ingham, April 20, 2005.

279   "Spiritual Leaders Seek to Heal Divisions," *Vancouver Sun*, February 19, 2000, B24.

280   "Diocese May Be Involved in Vancouver Multifaith Plan," *Topic*, November 2004, and the Web site of the Diocese of New Westminster at www.vancouver.anglican.ca/Portal/Default.aspx? tabid=1&mode=Story&StoryId=59.

281   Author's interview with Ingham, April 20, 2005.

282   Author's interview with Ingham, March 23, 2005.

283   Ibid.

284   Quoted in "The Biological Basis of Homosexuality," December 1997, available at www.unix.oit.umass.edu/~kripston/homosexuality/conclusions.html, December 1997.

285   Cited in The Rt. Rev. Richard Harries's paper, "Human Sexuality," Anglican Consultative Council, 1996, PSA Biographical Collection, 12, I.

286   Cited in Anglican Church of Canada press release, "Human Sexuality: A Statement by the Anglican Bishops of Canada — 1997."

287   Ibid.

288   Author's interview with Ingham, March 9, 2005.

289   Ingham, Michael, "Unity, Diversity and Change," January 9, 1994, private papers.

290   Ibid.

291   Ibid and also, Douglas Todd, "New Anglican Bishop Told Job Won't Be Easy."
       Vancouver Sun, January 10, 1994.

292   Author's interview with Ingham, March 9, 2005.

293   Ibid.

294   Author's interview with Ingham, June 23, 2005.

295   Ibid.

296   "For God So Loved the World: Welcoming Gays, Lesbians and Heterosexuals in the
       Anglican Church of Canada," Ingham papers.

297   "Challenge the Status Quo," *BC Business*, August 2003, 19.

298   "There Are No Grounds for Discrimination in Jesus Christ," *The Anglican*,
       September 1996, 5.

299   Author's interview with Ingham, April 20, 2005.

300   Ingham, September 7, 2005.

301   Transcript of the information session conducted by the Diocese of New Westminster,
       at Anglican Consultative Council-12, Hong Kong, September 19, 2002, available at
       http://listserv.episcopalian.org/scripts/wa.exe?A2=ind0209c&L=virtuosity&D=1
       &H=1&O=D&P=2403.

302   Author's interview with Neale Adams, Communications Officer, the Diocese of
       New Westminster, June 23, 2005.

303   Rev. Canon Eric Beresford, consultant for Ethics and Interfaith Relationships for
       the Anglican Church of Canada and for the Anglican Consultative Council, in his
       presentation to New Westminster Synod 2004, May 15, 2004.

304   Ingham, Michael, "In Response to Motion 9 of the Synod of the Diocese of New
       Westminster, May 1998," Synod Office files.

305   *The Official Report of the Lambeth Conference 1998*. Harrisburg: Morehouse
       Publishing, 1999, 93-95.

306   "Anglican Bishop Backs Gay Struggle," *Vancouver Sun*, August 12, 1998, A3.

307   Ibid.

308   Author's interview with Ingham, March 23, 2005.

309   Quoted in "Ingham Caught Between Bishops, Diocesan Council," *Anglican
       Journal*, December 1998.

310   Ingham, Michael. "In Response to Motion 9 of the Synod of the Diocese of New
       Westminster, May 1998," Synod Office files, 3.

311   Ibid, 4.

312   Ibid.

313   Ibid, 6.

314   Quoted in "Time Favours Gay Unions, Say Two Top Anglicans," *Vancouver Sun*,
       January 18, 1999.

315   "B.C. Bishop's Same-Sex Rite Threatens Rift in Church," *National Post*, December
       26, 2000.

316   Ibid.

317   "Dialogue on Same-Sex Unions," Synod Convening Circular 2001, 105-148.

318   "Anglicans Revisit Same-Sex Issue," Lower Mainland *BC Christian News*, May
       2001, 1.

319   Quoted in "Synod Vote to Ask for Blessing of Same-Sex Unions," *Topic*, June 2001.

320   Ingham, Michael, Announcement after the vote on Motion 9 at the Synod of the
       Diocese of New Westminster, June 2, 2001, Synod Office files.

321   Author's interview with Ingham, June 23, 2005.

322   Ibid.

323   Essentials to Steve Schuh, May 21, 2001 (e-mail).

324   Author's interview with Ingham, June 23, 2005.

325   "Questions and Answers about the Blessing of Same-Sex Unions," Web site of the
       Diocese of New Westminster, www.anglican.vancouver.ca.

326   "Synod Debates the Blessing of Same-Sex Unions," Web site of Diocese of New
       Westminster, www.anglican.vancouver.ca.

327   Ibid.

328   "Praise for Synod from Metropolitan David Crawley," Web site of the Diocese of New Westminster, www.anglican.vancouver.ca.

329   Author's interview with Neale Adams, Communications Officer, the Diocese of New Westminster, June 23, 2005.

330   Snail mail and e-mail sent to Synod Office, Diocese of New Westminster, 2001–04.

331   Ibid.

332   Quoted in "A Great Diverting of Energy," *Maclean's*, December 28, 2003.

333   Ibid.

334   Ingham's rebuttal in Hong Kong, quoted in McCullum, *Radical Compassion*, 515-16.

335   "Archbishop of Canterbury Singles Out Diocese at Meeting in Hong Kong," Web site of the Diocese of New Westminster, www.anglican.vancouver.ca.

336   Quoted in McCullum, *Radical Compassion*, 512.

337   Quoted in "In Blessing Gay Unions, Bishop Courts a Schism," *New York Times*, July 5, 2003.

338   Ibid.

339   Hambidge, Douglas. E-mail to author, July 8, 2005.

340   Quoted in "Dissident Priests Could Even Face Excommunication," *Globe and Mail*, October 28, 2003.

341   Quoted in "Disciplinary Charges a Last Resort, Bishop Says," *Globe and Mail*, October 29, 2003.

342   Ingham interview, September 7, 2005.

343   Quoted in "Anglican Split Deepens over Gay Bishop," *Globe and Mail*, November 4, 2004.

344   "Reclaiming Christian Orthodoxy," available at the Anglican Communion Web site, www.anglicancommunion.org/acns/articles/36/25/acns3648.html.

345   Letters to the editor, *Topic*, November, 2003.

346   "Challenge the Status Quo," *BC Business*, August 2003, 19.

347   Ibid.

348   Author's interview with Ingham, March 9, 2005.

349   Quoted in "Tyrant. Dictator. Heretic. . ." *Vancouver Sun*, February 21, 2004.

350   Author's interview with Ingham, March 9, 2005.

351   Quoted in "Task Force Proposes Alternate Bishops," *Anglican Journal*, April 2004.

352   Quoted in "Diocesan Council Considers Report of The Primate's Task Force on Adequate/Alternative Episcopal Oversight for Dissenting Minorities," http://www.samesexblessing.info/ Default.aspx?tabid=86.

353   Quoted in "Cool Reception Given Task Force Report," *Topic*, April 2004.

354   Quoted in "Diocesan Council Considers Report of The Primate's Task Force on Adequate/Alternative Episcopal Oversight for Dissenting Minorities," http://www.samesexblessing.info/ Default.aspx?tabid=86.

355   Quoted in "Bishops Delay Oversight Decision," *Anglican Journal*, May 2004.

356   Quoted in "Dissident Priests Asked to Vacate Church Buildings in New West," *Anglican Journal*, September 2004.

357   *Topic*, May 2004.

358   Author's interview with Harrison, June 23, 2005.

359   Ingham interview, September 7, 2005.

360   Quoted in "Back from the Brink," Web site of New Vision, www.churchinfoweb.com/newvision, June 4, 2004.

361   Ingham interview, September 7, 2005.

362   Author's interview with Steve Schuh, president of Integrity Vancouver, May 13, 2005.

363   The Lambeth Commission on Communion," *The Windsor Report 2004*, October 18, 2004, 51-57.

364   Quoted in "Synod to Consider the Windsor Report," *Topic*, November 2004.

365   Press release, Integrity Canada, October 19, 2004.

366   Quoted in "Bishops Unanimously Commend Report for Study," *Anglican Journal*, December 2004, 6.

367   Quoted in "Clergy Hope for Reconciliation," *Topic*, March 2005, 1.

368   Quoted in "Life in New Westminster," *New Vision* Web site, www.churchinfoweb.com/newvision.

369   Quoted in "Hutchison Brings Canadian Response to *Windsor Report* to Global Primates," *Anglican Journal*, March 2005, 1.

370   Statement by Bishop Michael Ingham, Diocese of New Westminster, February 25, 2005, Web site of Diocese of New Westminster, www.vancouver.anglican.ca.

371   The final version of "The Diocesan Response to the Windsor Report" can be found at: www.vancouver.anglican.ca/Portal/Portals/0/DownLoads/WindsorResponse 2005FINAL.pdf.

372   "Synod Votes to Limit Blessings in the Diocese," *Topic*, June 2005, and the diocesan Web site.

373   Chaplin, Ron, and Patti Brace, "Presentation by Integrity Canada," www.integrity-canada.org/cogs_5-6-2005.html.

374   "Canadians Will Not 'Participate Fully' in International Meeting," *Anglican Journal* Web site, www.anglicanjournal.com, posted May 8, 2005.

375   Author's interview with Ingham, June 23, 2005.

376   "Canadians Will Not 'Participate Fully' in International Meeting," *Anglican Journal* Web site, www.anglicanjournal.com, posted May 8, 2005.

377   *The Report of the Primate's Theological Commission of the Anglican Church of Canada on the Blessing of Same-Sex Unions*, May 2005, 16.

378   Ibid.

379   Author's interview with Ingham, June 23, 2005.

380   Author's interview with Elliott, July 11, 2005.

381   Sermon of the Canadian primate, Archbishop Andrew Hutchison, at the 103rd Synod of the Diocese of New Westminster, May 13, 2005. See also, Ferguson, Julie H., "I Stand with Your Bishop," *Topic*, June 2005.

382   "Synod Votes to Limit Blessings with the Diocese," Web site of the Diocese of New Westminster, www.anglican.vancouver.ca, posted May 15, 2005.

383   "True Reconciliation to Take Will, Intention . . . and Time," *Topic*, May 2005.

384   Author's interview with Steve Schuh, president of Integrity Vancouver, May 13, 2005.

385   "Synod Votes to Limit Blessings with the Diocese," Web site of the Diocese of New Westminster, www.anglican.vancouver.ca, posted May 15, 2005.

386   Ibid.

387   Remarks of the Canadian primate, Archbishop Andrew Hutchison, at the 103rd Synod of the Diocese of New Westminster, May 14, 2005.

388   Ferguson, Julie H., "I Stand with Your Bishop," *Topic*, June 2005.

389   Remarks of the Canadian primate, Archbishop Andrew Hutchison, at the 103rd Synod of the Diocese of New Westminster, May 14, 2005.

390   Quoted in "Canadians to Sit on Sidelines of Meeting," *Anglican Journal*, June 2005.

391   Author's interview with Ingham, March 23, 2005.

392   Ibid.

393   Quoted in "Relinquishing the Illusion of Church Unity," newsletter of Integrity Vancouver, Spring 2005.

394   "Vengeance in the Air as Churches Face Expulsion," *The Guardian*, June 22, 2005, www.guardian.co.uk/uk_news/story/ 0,3604,1511616,00.html.

395   Elliott, The Very Reverend Peter, Dean of Christ Church Cathedral, Vancouver, "Text of Remarks to the ACC Meeting in Nottingham," Web site of the Diocese of New Westminster, www.anglican.vancouver.ca.

396   Quoted in "Vancouver Priest Comes Out, Calls for Dialogue, " *Vancouver Sun*, June 22, 2005, A4.

397   "Dean Sees Worldwide Support for Inclusive Anglicanism," Web site of the Diocese of New Westminster, www.vancouver.anglican.ca/Portal/Default.aspx?tabid= 1&mode=Story&StoryId=195.

398   Ibid.

399	Author's interview with Harrison, June 23, 2005.
400	"Conservative Anglicans' Church Plan Revealed," *The Guardian*, June 15, 2005, available at www.guardian.co.uk/uk_news/story/ 0,1506674,00.html.
401	Ibid.
402	An open letter from Archbishop Akinola, reported in "Nigeria's Anglicans Snub Mother Church," *Vancouver Sun*, September 21, 2005.
403	"The 2003 Watchlist," *Maclean's*, January 20, 2003, 27.
404	"Challenge the Status Quo," *BC Business*, 19.
405	Todd, Douglas, "Tyrant. Dictator. Heretic. Totalitarian. Revisionist. Maverick. Renegade," *Vancouver Sun*, February 21, 2004.
406	Author's interview with Somerville, September 2, 2004.
407	Ibid.
408	Ibid.
409	Author's interview with Hambidge, May 11, 2004.
410	Author's interview with Judge Spencer, former Chancellor of the Diocese of New Westminster, August 10, 2004.
411	Author's interview with Ingham, June 23, 2005.
412	Author's interview with Ingham, April 7, 2005.
413	Author's interview with Ingham, March 23, 2005.
414	Ibid.
415	Author's interview with Ingham, March 9, 2005.

INDEX